FRANCE UNDER THE BOURBON RESTORATION
1814–1830

JULY 28, 1830

DELACROIX

FRANCE UNDER THE BOURBON RESTORATION

1814–1830

BY

FREDERICK B. ARTZ

NEW YORK

RUSSELL & RUSSELL · INC

1963

REISSUED, 1963, BY RUSSELL & RUSSELL, INC.
BY ARRANGEMENT WITH FREDERICK B. ARTZ
L. C. CATALOG CARD NO: 63—11027

PRINTED IN THE UNITED STATES OF AMERICA

TO

MY FATHER AND MOTHER

PREFACE

THIS book proposes no particular thesis. Although it doubtless reflects the middle-class Liberalism of the author, its sole purpose is to present the life and activity of the years 1814 to 1830 in their various aspects, and thus to contribute to a better understanding of an important period in French history that has been long neglected. I have tried to do for the Bourbon Restoration what a number of works of the type of Lowell's *Eve of the French Revolution* have done for the Ancien Régime. For the discussion of political conditions it was necessary to depend on newspapers and on police and prefectoral reports in the Archives Nationales in Paris, while for the other chapters I have found it more possible to base an adequate narrative on the great mass of studies that have appeared in the century since the July Revolution of 1830. An extended bibliography of this material appears at the end of the book.

I am deeply indebted for advice and suggestions to a large number of persons: to R. H. Lord, A. C. Coolidge, and Irving Babbitt of Harvard, who first called my attention to this field of studies; to M. Marion of the Collège de France, who graciously allowed me to draw on his vast store of knowledge of the period; to Georges Weill and Léon Cahen of the *Revue d'histoire moderne;* and to that generous friend of all historical students who have worked in France, M. Schmidt of the Archives Nationales in Paris. The whole manuscript was read by my colleagues R. H. Stetson, R. S. Fletcher, D. R. Moore, and Andrew Bongiorno, and also by W. L. Langer of Harvard, by Miss Louise Roberts of Tulane University, and by Miss Dorothy L. Mackay of Duke University. A grant from the Social Science Research Council enabled me to complete the research for the work in France. The material contained in Chapters III and IV was discussed in a seminar I gave at Harvard in the fall of 1930, and I am indebted to a number of my students for suggestions.

F. B. A.

CAMBRIDGE, MASSACHUSETTS
January, 1931

CONTENTS

ERRATA

Page 23, line 7, after *silence* add *and*; line 9, a period after *elections*, and suppress rest of sentence
Page 37, line 21, read *country*
Page 46, line 2, suppress *and*
Page 47, line 3, read *four* for *six*
Page 89, footnote 2, read *Ardèche*
Page 125, line 1, read *France*
Page 128, line 3, end of line, add dash
Page 137, line 13, read *Medicine*
Page 192, line 22, for *Voltaire* read *Sedaine*
Page 195, footnote, line 8, for *ella* read *elle a*
Page 203, line 9, read *Abbeville*
Page 211, last line, read *1803*
Page 214, line 17, after *Belgium* add *and England*
Page 238, line 14, read *1830*
Page 241, line 24, after *line* add *that*; line 25, suppress *in 1826. It*
Page 248, line 13, after *the* add *close of*
Page 265, last word, read *It*
Page 268, line 17, read *échevelée*
Page 297, line 15, for *her* read *his*
Page 342, line 21, read *Bernardin*
Page 387, line 8, read *Schubert*

LIST OF ILLUSTRATIONS

FRANCE UNDER THE BOURBON RESTORATION 1814–1830

INTRODUCTION

ALTHOUGH a century has passed since the "July Days of 1830," it is only in recent years that the place of the Bourbon Restoration in the history of France and of modern Europe has been justly estimated. The striking changes made by the Revolution overshadowed by their greatness the period after Waterloo, and later generations imagined that the years 1815 to 1830 were as unimportant as they were certainly undramatic. It long remained a common belief that the sun of France had set, and men assumed that her leadership had passed to other peoples.

In reality, the influence of France was not ended by the downfall of Napoleon. The assumption that she was exhausted is not borne out by a study of the period. The French people still possessed tremendous energy, which was soon turned to the reconstruction of political and social institutions and to the founding of new schools of philosophy, art, and literature. And beyond her own borders, the states that Napoleon had ruled by the sword continued after 1815 to be influenced profoundly by French ideas and French experience.

In the internal development of France the period is a very significant one, for it afforded the French people their first extended experience in self-government. This new political order, inaugurated by the Charter of 1814, was a patent imitation of the English parliamentary system, and if it proved in practice a rather ill-adapted copy of its English model, it was nevertheless, for the liberated middle class, a valuable school of politics. The modern form of parliamentary government in France, the system of political parties, and the electoral regime all date in their practical workings from the political experiments and failures of these years.

The economic and social movements of the period, unlike the political, were not peculiar to it; they were, rather, part of a gradual economic transformation that took place between 1750 and 1850. In spite of many industrial changes, the France of the Restoration was still primarily an agricultural country. Her commonest social type was the small proprietor, conservative in religion and politics, fearful of both revolution and reaction, and living under conditions that had not changed greatly since the close of the Middle Ages. The traditional class lines of an old and essentially rural society were blurred but not destroyed. The larger towns were developing small manufactures, but the reluctance of the French to make large investments, and the lack of adequate means of communication, retarded this development.

The influence of the industrial bourgeoisie, though it had made gains at the expense of the aristocracy and the clergy, was still limited by the presence of these old and powerful groups. The tendency of business to dominate all classes and to impose its philosophy of life on every social group was only just appearing. In both town and country it was the advent of the railroad after 1830 that marked the real transition between the old social order and the new. Balzac's novels show, however, that the towns were coming more and more into the hands of the middle class, and that a grasping bourgeois desire for money was more common than it had been in the eighteenth century. It was, moreover, among the hard-working and self-reliant bourgeoisie, rather than in the Church or in the official circles of the government, that the deeper purposes of the nation were taking form.

Intellectually the decade from 1820 to 1830 is one of the richest in the last century and a quarter of French history. This generation of the eighteen-twenties, which had not shared actively in the stirring events of the Revolution and the Empire, turned its back on old controversies and began a series of new movements which in one form or another still dominate the intellectual and artistic life of France: the Liberal Catholicism of Lamennais, the Eclecticism of Victor Cousin, the Positivism of Auguste Comte, the Socialism of Saint-Simon and Fourier, and the Romanticism of Hugo, Delacroix, and Berlioz. It seems clear that the period of the Bourbon Restoration stands next in importance to that of the Revolution in the evolution of modern France.

In the general currents of European life France assumed a much more important rôle than might have been expected of a defeated nation. It is true that, in the great movement of European thought known as Romanticism, France after 1800 played the leading part only in painting. Delacroix, and after him the French Romantic landscape painters, had as innovators no equals in Europe. In the field of music, France is second to Germany, though Berlioz is undoubtedly a figure of first-rate importance in the development of modern orchestral music. In literature, the French Romantic School is inferior to both the English and German schools. As European figures in the earlier part of the nineteenth century, Byron and Scott, and Goethe and Schiller, far outrank Lamartine or Victor Hugo or any of their contemporaries. The one literary genre in which France took the lead was in the writing of history, but even in this German scholarship was developing methods of criticism and research that have done much to discredit the best work of Guizot and of Michelet. Nevertheless, in literature and music, while France was not the leader, her influence was everywhere felt, and her achievements recognized.

The European influence of France was primarily political and economic. The French government after 1815 was the most liberal among the larger states on the continent, and although France was behind England in her political development, she seemed to the oppressed liberals in nearly every land, from Spain to Russia, a shining example of how an enlightened people might create a free government, a free press, and an educated middle class. Paris represented to many European Liberals the counter-blast to Vienna, from whence emanated Metternich's system of relentless oppression. Paris in these years was full of political exiles who were later to return to their own peoples bringing back the gospel of Liberty, Equality, and Fraternity.

In economic organization France after 1815 was far in advance of her continental neighbors, Germany, Italy, and Spain. Again she was, in this regard, inferior to England; but as in the case of politics, France's continental influence surpassed that of England, whose more remote geographical position and still more remote manners and ideas made her seem less attractive to foreigners. In the field of social and economic thought the influence of France was of first importance. Such diverse modern programs of reform as those of Industrial Democracy, of the Coöperation Movement, and of all the shades of Anarchism, Socialism, and Communism reflect the influence of the economic theorists of the Restoration. From Waterloo to the Coup d'Etat of 1851 France was the leader in the whole political and economic life of the Continent — a position of which she had been in possession since the Age of Louis Quatorze.

CHAPTER I

THE BEGINNINGS OF A MODERN PARLIAMENTARY GOVERNMENT IN FRANCE

I. THE RESTORATION: A POLITICAL NARRATIVE

THE Restoration was the first extended experiment in free and representative government that France had known. From the beginning of the Revolution in 1789 one regime after another had been tried, constitutions succeeding each other with bewildering rapidity. Finally with the fall of Napoleon the distracted country entered on a more peaceful and a freer political life. For the first time in French history there appeared, with some degree of permanency, modern political parties, a modern type of electoral system, and the sort of modern parliamentary government that we have come to associate with a democratic regime.

This experiment was undertaken under most unfavorable conditions. Lack of experience and the rancorous hatreds created by the Revolution made nearly any continuity of policy very difficult. The Revolution had created such a fundamental cleavage in French society that not until 1870 was it possible to establish any government that lasted longer than two decades. Alongside the old "alliance of the throne and the altar" there had arisen since 1789 a new alliance of free thought and democracy. "One party," writes Louis Blanc, "desired that the nation should be agricultural, that the old system of large proprietorship be reconstructed by means of entails and the right of primogeniture, that the clergy should be indemnified out of the forests of the state, that the administrative centralization of the Revolution be abolished, that the country, in short, should be brought back to the aristocratic and clerical regime of which the bourgeoisie had undermined the foundations. The bourgeoisie, in turn, wanted freedom in trade, and full social and educational opportunities. The aristocrats consisted of scions of old families and dignitaries of the Church. To the bourgeoisie belonged bankers, manufacturers, the holders of national property, physicians, and lawyers."[1] The Restoration was thus inevitably an age of extremes. Ultramontanes and atheists, absolutists and democrats, men who had joined the camp of the Emigrés at Coblenz and men who had sat in the Convention and voted for the execution of Louis XVI, met in the Chambers and in society, and many of them seemed more ready to begin the Revolution over again than to try to live in peace. Under such circumstances it is not surprising that this government lasted only fifteen years.

The sudden collapse of the Napoleonic Empire in 1814 found both the French and the Allies who had defeated Napoleon quite unprepared; and it was, to some degree, mere chance that they brought back the Bourbons. Castlereagh, Metternich, and the Emperor Alexander, in whose hands the situation lay, were quite

1 L. Blanc, *History of Ten Years*, tr. London, 1844, I, 37.

uncertain what to do. Various plans for a new French government were discussed. No one could discover among the French any enthusiasm for the Bourbons. A monarchy under the Duc d'Orléans, Bernadotte, or Eugène Beauharnais, and even a republic, were considered. The allied Powers seemed to be waiting for some manifestation on the part of the French people. Well aware of this, Talleyrand and Vitrolles, an agent of Louis XVIII and his brother, the Comte d'Artois, organized on the streets of Paris a noisy demonstration in favor of the Bourbons. This helped to turn the tide. In many ways, the decision was in Talleyrand's hands. The Allies trusted him and would negotiate with him. Here, as through his whole career, Talleyrand showed an extraordinary aptitude in grasping the situation. This "silk stocking filled with mud," as Napoleon had called him, had that unerring insight that made it possible for him to know today what everyone else would be thinking tomorrow. Largely on his word, the Allies accepted Louis XVIII. Soon the Senate, the Municipal Council of Paris, and various other official groups voted for the return of the old royal family as most likely to secure peace. In the midst of this distress and uncertainty, Napoleon was sent to Elba, Louis returned from England, and after an exile of a quarter of a century the Bourbon monarchy was restored.

At once everyone was wondering what the new King would do. Who were these almost forgotten Bourbons of whom the press of the Empire had been forbidden to say a word? Already the King's brother, the Comte d'Artois, and a large group of returning Emigrés were bringing pressure on the new monarch to start a counter-revolution at once. It was of this group, rather than of the returning King, of whom the remark was true that "the Bourbons had learned nothing and had forgotten nothing." Louis XVIII was not slow in declaring himself in favor of compromise. He was getting old, and his health was bad. He could hardly walk because of his weight and the gout, and evidently, like Charles II of England, he had "no intention of going again on his travels." He had a fair comprehension, too, of what the events of the years 1789 to 1814 meant. On the way from England he had been presented with a statement from the Senate saying that France must have a constitutional government. In view of this demand, Louis hastened to issue a proclamation from Saint-Ouen promising not to disturb anyone for his opinions, and promising also to grant a constitution that would assure the payment of the public debt, freedom of the press and of religion, and would guarantee full property rights to those who had purchased national lands during the Revolution. This declaration seems to have caused general satisfaction. The new King entered Paris in May, 1814, and took up his residence at the Tuileries.

The committee appointed by the King to draw up the Charter included nine senators, nine deputies, and four ministers, all of whom were men of moderate opinions who had served the state under Napoleon. After six days of deliberation, the famous document was ready. It embodied the promises made at Saint-Ouen, establishing for France a parliamentary government more or less on the model of that of England, and maintaining the chief features of the Napoleonic administrative system. For the rest, the document was vague, and full of contradictions. These last were made worse through the King's attaching a curious preamble in which he announced that the Charter was his gift to France, and that it had been "granted" in the "nineteenth year of our reign." Only time and experience could reveal what the Charter was to mean. The mass of the population was apathetic to these changes. The French seemed to be willing to accept anything that would assure peace and would guarantee that there would be no return to the Ancien Régime. Louis XVIII had at least made public acknowledgment that the new society which had issued from the "Declaration of the Rights of Man" would not be destroyed; and so the return of the Bourbons was accepted.

During this First Restoration (1814–5) the only active party in France was that headed by the Comte d'Artois. He established himself in the Pavillon de Marsan in the Tuileries, and his circle became a kind of invisible government. He prided himself on being surrounded by men who had never served any of the Revolutionary regimes and had been out of France or living in retirement for the last quarter-century. How poorly such a group could understand the interests and ideas of a nation that had passed through all the experiences of the Revolution and the Empire is self-evident. Their ignorance, however, was even exceeded by their prejudices. The violent Royalism and reactionary views of this group, who soon came to be known as the Ultra-Royalists or the Ultras, made them hated and mistrusted by most reasonable men. In 1814, as the only organized political group in the exhausted and distracted country, they unfortunately were in control of the situation. Their agents went about through the provinces securing support for their program from the municipal councils. Soon the country was in the grip of reaction. The exaggerated statements made by these Ultras and by some of the higher clergy, especially their threats that the government would take back the clerical and noble lands sold during the Revolution, frightened many, and brought serious discredit on the government of Louis XVIII even before it was under way.

Other ill-timed acts exaggerated the situation. To save money the army was greatly reduced, and many officers who had distinguished themselves in the campaigns of Napoleon were put on half pay. They were further annoyed by being forced to live in their native towns and by being kept under continual surveillance by the police. Disgruntled officers were soon scattered all over France, sowing hatred against the Bourbons. They remained important sources of opposition to the government all through the Restoration. At the same time the national educational system,—the Université de France,—established by Napoleon and one of the great achievements of the Revolution, was threatened with abolition. In the meantime, the allied agents in Paris, the Duke of Wellington and the Russian ambassador, Pozzo di Borgo, were meddling in French affairs. Louis XVIII and his new regime seemed nowhere to find friends.

Little wonder, then, that when Napoleon came back from Elba in May, 1815, he was enthusiastically received, at least by the army. In twenty days he carried the tricolor from the Riviera to Paris. In nearly every town he was greeted with tales of the popular fear of restoring the Ancien Régime, and with bitter denunciations of the priests. Louis XVIII fled to Ghent, and Napoleon hurriedly set about reorganizing his government. He soon found that he could not hope to remain in power unless this government were liberalized. With a certain shrewdness, too, he realized that, having been put under the ban by the European monarchies, and facing in France the hatred of the clergy and many of the nobility, he could only hope to hold his power by again arousing the old revolutionary ardor of the masses. So he called in Benjamin Constant to prepare an "Acte Additionnel" in imitation of the Charter of 1814. The document, the sixth constitution France had known since 1789, provided for a responsible ministry, jury trial, and liberty of the press. This makeshift was presented to the French people through a plebiscite in which only about a million bothered to vote. France was evidently weary of constitutions, and uncertain, too, of the desirability of this latest regime. Napoleon, realizing that the military problem would be even more difficult, turned to reorganizing his army. In the meantime, the Congress of Vienna, where the Powers were redrawing the map of Europe, had broken up, and the allied armies were hastily reassembled. In June, 1815, Napoleon pushed north into Belgium to defeat the English army under Wellington before Blücher and the Prussians arrived. His plan failed at the last moment, and the result was the defeat of Waterloo. Driven back to Paris, he abdicated a second time. Louis XVIII returned from Ghent, and the fallen Emperor was soon on his way to Saint Helena.

Louis was now determined to do all in his power to maintain a regime that would "heal the wounds of the Revolution." The spectacle of a gouty old gentleman, a Voltairian dilettante of the Ancien Régime, arriving in his capital "in the baggage of the Allies" and laboriously ascending the throne of the great Emperor savored of the ridiculous. But the new monarch was clear-eyed, and he proposed to carry out the promises made in the Charter. "The system I have adopted," he declared, "is based on the maxim that I will never be the king of two peoples, and to the ultimate fusion of these all the efforts of my government are directed." To harmonize the old France of Royalism and Catholicism with the new France of democracy and free thought was a difficult program. The new monarchy was disliked by a host of Liberals and Bonapartists, now temporarily reduced to silence. The Ultras, equally displeased with the King's conciliatory ideas, were soon doing all they could to discredit his policy. At the same time France was faced with bankruptcy, and by the terms of the Treaties of Vienna was obliged to relinquish territory along the eastern frontier, to assume the payment of a huge indemnity, and to support an army of occupation for five years. Until 1818 a weekly meeting of the representatives of the Allies was held in Paris, and there was continual interference in the government from this source. The new government was everywhere beset with difficulties.

The King showed surprising willingness to make concessions, to try to forget the past, and even to use men like Talleyrand and Fouché, whom he personally despised. In spite of his attitude, however, a White Terror broke out in 1815. Bccause of the surprising ease with which Napoleon had again made himself master of France, the Ultras were convinced of a great plot of Liberals to overthrow the new monarchy. One half of France was spying on the other half. Men who were prominent in the Revolution, Protestants, and Bonapartists were murdered by Royalist mobs in the Vendée, Brittany, and the South of France. Marshal Ney and a number of other officers who went over to Napoleon in 1815 were given summary trials and executed.

In the midst of this bitter Royalist reaction, the first elections for the Chamber of Deputies were held. The result was the election of a reactionary Chamber, called by Louis XVIII in a moment of amiable enthusiasm the "Chambre Introuvable." Before they had finished their short session he must have regretted the expression! The first result of the election was the resignation of the temporary Talleyrand-Fouché ministry and the formation of a ministry of moderate Royalists under the Duc de Richelieu (1815–8). Richelieu was an honest and able administrator who had lived in Russia as an exile for a generation. He did not understand the French situation, but he agreed with the King as to the desirability of a policy of moderation, a policy of "royalizing the nation and of nationalizing the monarchy." The most interesting member of this ministry, besides Richelieu, was Decazes, brought in to please the King. Louis liked Decazes personally, and he appreciated Decazes' ability to relieve him of tiresome details. The King had a comical turn of mind, and he seems first to have become attached to Decazes when the latter, as Minister of Police, told him amusing stories of the seamy side of the lives of certain notables. Louis, moreover, always had to have someone about with whom he could gossip. This confidant from 1815 to 1820 was Decazes, who shared fully Louis XVIII's policy of moderation.

The Richelieu ministry and the King soon found themselves blocked by the Ultra-Royalist majorities in the legislative Chambers. Moved by the most reactionary ideas, the Chambers passed a series of ill-advised laws, chief of which were a bill banishing a large number of men prominent in the government of the Empire, a law muzzling the press,— no session of the Chambers during the Restoration passed without some changes in the press laws and in the electoral system,— and a law establishing special courts in each department to try treason cases. These Cours Prévôtales soon achieved a disreputable notoriety which seriously interfered with Louis' policy of conciliation. Suspected persons were arrested and held for weeks without trial. Semi-military

CARICATURE OF THE DUC DE RICHELIEU

methods of trial were used, and fines and terms of imprisonment were imposed in wholesale fashion. The worst abuses were in Grenoble, where an insurrection in the garrison was put down in the most brutal fashion. For a time there was hardly a middle-class family without some member who saw himself threatened in his fortune, his liberty, or his life. It was a great relief to the country when in 1817 Richelieu induced the Chambers to abolish these courts.

The Chambre Introuvable proved so reactionary that on the advice of the allied Powers, who feared that it would start a new revolution, Louis XVIII dissolved it by royal decree in 1816. These violent Ultra-Royalists had done nothing to alleviate the burdens under which the country was groaning, and they had shown clearly enough that their aims and aspirations were distinct from those held by the great mass of their fellow countrymen.

The next four years, 1816 to 1820, were, from the point of view of politics, the calmest of the Restoration. New elections returned a Chamber of Deputies of a much more Liberal stripe, and the King and the Richelieu ministry carried through a program of moderation. In both Chambers they had the backing of a large group of Constitutional Royalists and a group of moderate Liberals. At the extreme right and left of the Chambers sat a few bitter Ultras, and a number of determined enemies of the dynasty, all of whom hated the Charter and would probably have been willing to overthrow the government. For the time being, the situation was in the hands of the Center, a coalition of men who, though they were not in entire agreement, believed in supporting the King and the Charter. This group, under the leadership of the Richelieu ministry, passed a more liberal electoral law (1817), calculated to give greater power in the elections to the middle class. They also reorganized the army on a more democratic basis, obtained the liberation of the occupied territory by paying off the indemnity to the Allies (1818), and passed a more reasonable press law. The ministry and the coalition of the Center were bitterly but ineffectively opposed by a coalition of the Extreme Right and Extreme Left who had absolutely nothing in common except a desire to overthrow the ministry. The payment of the indemnity, the liberation of French territory, and the reception of France into the Court of Powers at the Congress of Aix-la-Chapelle were largely the work of Richelieu. The Ultras carried their hatred of Richelieu and his ministry to the point of urging the allied Powers to continue to occupy France and to refuse to accept the indemnity. This action so discouraged Richelieu that he resigned in 1818, and the King re-formed the ministry under Dessoles and his favorite, Decazes (1818–20). The Ultras continued to do everything in their power to exasperate the new ministry. Perhaps their most exaggerated action during the years 1815–20 was the organizing of what appeared to be two revolutionary outbreaks, one at Lyons in 1817 and one in Paris the next year. Both were attempts to frighten Louis XVIII into adopting their program. In spite of the manipulation of the elections by the prefects, many of whom were Ultras, the annual elections to the Chamber of Deputies kept up a steady majority in the Center. The Ultras and the Extreme Left remained always in the minority until after 1820. This Center coalition assured peace, at least for the time being.

The sessions in the Chambers, however, grew each year more acrimonious. Parliamentary oratory in France has, in spite of this, probably never since stood on so high a level. The most masterful addresses of the Right Center were those of de Serre, a loyal friend of the monarchy but the enemy of the Ultras. Chief among the speakers of the Left Center was Royer-Collard. The liveliest sessions were those in which fanatical Ultras like La Bourdonnaye and radicals like Manuel on the slightest excuse rose to re-fight the battles of the Revolution. Fundamental principles of government have probably at no time in nineteenth-century France been so thoroughly debated as in these legislative sessions of the Restoration. The debates in the Chamber of Deputies were printed in the *Moniteur* and commented on in the political press, and the reading public followed this parliamentary war with lively interest. All this, comparatively speaking, was a new experience for the French people.

The program of moderation went to pieces in 1820. Partial elections, one of which in 1819 brought to the Chamber of Deputies the notorious regicide, Abbé Grégoire, were returning more Liberals.[1] This frightened

1 Grégoire's famous remark that "kings are in the moral order what monsters are in the physical" had given him great notoriety. The election of no Frenchman to the Chamber of Deputies could have seemed more of an affront to royalty.

the King and drove him more into the hands of the Ultras. The son of the Comte d'Artois, the Duc de Berri,— the only member of the royal family likely to have a male heir,—was murdered by a fanatic[1] one night as he was leaving the opera. This attempt to end the dynasty failed, however, as only a few months later the Duchesse, his wife, gave birth to a son. The rage of the Ultras over this assassination was so violent that Louis XVIII was obliged to dismiss Decazes, on whom, most illogically, the Ultras were trying to place the blame for the murder, and to recall the Duc de Richelieu. This second Richelieu ministry lasted until 1822, when a combination of Ultras and Liberals overthrew it and the King felt forced to form a new ministry under a Royalist of more pronounced ideas, the Comte de Villèle. The effort to reconcile Royalism with Liberalism had by 1820 ended in failure. This attempt was, however, prolonged until 1829, though clearly enough after 1820 the monarchy moved toward absolutism, while the nation moved toward revolution.

The last four years of the reign of Louis XVIII (1820–4) found him more weary and broken in health. He fell almost entirely under the influence of Madame du Cayla, an agent of the circle of the Comte d'Artois who supplanted Decazes as the King's confidant. She was a witty woman and a most appreciative listener, and the aging King was now more than ever ready to neglect the routine of business for the company of an entertaining companion. Madame du Cayla worked

1 Louvel.

continually to win the King over to the views of the Ultras. In the meantime the situation fell into the control of the Comte d'Artois, who was now merely awaiting the day when he would be king. The chief acts of the second Richelieu ministry (1820–2) were the passage of a severe law of press censorship which practically reduced the Liberal press to silence, a new electoral law calculated to give the government agents a greater control in elections, and the dramatic and forcible expulsion of the Liberal orator Manuel from the Chamber of Deputies. The next elections showed the results of the new electoral law. Royalists of a more conservative sort were returned in such large numbers that Louis XVIII again felt obliged to part with Richelieu and, as we have seen, to form a cabinet under Villèle, who remained head of the ministry until 1827, the longest of all the prime ministries of the Restoration.

This growing power of the reactionary element in the government drove the Liberals to conspiracy, and the years 1820–2 saw the appearance of the Carbonari in France, with a number of abortive uprisings against the government. The army had earlier been the great stronghold of Republicanism and, since 1815, of Bonapartism, and it was there that revolutionary plots developed. A series of insurrections in the garrisons of Belfort, Saumur, Toulon, and La Rochelle was organized, but all failed miserably. At La Rochelle four young sergeants who refused to answer any questions met their death so heroically that they have ever since been regarded by all French radicals as the great martyrs of liberty of the Restoration. The high social and political position of some of the chief conspirators, among them Lafayette, made the government afraid to conduct a thorough investigation of the whole movement. Nevertheless by 1822 the Carbonari had failed because of the almost complete indifference on the part of the general populace. Dislike of the government was undoubtedly greatly on the increase, but it had not yet reached the stage where the French people were willing to risk a revolution.

In 1823, at the Congress of Verona, France agreed with the Powers of the Holy Alliance to put down a rebellion in Spain and restore the Bourbon king to power. The French expedition under the Duc d'Angoulême, the nephew of Louis XVIII, met with almost no opposition from the Spanish rebels. The terrible reaction that followed the restoration of the Spanish king, with its wholesale executions, as well as the general ease of the conquest, took from the French government all the credit Louis XVIII and Villèle had hoped to derive. Like the help given to the Greeks in the War of Independence in 1827, and the French seizure of Algiers in 1830, it all seemed but a pale reflection of the military glories of the Empire. The foreign policy of the Restoration appeared feeble and ridiculous.

The closing years of the reign of Louis XVIII were marked by a series of interesting movements outside of politics. The Church was carrying on a great though ill-advised campaign of evangelization, through the Missions de France and the Congrégation — a work which aroused the violent animosity of the Liberals. A whole series of new intellectual movements were developing or had their beginning during these years. Eclecticism, Liberal Catholicism, Romanticism, Positivism, and the beginnings of modern Socialism were movements which mark the Restoration as one of the most fecund periods in the history of French thought. A new generation which had not lived through the Revolution was asserting itself. Full of ardor, confident of its powers, and bringing new solutions to old problems, this generation was still too young to express itself in politics, and was obliged to spend its energy in writing and discussion. As Jouffroy wrote in the *Globe* in 1824, "A new generation has arisen, and already the children have outstripped their fathers, the emptiness of whose doctrines they clearly see."[1] Economically the country was prosperous, and everywhere there were signs that a new society was forming. In the face of this the government only grew more reactionary.

The accession of the Comte d'Artois, as Charles X, in 1824, meant the triumph of all the forces of the Ancien Régime. In 1814 Louis XVIII had said, justly, that the fate of the monarchy depended on whether he survived his brother — an observation that reminds one of the remark which Charles II of England is said to have made to his brother, later James II: "James, they will never kill me to make you king!" Charles X, as Sorel says, "had all the qualities required for gaily losing a battle or for gracefully ruining a dynasty, but none

1 S. Charléty, *La Restauration* (1921), p. 199.

needed for managing a party or reconquering a country."[1] As the Comte d'Artois he had always looked on the Charter as a temporary concession, and at the beginning of the Restoration had said that he hoped soon for a return to the "natural order of things." Now at the age of sixty-seven, as Charles X, he was not likely to change his ideas. One of the first public indications of his views was the coronation at Rheims in 1825. Here the French were treated to a spectacle of the most elaborate mediæval mummery. Their attitude was well set forth in Béranger's popular verses, "Charles le simple." On that coronation day at Rheims it seemed to many, in spite of the King's oath to defend the Charter, that the Revolution had been but an unimportant incident in the history of France, even the memory of which would soon be effaced.

The Chamber of Deputies, owing to the government's control of elections, made possible by the electoral law of 1820, was now dominantly Royalist, though each new election was to bring in more Liberals until by 1827 they were in the majority. The Comte de Villèle remained head of the ministry. He was a pronounced Royalist, but even his Royalism was frequently insufficient to suit the King and a large group of ardent Ultras. Villèle was primarily a financier, and while for five years he gave the country an honest and efficient administration, he was in no wise a statesman, or even a skilled parliamentarian. In matters of general policy he was out of touch with the country, and he was always too

1 A. Sorel, *L'Europe et la Revolution française* (1885–1904), II, 173.

willing to give in to the King. His program after 1824 was not primarily a political one. On the contrary, he and the Royalists aimed chiefly at a general social and religious reorganization that would move toward something of a reconstruction of the Ancien Régime. Landed property on a large scale was to be reëstablished by indemnifying the Emigrés and by enacting a law of primogeniture, while the moral and social power of the Church was to be restored through the reëstablishment of the religious orders and the reconstitution of the Church's old control of education. Villèle realized, however, better than some of his fellow Royalists that there were limits beyond which it was impossible to go. His royalism was, as Matthew Arnold later said of his own liberalism, "tempered with experience and renouncement." Villèle soon found his ministry attacked, as indeed was every ministry of the Restoration, by a group of Ultras and by the Liberal leaders of the Left. Even under Louis XVIII no middle ground had been found on which a stable regime could stand. Now the monarch had given up a policy of conciliation, and was staking everything on an attempt to reëstablish the Ancien Régime. With such a program there could hardly be a partial success. From 1824 on the only alternative was the Ancien Régime or revolution.

Villèle, whose judgment was always better than that of Charles X, realized that it was impossible to restore all the noble lands without overthrowing the Charter with its guarantee of the land settlement of the Revolution, and this he was not willing to do. So he decided on a program of indemnification "to close the last wounds of the Revolution." The debates on this indemnification bill lasted off and on for two years, and were among the bitterest of the Restoration. A law was finally passed which indemnified the nobles to the extent of a thousand million francs, the money to be raised largely by reducing the interest on government bonds from 5 to 3 per cent. Most of the holders of these bonds were among the middle class, who found themselves despoiled to pay the nobles. The result was rather a reopening than a healing of the "wounds of the Revolution." The further attempt to form a more powerful landed class through a law of primogeniture met with rejection by the Chamber of Peers. The peers on several important occasions showed more judgment of what was and what was not possible than did the deputies. The Duc de Broglie, in speaking of this law, said truly, "This is no law, but a manifesto against society." The failure of the Chambers to pass the bill was greeted in Paris with a general illumination of the city and with great popular rejoicing. Similar manifestations followed the rejection by the Chamber of Peers of a law which would practically have abolished all except a few newspapers — a law named by one of the ministers "the law of justice and of love." The cries of "Long live the Chamber of Peers!" "Down with the ministry!" and "Down with the Jesuits!"—the first rumblings of revolution — were heard in the streets of Paris.

During these years the ministry and the King were giving their fullest support to the Church. The clergy were allowed to interfere more and more in educational matters, bishops were appointed to a number of high positions in the state, and the government did all in its power to further the work of the Missionaries. To please the Church, Villèle tried to carry through a bill that made certain thefts in a church, when "done in hatred of religion," punishable with death. This Law of Sacrilege was again the occasion for hot debates. The ministry realized that cases of this sort would be rare, but Villèle was determined "to raise a monument of piety." In discussing the bill, Bonald declared that to punish the sacrilegious person with death was after all but to send him before his natural judge. It must have seemed to some of those who heard him that the spirit of the Inquisition hovered over the deliberations. The bill was finally passed, but it was never enforced. This series of laws trying to restore the Ancien Régime raised a perfect tempest in the press. The Comte de Montlosier rained down pamphlets against the Jesuits, the Missionaries, the Congrégation, and the ministry. The Liberal papers went to the limits of denunciation, for which many of them were fined.

The answer of Liberal opinion to this program of the ministry was to rally around the Charter and the traditions of the Gallican Liberties of the French Church. The attempt of the Liberals to bring changes by conspiracy and revolution had been given up, and now it was always on the basis of the Charter and by parliamentary means that they tried to bring about reforms. They were carrying out a great program of influencing opinion through the press and of working to reduce the government's control in the elections. In the midst of a torrent of denunciation of the King and the ministry, Charles X in 1826 made himself even more unpopular by appearing in religious processions connected with the Papal Jubilee, and by abolishing the National Guard. When the King was reviewing the National Guard, some of the men called out, "Down with the ministers and the Jesuits!" The King was very angry, and promptly dissolved the organization which was the pride of the bourgeoisie and their guarantee against tyranny. This action was received with deep indignation all over the country.

The large gains made by the Liberals in the elections of 1827 further frightened Charles X. He thereupon dissolved the Chamber of Deputies and called for new elections. The result was an even greater victory for the Liberals. The Liberals were also winning striking victories in the courts, where their newspapers charged with making illegal attacks on the monarchy, the ministry, and the Church were in many cases dramatically acquitted. Early in 1828 Villèle gave up and resigned. By this time it was evident that it was war to the death between the Ultras and the Liberals. The Center parties were greatly reduced in numbers, and the situation had drifted into the hands of the extremists. The best opinion of the country, as represented by the French Academy, the magistracy, the professional classes, and the press was now definitely alienated from the King. Revolution was on the horizon.

Charles X, in 1828, seeing that he could not control the Chambers, seems to have decided on a coup d'état, but, aware that he must for the time being await the occasion, he appointed a moderate ministry under Martignac. This ministry dragged out its sorry existence a little over a year (1828–9). The King never really gave it his support. On the other hand, it never succeeded in gaining the backing of the Liberals, though Martignac honestly tried to placate them. Guizot, Villemain, and Cousin were restored to their teaching positions which they had lost in 1822 at the accession of Villèle, a number of notoriously reactionary Ultras were dismissed from the civil service, a more moderate press bill was passed, and laws against the Jesuits and the clerical control of primary education were passed. But Martignac suited neither extreme. The Liberals regarded him as a straggler from Villèle's party, and refused to support an excellent law for administrative decentralization, merely because the ministry proposed it. At the same time, the Ultras looked on Martignac as a dangerous compromiser. The old Center coalition had by 1829 practically disappeared, and, gaining no following from either Right or Left, Martignac resigned.

Charles X was evidently trying to prove that nothing would please the Chambers, and that all attempts to reconcile royal with constitutional government were doomed to fail. And from the King's point of view they were doomed. In every other case since 1816, when the ministry and the majority in the Chambers were at variance the king had yielded to the majority and selected a new ministry. The monarch now refused to recognize the principle of ministerial responsibility, and decided to select a cabinet suitable to himself. For over a year he had been negotiating with the Prince de Polignac, who in turn had been trying to form a ministry. But Polignac's attempts to get prominent men to serve in such a combination were always met with refusal. Polignac was probably the most hated Ultra in France. Son of a favorite of Marie Antoinette, it was said of him that "he carried proudly the burden of his family's great unpopularity." His very name was a battle cry. In 1816 he had refused to swear allegiance to the Charter, and he was known as a prominent member of the Congrégation. No one had any faith in his capacities or his ideas. Not until August, 1829, was Polignac able to get a cabinet together. It was a strange collection, which included La Bourdonnaye, the noisiest and most boastful Ultra in the Chambers, and Bourmont, who had betrayed Napoleon at Waterloo. "Coblenz, Waterloo, 1815," as one of the Liberal journals declared, "squeeze, press the ministry as you like; you will wring from it nothing but national dangers and humiliations." On reading the news, Royer-Collard remarked, "Decidedly Charles X is still the Comte d'Artois!"

A wave of popular resentment swept over the country. The appointment of this ministry was considered a declaration of war on French society. The Liberal society Aide-toi, le Ciel t'aidera, organized in 1827, became more active. The newspapers on both sides grew more violent. Associations for the purpose of refusing to pay taxes in case the King should try to use unconstitutional methods of government were formed in many parts of France. The excitement in Paris, and to some extent through the provinces, was intense. The *Globe* became a political journal, and in January, 1830, the young Thiers founded the *National*, which was soon preaching the necessity of a "French 1688." The program of the Liberal press, as stated by Thiers, was "to shut up the Bourbons inside the Charter. They will be sure to jump out the window." The *National* carried on a clever propaganda. Thiers knew that the middle class would resent any violation of the Charter. It was quite possible, however, that their fears of revolution would prove stronger than their devotion to the Constitution. They must thus be convinced that not only were the Bourbons a menace to existing institutions, but that their expulsion need not entail social or economic convulsions.

The legislative session of March, 1830, devoted its chief attention to framing its replies to the address of the King. The answer of the Chamber of Deputies was so displeasing to Charles that he dissolved the Chamber and called for new elections. Most of the 221 members who had voted for the firm answer to the King's address were returned. Both Chambers were evidently set against the royal policy and the ministry. Even the news of the capture of Algiers, which the King hoped would create enthusiasm for the monarchy, was without effect. If Charles X now refused to yield, his only alternative was a coup d'état.

Until this moment the conflict between the King and the Chambers had never been clear-cut. A tacit compromise between royalty and liberty had been maintained for fifteen years. The old royal power, however, while keeping its outward forms, had in reality been transformed. The new principle of liberty had been steadily making progress. So far the position of neither side had been very explicitly set forth. Now for the first time the supporters of the principle of constitutional monarchy and the supporters of the principle of absolutism had each clearly announced their full pretensions. From the tactical point of view, Charles was making the supreme mistake of putting himself in such a position that the official rejection of the ministry also fully involved the rejection of the King.

The ministry and the King realized after the elections of 1830 that some action must be taken. Various projects were debated in the cabinet meetings. Finally a series of ordinances was decided upon, in spite of warnings from Nicholas I of Russia and Prince Metternich. The ordinances were published in the *Moniteur* of July 26, 1830. The first suspended the liberty of the press by requiring for all newspapers a fresh authorization from the government every three months; the second dissolved the newly elected Chamber of Deputies, which had never met; the third reduced the number of deputies, and cut down the electorate from 100,000 to 25,000; while the last ordered new elections. In the strictest letter of the law, Charles X and Polignac could find justification for these measures in the ambiguous phraseology of the Charter, especially in Article 14, which said "that the King might make the necessary regulations and ordinances for the execution of the laws and for the safety of the state." All the four ordinances were concerned with matters that had been regulated by royal ordinance before, and no mention was made in the ordinances of abolishing the Chambers or the Charter. The country, however, understood these ordinances in a very different sense.

Paris was soon in revolt. The police tried vainly to break up public meetings in the streets, and to stop the publication of the Liberal papers. A group of journalists under the leadership of Thiers published a collective protest against the ordinances. This was quickly circulated and placarded about the city. The cabinet had made no adequate provision for the defence of Paris. Polignac had assured the King that the nation was prosperous and was not interested in parliaments and electoral laws, and that there would be no trouble. Most of the troops were in Algeria or in the French provinces. When disorder broke out in the city the garrison was unable to control the situation. The closing of most of the retail stores and the factories turned hundreds of men on to the streets. In many cases the employers either armed their workers or else urged them to arm themselves. This large number of men suddenly out of work and now roaming the streets was a determining factor in carrying through the revolution. These workingmen were joined by groups of students from the Ecole Polytechnique, the Ecole de Médicine, and the Ecole de Droit. Committees were hastily formed to arouse the various sections of the city. Paving blocks were torn up to form barricades, and the soldiers found it difficult to get through the streets. The population threw down missiles from the windows, and shot at the government troops from the roofs. On July 28, two days after the appearance of the ordinances, the insurgents had captured the Hôtel de Ville and the tricolor floated from the towers of Nôtre Dame. On the twenty-ninth a group of Republicans set up a provisional government at the Hôtel de Ville and reëstablished the National Guard under Lafayette. The King was staying at Saint-Cloud, and, failing to retake the city, the royal troops were ordered to move out there to join him.

On the twenty-ninth the situation was still uncertain. Would the Republicans, who had almost no following in the country, be able to maintain their provisional government? The morning of the thirtieth Parisians awoke to find the city placarded with bills suggesting the Duc d'Orléans, the King's cousin, as a candidate for the throne. The statement had been drawn up by Thiers. In the meantime, Talleyrand, still the prince of negotiators, had not been idle. Through his efforts the Diplomatic Corps in Paris refused to side with Charles X even after it was known that he had withdrawn the ordinances. Talleyrand hurried out to Neuilly, and succeeded in getting the Duc d'Orléans to agree to come to Paris and to accept the headship of the government offered him by a group of Liberal deputies who had been meeting at Laffitte's house. The Duc came into the city, mounted a horse, and, carrying the tricolor, proceeded through a dense crowd to the Hôtel de Ville. Here he was greeted by Lafayette, proclaimed by the crowd, and reluctantly accepted by the provisional republican government as king. "We give in because we are not strong enough," said one of the young Republicans. "Next time it will be different!" — an interesting prediction of what was to happen in 1848.

On the second of August Charles X abdicated in favor of his grandson, the Comte de Chambord, and tried to open negotiations with the government in Paris. Failing this, and fearing violence, he started for the coast, from whence he proceeded with his family to England. In the meantime the Duc d'Orléans had taken the title of "King of the French People." In a few days the government of Charles X had collapsed, the "French 1688" had been accomplished almost without loss of life, and the Bourbons were again in exile. In every county in Europe the Liberals were thrilled with the news of the first successful revolution since 1815.

II. THE CHARTER, THE CENTRAL GOVERNMENT, AND THE LOCAL ADMINISTRATION

Behind the strife of political parties which led to the downfall of the government of the Restoration lay fundamental contradictions in the Charter of 1814. Louis XVIII, rather than appear to receive his throne from the French people, had himself granted a constitution. The text of this curious document shows in every part its hasty construction and its spirit of compromise. The preamble, added at the last moment, after the rest of the Charter was framed, was wholly in the spirit of the Ancien Régime. Dated by Louis XVIII "1814, and of my reign the nineteenth year," it spoke of the Charter as "a concession and grant of the King," who, although all authority resided in his person, had nevertheless decided to follow in the footsteps of his ancestors, and as "the communes had owed their freedom to Louis VI, and the extension of their rights to Saint Louis and Philip the Fair, as the judicial order had been established and developed by the laws of Louis XI, Henry II, and Charles IX, and finally as Louis XIV had regulated all parts of the public administration," so he, Louis XVIII, now granted new institutions to France. One would imagine that there had never been a Revolution or an Empire in France. Louis XVIII was evidently determined, at any cost, to save the face of the monarchy and to make it appear that the old theory of the divine right of kings still held good.[1]

The Charter itself contained important compromises with the theories of democracy. It declared that the king possessed all executive power, that he should com-

1 Ruggiero, in his *History of European Liberalism* (Oxford, 1927), pp. 159–160, makes the shrewd observation: "A legal difference between the revolutionary constitutions and that of Louis XVIII consists in the fact that the latter speaks not of the rights of man in general but of the rights of Frenchmen in particular; this follows from the principle of the sovereignty of the monarch, for within the limits of his realm any monarch may issue whatever ordinances he thinks best."

mand the army and navy, declare war, make treaties, and appoint to all positions in the civil service. The legislative power, on the other hand, was to be exercised partly by the monarch, who had the right to propose all laws, and partly by a two-chambered legislature made up of an hereditary Chamber of Peers, appointed by the king, and an elective Chamber of Deputies. Here the framers were greatly influenced by the English parliamentary regime. The Chambers, although they could not propose laws, might petition the monarch to make a law. The Chambers could accept or reject the proposals of the king, but they could not amend them without the royal consent. No taxes could be levied without the consent of the Chambers; all money bills went first to the Chamber of Deputies. Equality before the law, freedom of the press, the right of fair trial, and religious freedom were all proclaimed, although in a vague and unsatisfactory way. Purchasers of national lands were assured of their rights. Napoleon's law codes, his Concordat with the Church, his nobility and Legion of Honor, and his local administrative system were recognized. No provision was made for revising the Charter.

On examining the Charter more closely one finds that for nearly every provision there was some contradiction. The preamble, as we have seen, was based on the idea of the monarch's divine right. The Charter itself recognized the revolutionary principle of the sovereignty of the people. Freedom of worship was granted, but Catholicism was defined as "the religion of the state."

Liberty of the press was promised, but it was laid down that "laws would be introduced to correct its abuses." The Chambers were supposed to be a law-making body, but they could not initiate laws, and the King was also empowered to make "ordinances for the execution of the laws and for the safety of the state." Would the government established by the Charter be a limited or an absolute monarchy? To whom would the ministers be responsible? Or, in other words, would the Chambers merely replace the old Parlement de Paris as a protesting body in cases of royal tyranny, or would they really govern the state as in England?

Apparently the Chamber of Deputies, according to the letter of the Charter, did not represent the right of the people to take part in the government. It represented rather the willingness of the king to consult the opinions of his subjects. The ministers were not, then, delegates of the majority, but officers of the king charged with the execution of his personal policy. The tendency from 1815 to 1830 was to interpret the Charter in a liberal sense, and definitely to move toward a responsible ministry modeled on the British cabinet system. By 1830 this idea of a responsible ministry had won almost universal acceptance, so that when in 1829 Charles X, in appointing the Polignac ministry, claimed that he was within his rights according to the Charter, no one, except a few Ultras, thought he was acting in good faith. Clearly, in the matter of a responsible ministry, as in other matters, the Charter had come by 1830 to mean something quite different from what it had meant in 1814 — one of the many cases in constitutional development where usage and interpretation profoundly modify the letter of the law. Fundamental questions which showed both the vagueness and the contradictions of the Charter came up continually during the Restoration, until, failing a peaceful solution, they were settled by force in the Revolution of 1830. Through all the debates each side was able to and did justify itself by the Charter, though neither side could ever fully prove its point. Regarded, however, from the point of view of the period, the Charter was the most liberal instrument of government that existed anywhere on the continent.[1]

At the head of the state — according to the Charter — stood the king. His views and his capacities played a very large rôle in the government, for he was in no sense the mere figurehead which the English king had become. Louis XVIII, as we have seen, was indolent and not inclined to take the initiative, though at least until 1820 he was firm in his determination to abide by a policy of reconciliation. Charles X took a much more active part in affairs. Unlike Louis XVIII, he attended all the meetings of the cabinet and engaged actively in the discussions. He insisted, too, that his son, the Duc d'Angoulême, attend these meetings. Charles made the serious mistake of identifying himself with one party — a party, too, that was in a hopeless minority in the state. He also compromised his position by entering too actively in the affairs of the government. Both

1 With the possible exception of the Polish Constitution.

by temperament and by conviction Charles X was much less fitted to rule a kingdom than his brother, Louis XVIII.

In theory, the king acted through a Council of State which included the ministers, the princes of the royal family, and a group of persons appointed by the king. In practice, this body met rarely, and appointments to it were considered largely honorary. It gradually increased in size until by 1830 there were thirty members.

The real central governing body was the cabinet. Usually, though not always, the ministers, as in England, were members of one of the Chambers. They were allowed by the Charter to speak in either Chamber whenever they chose to do so, though in practice a minister almost always limited himself to addressing the Chamber of which he was a member. A curious usage prevailed of hiring men, often not members of either Chamber, to plead some law which the ministers might, for one reason or another, prefer to have so presented. These "Commissionnaires du roi," as they were called, were usually lawyers, selected for their unusual ability as orators. Guizot served several times in this capacity. Though the Charter, strangely enough, said nothing about it, the ministry represented the party in power in the Chambers. The only exceptions to this were in the case of the first Richelieu ministry, maintained by Louis XVIII against the wishes of the Chambre Introuvable (1815–6), and the Polignac ministry (1829–30), appointed by Charles X with the deliberate intention of flouting the views of the Chambers.

The legislative power, invested by the Charter in the king and in a two-chambered legislature, expressed its will not only by votes on individual laws, and by general favor or hostility to the ministry, but also by an annual address which after 1820 became a regular way of reviewing, criticizing, and commenting upon the whole policy of the government.

The Chamber of Peers was created to furnish an aristocratic power in the government similar to that exercised at the time by the English House of Lords. The members were chosen by the king, and the positions were hereditary. The membership was several times increased until by 1830 there were 335 peers. In the selection of the members a deliberate attempt was made to unite the old nobility with that of the Empire. Most of the members were old, and their talents were military and administrative rather than parliamentary. Unlike the deputies, who received no pay, the peers received a fixed salary of 30,000 francs a year. Their meeting place was the Luxembourg Palace. The sessions were secret, and the debates did not appear in the *Moniteur*, as did those of the Chamber of Deputies. Hence the reading public took little interest in their activities. The peers always wrote their speeches, and even the members themselves often complained that the meetings were dull. It was the custom to make fun of the Chamber of Peers. Chateaubriand speaks of the peers as "those old men, the dried-up débris of the Old Monarchy, the Revolution, and the Empire," and another compares the Chamber of Peers to a "sort of cemetery where are interred the nonentities in favor with the king, and the able men of whom the king is afraid."[1] The wholesale creation of new peers — Decazes created 73 in 1819 and Villèle created 67 more in 1827 — did not help to improve the popular respect for this Chamber. Yet its vote often represented the real views of the country much better than did that of the Chamber of Deputies, which was usually elected under the influence of some flurry of opinion. The presence of former generals and officials of the Empire probably accounts for the greater Liberalism of the upper house — a Liberalism which in their vote on the Bill of Primogeniture and the "law of justice and of love" under Villèle blocked the program of the Ultras.

Though an elective body, the restriction of the fran chise and the government's manipulation of the elections kept the Chamber of Deputies from being truly representative. Moreover, many of the deputies were public officials. In 1830, 142 of the deputies elected were already public functionaries. There was clearly a tendency for many of the deputies to make advancement in the civil service a condition of their vote for the bills proposed by the ministry — a thoroughly bad practice. But this was not all. Under the existing system of local administration every local interest in the departments depended on the central authorities, and it was too often some very secondary local interest that determined the votes of both the electors and their

1 G. Weill, *La France sous la monarchie constitutionnelle* (2d ed., 1912), p. 13.

deputies. A commune wanted a grant for the repair of its church or school, an individual wanted a scholarship for his son or a decoration for himself, and these advantages could only be obtained directly through the central government. It was on condition of demanding them, therefore, that a deputy was returned to the Chamber, and on condition of obtaining them that the deputy gave his vote to the ministry. Nevertheless, as the Chamber of Deputies was in many ways a new institution in France, and as the *Moniteur* published its speeches in full, it was a far more important element in the movement of public opinion than was the Chamber of Peers.

The quality of the debates in the Chamber of Deputies has never been higher, and its discussions were often of fundamental interest. The speeches were prepared beforehand, though very rarely read from manuscript. Only in the last years of the Restoration did improvisation become common. The custom of having the speakers always come forward to the tribune beneath the president's desk helped to keep a certain dignity in the sessions, although sometimes a regular battle occurred when three or four speakers were struggling to get into the tribune. When it was known beforehand that an important question was to be argued, the members who wished to speak inscribed their names in the president's book, and when the session opened they were called on to speak in the order in which they stood on the list. Much of the work of each session was done in ten or twelve committees called "bureaux," to one or another of which all the members were assigned by lot. Each month or six weeks and the bureaux were re-formed.

From the Left the orators spoke of the "hydra of reaction"; on the Right they glorified "the ancient tradition of the wisdom of our kings." The old war between the Ancien Régime and the Revolution constantly reappeared through all the debates. If all the parties involved had been willing to remain within some common ground of legality, a compromise might have been arrived at that would have been more conducive to the dispatch of parliamentary business. But the respect for legality after so many violent "journées" and coups d'état was never very sure. Each group accused its adversaries of the blackest designs. The Left saw the Ultras always ready to call in foreign aid and to restore the Ancien Régime. The Right had a terror of secret societies, the Freemasons, and "les sectes révolutionnaires." The fighting of old battles often blocked the passage of bills for months. The French have been slow in learning to govern themselves. This opportunity of self-government during the Restoration was thus, in spite of many shortcomings, a very valuable political experience for the French people.

The modern political system of France dates from the Restoration; her administrative system dates from the period of the Revolution and the Empire. In 1815 the government of Louis XVIII merely accepted this existing administrative system, every part of which was characterized by extreme centralization.[1] The country

1 Taine says that "centralization in France has improved only the dramatic, conversational, and culinary arts" ! (H. Taine, *Voyage en Italie*, I, 101.)

had been divided during the Revolution into eighty-three departments, each of which in turn had been cut into about six arrondissements. Each arrondissement was further divided into ten or twelve cantons, and the cantons, finally, were made up of a varying number of communes. The only variations in the system were in the case of the city of Paris and the Department of the Seine. Here the positions of prefect of the department and mayor of the city were held by the same man, while the municipal council and the departmental council were identical. The central government appointed prefects of the departments, who in turn appointed the departmental councils, the councils of the arrondissements, and finally the local mayors and town councils. All these local councils of the departments, the arrondissements, and the communes — the canton was a judicial district — were purely deliberative assemblies, from time to time giving advice which the government could use or ignore, as it chose. The general council of the department was a body of local notables called together by the prefect for a few days each year to discuss with him the needs of the department. After this short meeting, the prefect was again free to carry on his administration under the sole control of the central government.

In speaking of the system, Royer-Collard characterized it well: "It has made us a people of administrés in the hands of irresponsible functionaries."[1] The system was originally established on the theory that the nation

1 *Moniteur*, Jan. 23, 1822.

was incapable of self-government. The Liberals, after 1815, wanted local self-government as a necessary complement to national self-government. The Royalists also favored local self-government, because they imagined that in such a regime local interests would entirely dominate the political life of the country, and through indifference a greater absolutism might be allowed in the central government. Parliamentary discussions of decentralization in 1821 and in 1828 came to nothing, though in 1821 an ordinance allowed the prefects themselves to settle more departmental affairs directly, and save time that earlier had been wasted in sending everything to Paris for approval.

The prefects were most of them old Royalists out of touch in their whole experience and ideas with the districts they administered, and thus they were bound to misrepresent conditions in the numerous and often absurdly detailed reports which they sent up to the Ministry of the Interior. The prefects, also, were moved about too often,— every two or three years,— so they never really came to understand the local situation. The whole system was in the hands of these government appointees, so that the word "fonctionnaire" became a synonym for laziness, ignorance, and inefficiency, for an exaggerated sense of self-importance, and finally for absurd flattery of the power next higher up. All this was favored, too, by the desire of the French for security and for a steady income. The system was honeycombed with patronage. Positions in postoffices and in tobacco shops, and decorations, were unblushingly used to gain favor. The use of the prefects in controlling the electoral machinery was also in line with the government's conception of the work of the local administrator. An excellent self-portrait of a prefect is furnished in a letter of the Prefect of Corrèze to the Minister of the Interior on December 16, 1829:

> In the midst of all these political changes, my system is to distract those who might make trouble, rather than to combat them, to absorb them in local interests and activities, and so to overcome the bad influences of Paris which reach us through the newspapers and through the stream of corrupted youth whom the schools of Paris scatter each year through the provinces.[1]

The novels of Stendhal and of Balzac abound in excellent portraits of the types of functionary of the Restoration.

Hand in hand with the prefects and their appointees worked the police, who played a great rôle during the Restoration, prying everywhere, bribing domestics, stirring up trouble as agents provocateurs, and keeping an enormous amount of more or less reliable information on thousands of individuals. The history of the police during the Restoration is still to be written, but the huge mass of the material in the Archives in Paris bearing on their work from 1814 to 1830 gives some suggestion of the extent of their activity. Without the police and without the prefects and their control of the situation the Restoration could not have lasted even as long as it did. Indeed, the police, and the local administration in general, did much better work in helping to per-

1 Arch. Nat., F[7]. 6776.

petuate a system than in administering the government of the nation. Their importance to the Restoration is well stated in a famous pamphlet of Chateaubriand. "A bishop, an army commander, a prefect, a procureur of the King, a police commandant — if these are for God and for the King, I will answer for the rest."[1]

III. POLITICAL PARTIES AND THE ELECTORAL SYSTEM

The Charter, in providing for a parliamentary regime, assumed the formation of political parties. These soon appeared, and, like all modern party divisions on the continent, they took their names from the seating in the Revolutionary assemblies, the Right, the Right Center, the Left Center, and the Left. It must, however, be understood at the outset that there were no sharp boundaries between parties, and members passed back and forth from one group to another. Party formation after 1815 was slow, and close party organization hardly existed until the close of the Restoration. Moreover, the word "party" at this time was still synonymous with faction and meant intrigue and underhanded methods. Only gradually did the word come to have the meaning we attach to it. There was, nevertheless, always a tendency to follow the leadership of eminent men, and it is in that sense rather than as organizations with established usages and traditions that the political parties of the Restoration must be conceived. The divisions indicated in what follows should be understood as representing tendencies rather than absolute

1 Chateaubriand, *La monarchie selon la Charte* (1816), p. 16.

1820

THE PAST THE PRESENT

differences. Modern French politics since 1815 have at all times shown this fluidity and this tendency to form and re-form many small parties.

The Right, which in 1815 gave itself the name "Royalist," came soon to be known generally as the "Ultra-Royalist" or "Ultra" party. This party derived its philosophic justification from the writings of Bonald and Joseph de Maistre. All power, according to their theocratic argument, is derived from God, and political society is His work, not the invention of man; least of all is it based on the absurd social contract of Rousseau. Men are by nature unequal — even if, as Bonald says, the Charter of 1814 affirms that they are equal; and God has constituted kings to govern them and the Church to lead them out of their inherent selfishness and sin. All attempts to interfere with this work are attempts to interfere with the purposes of God. Under king and bishops society should be organized as a hierarchy, so that from the nobility to the "corporations de métier" all families and persons would find their proper places as they had under the Ancien Régime.

Tyranny was to be prevented by a strong magistrature, a much more effective method of control than by an elective chamber which was at the mercy of the king, who could dissolve it, and of the whim of the electors, who would always be changing it by election. The political philosophy of the Revolution, these theorists maintained, had been refuted by the course of the Revolution itself. The attempt to put these principles into action had issued in disaster and tyranny. Realizing this, de Maistre made the sound observation that the organization of a state must follow the actual existing distribution of power, a distribution which is not changed though dilettante politicians alter it upon a sheet of paper. These reactionaries, like almost all the thinkers of the time, failed, however, to see the constructive side of the Revolution. In 1815, to nearly everyone the Revolution still meant only the guillotine, the nonsense of the worship of the Supreme Being, civil and foreign war, the misery of a ruined currency, and finally defeat and anarchy. Bonald, de Maistre, and Ballanche, a third theorist of the group, carried this fear of the Revolution to its very limits, and, not content with denying what Voltaire and Rousseau had affirmed, they went to the extreme of reaffirming all that they had denied. Reaction and repression seemed to them the first need of society. The tone of this polemic is shown in de Maistre's famous Eulogy of the Executioner. "All greatness, all power, all order, depend upon the executioner. He is the tie that holds society together. Take away this force and that very moment order is suspended by chaos, thrones fall, and states disappear."[1] These philosophers idealized the Ancien Régime and failed utterly to understand the tremendous gap between its ideals and potentialities and its sordid, vicious realities in the days of Louis XV and Louis XVI.

The school of the Swiss writer Haller, whose translated works circulated widely in France after 1820, while holding no such religious opinions, arrived politically at

1 G. Brandes, *The Reaction in France* (1903), p. 101.

the same conclusions. Institutions, according to this doctrine, must develop slowly and naturally, and all attempts to break sharply with the past, especially such attempts as those of the eighteenth-century Philosophers to remake society by reason alone, are bad, and bound to cause anarchy — a line of argument resembling that of Edmund Burke in his *Reflections on the French Revolution*, which appeared in several French editions before 1830.

Most of the members of the Right were either dignitaries of the Church or men of noble origin, and in reality their views were determined far more by their social and economic situation than by any appeals to political philosophy. Their practical program consisted largely in making war on the Revolution and in attempting to undo all its legislation. The most extreme always demanded the restoration of feudal rights, the abolition of the Napoleonic Concordat and the reconstitution of the church of the Ancien Régime, strict censorship of the press, and in general a return to the era before 1789. This group was responsible for some of the excesses of the White Terror of 1815, the notorious Cours Prévôtales of the early years of the Restoration, the traitorous appeal to the Duke of Wellington in 1818 to continue the allied occupation, for no other reason than to vent their rage on the moderate ministry of the Duc de Richelieu, the defeat of "l'enseignement mutuel" as a means of extending state education, the growing monopoly of education by the Church, the reactionary Electoral Law of the Double Vote (1820), the Laws of Sacrilege and of Indemnification, the expulsion of the Liberal, Manuel, from the Chamber of Deputies and of various well-known professors, including Villemain, Guizot, and Victor Cousin, from the Université, the disbanding of the National Guard, and finally the Coup d'Etat of 1830.

Their tactics consisted always in trying to show that the country was honeycombed with revolutionary conspiracies and that the monarchy was on the verge of a collapse. Such views, however, did not prevent these Ultras from doing a good deal of conspiring themselves. "The violence of this party," says the Duc de Broglie, "both in the Chambers and out of it, at the tribune and in the galleries, in trousers or petticoats, recalled feature by feature the worst days of Robespierre and the Convention."[1] To them the Restoration was a victory. They were willing to receive support from any group, and in many cases united with the Left in order to embarrass the ministry in power. They were like the revolutionaries of the Extreme Left in that they would have liked to overthrow the Charter. They were often more royal than the king and more Catholic than the Pope. They were always, after 1816, in a minority in the Chambers. The Ultras were the first group to organize as a party and to hold private meetings of their deputies to discuss policies and prepare a program. They were also the first to organize political committees in the provinces, and though they objected strenuously to the organization of the Liberal groups after 1817, they had set the example.

1 G. Lowes Dickinson, *Revolution and Reaction in Modern France* (1926), p. 75.

These Ultras had a great dislike for Louis XVIII. He seemed to them a shameful figure of a monarch, who, after having encouraged his loyal subjects to emigrate, had after 1815 reserved many of his favors for men who had been enemies of the monarchy. They looked upon him as a "Crowned Jacobin, a King Voltaire," who had imported a monstrous English Charter into France. Charles X, both as Comte d'Artois and as king, was the real leader of this group — which accounts for its rapid rise in power after 1824. Back in the early years of the Revolution the Comte d'Artois had hired pamphleteers to write disrespectfully of his brother Louis XVI, whom he considered too mild. After 1815 he made the same objections to Louis XVIII. From 1789 to 1824 he had truly "learned nothing and forgotten nothing." By 1829 the Ultras, whose principles the Polignac ministry fully represented, had come to be a weak and dying party whose position was maintained only through the personal influence of the King and the abuses of the electoral system. Speaking of this group in 1829, one prefect said: "These Ultras are nothing any more, either in numbers or in influence. A few ecclesiastics and a few old men — that's about all that is left of them today."[1]

The party of the Right Center, though still Royalist, was made up of men of more moderate opinions. They desired if possible to reconcile the monarchy to the Charter and a parliamentary regime, but they were averse to any great extension of the terms of the Charter

1 Arch. Nat., F^7. 6770. Prefect of the Meuse to the Minister of the Interior.

and were determined to maintain a strong kingship. They wanted to develop a conservative, hereditary, and landholding aristocracy, to raise the property qualifications for voting, to reinforce the clergy, though not to excess, and to curb the press, though not suppress it. These men of the Right Center were sincere in their devotion to the Charter and in their desire to "heal the wounds of the Revolution." They were accused by the Ultras of sacrificing the monarchy to the principles of liberty, and by the parties of the Left of sacrificing the great gains of the Revolution in their determination to strengthen the monarchy. Chateaubriand and de Serre were the most able men of this Right Center. This party furnished all the leaders of the Restoration ministries except the last one. The party was made up of quiet, conservative men generally inclined to vote for the government in power because it was the government in power. Like the Right, this Right Center had no able orator, except perhaps de Serre. The whole group had, in a word, the habitual faults of all moderates — inertia and timidity. The leadership of the various Royalist groups after 1820 fell more and more into the hands of the extremists, and after 1824 the moderate elements assumed the attitude of looking on.

Between the Right Center and the Left Center stood a small independent group that voted sometimes one way and sometimes another, though after 1824 all of its members went over to the Left Center or the Left. In 1815 a satiric journal had dubbed this group the "Doctrinaires," and so they were generally referred to, usually with an accent of contempt. Despite their name, they had in reality no fixed doctrine. They pursued a compromise between the "Principles of 1789" and the "Principle of Legitimacy of 1815." Royer-Collard, the greatest thinker of the group, wrote to Guizot in 1823: "I never conceived the word Restoration in a narrow and literal sense, but I have always regarded it as meaning a certain general condition of society and government which will for the present assure in France order, justice, and liberty."[1] They looked on the Charter as the "juste milieu," the perfect compromise, and the natural consequence of the whole history of France. Their taste for abstract formulæ, and their pretenses of judging all things only by reason, and always from a superior position, annoyed their opponents both Liberal and Royalist. "They are only four in number," as a journal once remarked — "four who sometimes pride themselves on being only three, because it seems impossible to them that there could be four such heads in the world; and sometimes they are five, but that is when they wish to frighten their enemies by their number."[2] The Duc de Broglie, one of their number, once laughingly remarked that there was a place for all the Doctrinaires on Beugnot's famous sofa.

The only popular member of the group was Camille Jordan. The most able was Royer-Collard. Outside the Chamber of Deputies were Guizot, Barante, and Victor Cousin, and in the Chamber of Peers the Duc de

1 Charléty, p. 87.

2 G. Weill, *op. cit.*, p. 18, note.

Broglie, certainly among the ablest men of their generation. The intellect, the learning, and the oratorical powers of Royer-Collard made him the most respected statesman of the Restoration, though to some his manner seemed cold and pedantic. His philosophy of government was based on the division of the state into three powers working together to maintain an equilibrium: an hereditary monarchy, an hereditary peerage representing the necessary inequality of individuals, and finally a representative assembly to embody the element of equality, this assembly to be recruited from the middle class, the most representative and the most valuable force in the state. When any one of these powers became too strong, the equilibrium was upset. It is this belief in a balance of powers that explains Royer-Collard's policy of sometimes defending the king against the Chambers, and after 1824 of defending the Chambers against the encroachment of the monarch.

These Doctrinaires had no faith in revolutionary methods. They believed it would be possible, though only by slow degrees, to educate the country in the practice of self-government. They were thus at the same time both the opponents and the perpetuators of the Revolution — opponents of its philosophy and its ready-made methods, and perpetuators of that vital and positive modern influence for which in its wider aspects the Revolution still stands. The final result of the work of the Doctrinaires was to stimulate the growth of the whole Liberal cause.

The Left Center was made up of men of moderate

Liberalism. Like the Right Center, this group believed in the honest execution of the Charter, but it also believed that the Charter should be extended toward greater democracy. The Extreme Left, usually referred to as the Left, carried these views further, and in its ranks were some avowed enemies of the dynasty, Orleanists, Bonapartists, and a few Republicans. Most of the ablest men of the Chamber of Deputies had their seats on the Left, sometimes in the Left Center and sometimes with the Left, the division not always being very clearly marked. Benjamin Constant, Manuel, Laffitte, Casimir-Périer, Voyer d'Argenson, and Lafayette were the leaders. They were an able and interesting group. Lafayette was a generous, naïve man, the "Friend of Humanity." Though devoted too much to applause,— Jefferson had said of him, "Lafayette has a perfectly canine taste for publicity,"— he had become for the masses a great symbol of democracy. His great article of faith was the sovereignty of the people, and if it took a new revolution to achieve a democratic regime and to embody it in a constitution framed by a popularly elected assembly, he was willing to see such a revolution. Charles X once wisely remarked, "There are two men who have not changed since 1789, Lafayette and myself."

Benjamin Constant had the keenest intellect of the group. Born in 1767 and dying in 1830, he seemed to have all the intellectual and moral weaknesses of both the eighteenth and nineteenth centuries — a curious combination of Voltaire and René. An uneasy and unhappy man in private life, he was an able public speaker and a brilliant pamphleteer. His convictions as a Liberal were profoundly sincere. The hatred of the bourgeoisie for the Ancien Régime was embodied in Manuel, Laffitte, and Casimir-Périer. Manuel never failed to introduce into his fiery speeches all the most bitter memories of the Revolution. He was an extraordinary extemporizer, and he knew how to drive the parties of the Right into a veritable frenzy. Laffitte and Casimir-Périer were self-made financiers who had come up from the masses. Laffitte was the son of a carpenter of Bayonne. He had arrived in Paris almost penniless and had come to be the richest banker in France. He was a poor speaker, but he entertained lavishly at his home in Paris and at the Château de Maisons, and his fireside became the great rendezvous of all the malcontents. Voyer d'Argenson was an avowed Republican.

Besides these Liberal political leaders, there were two brilliant writers who did much to popularize the Liberal cause — Paul-Louis Courier and Béranger. Courier had been an officer in Napoleon's army, and before 1815 had become known as a grumbler against the Imperial Regime. Yet at the Restoration this man, who had always depicted the worst side of war, turned to worship national glory. Though he was in comfortable circumstances, and an accomplished Greek scholar, he loved to describe himself as a simple vinedresser and to speak from the standpoint of the people. The tyranny of some prefect, the ridiculous pretensions of a local noble, and above all the occasional fanaticism of the priests, were the inspiration of his attacks. He shows how imprisonment for six months without a proper trial, and misery, sickness, and death brought upon the children and other relatives of the accused, are the punishments for trifling offences. Forty gendarmes are sent to a village directly it falls under suspicion of Bonapartism. The suspected persons are taken from their beds and fettered like criminals. When he was sent to prison himself, Courier wrote: "It is not my cleverness, but my stupidity, which has landed me in prison. I had put my faith in the Charter, and I confess it to my shame."[1] He produced his effects in a few pages, apparently with naïve downrightness, but in reality with consummate satiric art. He was the master of a clear, finely chiseled style, and his pamphlets belong to the great tradition of French prose. His ideal of government, though never clearly defined, was a bourgeois democracy, and he was always praising Louis Philippe, the Duc d'Orléans.

A Liberal of much the same capacities and outlook was the poet Béranger, who began in 1815 to publish witty and satirical songs against the King, the nobles, and the clergy. Like the popular lithographers of the time, he excelled in depicting the stupid and cowardly Emigré, the hypocritical priest, the honest peasant, and the hard-working bourgeois. He contributed to the growth of the Napoleonic Legend by describing Napoleon as a lover of peace and the friend of the people. From 1815 to after 1830 Béranger was the most popular and widely read of all the poets of the time. His tech-

1 Brandes, p. 285.

nical mastery of simple verse forms and the aptness of his witticisms gave him a higher literary reputation in his own lifetime than he has had since. He was the perfect nineteenth-century expression of the same keen but narrow bourgeois spirit that in the Middle Ages had produced the fabliaux. His conventionality and his commonplace views, which seem limitations today, only helped his reputation during his own lifetime. Both Courier and Béranger gave great impetus to the growth of a bourgeois and at the same time Bonapartist type of Liberalism that has played a great rôle in modern France.

The Liberals were not organized until the elections of 1817. During the next years they did a great deal of conspiring. In 1818 a number of radical deputies and peers, including Lafayette, Dupont de l'Eure, Voyer d'Argenson, and Manuel, formed connections with several secret societies, L'Union, Les Amis de la Presse, and Les Amis de la Vérité. These secret societies, about which little is known, included some Freemasons and a large number of Napoleonic officers on half pay. Their program was vague. Some were Bonapartists, a lesser number were Republicans. All agreed in their hatred of the present regime and in their devotion to the tricolor. Several of these secret societies united to start a military uprising in Alsace in 1821, but it failed completely.

The death of Napoleon in 1821, and the developing legend of a Napoleon who was a Liberal, the friend of the people, and the lover of peace, brought the Bonapartists and Republicans closer together. As we have seen in the case of Béranger, men were coming to think of Napoleon affectionately as the man who "took the place of the weary sentinel," who sat with the peasant by his cottage door, who saved France from the Cossacks — the Little Corporal with the three-cornered hat and the gray coat. The younger generation, too, was dreaming of Napoleon. "The King of France," wrote Alfred de Musset, "sat upon his throne. And when boys talked of glory, the answer was, 'Become priests'; and when they talked of honor, the answer was, 'Become priests'; and when they talked of hope, of love, of energy and of life, it was still, 'Become priests.' "[1] France was bored and restless, and, while men forgot the miseries of the Empire, its glory grew in their memories and imaginations. Liberalism and Bonapartism were moving together.

In 1821 there was founded at Saumur a new secret society, the Chevaliers de la Liberté. This was soon united with the other secret societies into a large organization on the model of the Italian Carbonari. At the center of this French Carbonari society was "la haute vente," under which were "ventes centrales," and finally "ventes particulières," each composed of at least twenty members. All France was soon covered by the network of these societies. The recruits were largely soldiers, though many lawyers, doctors, and journalists joined the movement. No effort was made to affiliate the working classes. The prosperity which prevailed at the time, the general bourgeois fear of revolution, and the indifference of the peasants, kept the movement from

1 Alfred de Musset, *Confessions d'un enfant du siècle*, Ch. II.

gaining any great national following. Among the members were Lafayette and a group of deputies, Victor Cousin the philosopher, Thierry the historian, and Dubois and Jouffroy who in 1824 founded the *Globe*. Every member swore absolute secrecy and obedience to orders, and all agreed to keep ready a gun and fifty cartridges. The symbolism, which was elaborate and included secret passwords and handshakes, was all imitated from the Freemasonic lodges.

The program of the Carbonari was as vague as that of the earlier Liberal secret societies. They agreed in general on the expulsion of the Bourbons and the right of the people to choose the government they preferred. The best institutions were those that assured happiness to the greatest number. Their favorite books were Destutt de Tracy's *Commentaire sur l'esprit des lois* (1819) and Daunou's *Essai sur les garanties individuelles* (1818), both works representing an interesting combination of the ideas of de Montesquieu, Condillac, Diderot, Condorcet, and the English Utilitarian, Jeremy Bentham. A series of insurrections in various garrisons was the outgrowth of this activity. All were quickly put down, and by the end of 1822 the Carbonari as an organization had gone to pieces.

After 1822 the program of the Liberals became entirely a constitutional one, and the internal differences in the Liberal ranks were largely differences in their hatred of the Royalists. During the Restoration the Royalists had the advantages of a better organized philosophy of the state, as well as a more definite practical program. The Liberals usually had more able speakers. After 1822 the Liberal rallying cry was "Vive la Charte!" or, as Benjamin Constant told a gathering of students, "Vive la Charte, rien que la Charte, toute la Charte!" In much the same way these Liberals insisted on the Gallican Liberties of the French Church against the growing power and pretensions of the clergy. This ardent defence of the Charter against the Ultras and Charles X, and also the defence of the Gallican Liberties, were very clever political moves, in that they now made it practically impossible to accuse the Liberals of revolutionary designs. Their demands were not unreasonable. They wanted a middle-class, representative government, with respect for the freedom of the press, of religion, and of industry — in a word, the English regime, though some would have preferred it without the House of Lords. They were often curiously conservative in their fear of the masses. Carrel, one of the most advanced Liberals at the close of the Restoration, reproaches the Royalists for trying "to arouse within the nation another nation than the one which reads the papers and follows the debates in the Chambers, which commands industry and owns the soil."[1]

In 1827 a new Liberal society, Aide-toi, le Ciel t'aidera, was formed to supplement the work of the old Comité Directeur. The last was an organization which dates from 1817, and which circulated Liberal literature, though not of a revolutionary character. Guizot was at

1 Thureau-Dangin, *Le parti libéral sous la Restauration* (2d ed., 1888), p. 498, note.

the head of the new society in 1827, and a lively campaign was carried on to influence the electors. They were especially active in forcing the prefects to rectify the electoral lists. One prefect writes: "Nothing escapes their investigation. They have an immense network that covers all of France."[1] Among the same prefectoral reports are preserved many small handbills, distributed by the Liberal society and sent up to Paris by the prefects for the inspection of the Ministry of the Interior. These handbills follow a more or less fixed formula: a condemnation of the manipulation of the elections by the government, an attack on the ministers, a diatribe against the Jesuits, a call to elect Liberal deputies — all ending with an eloquent appeal for free government in the name of the Charter.[2]

The work of the Liberals also included an active campaign among the younger generation, particularly in Paris. The public lectures of Benjamin Constant at the Athénée were supplemented by the opening of reading rooms. These reflected clearly the widening interest in politics that came in the later years of the Restoration. From the provinces one of the prefects writes: "The Liberal journals that are in all the inns and cafés keep the young men continually agitated."[3] Liberalism, often of a Republican stripe, grew more marked in the schools. In 1819 at the Ecole de Droit, and in 1823 at the Ecole de Médecine, the students and some of the

1 Arch. Nat., F7. 6772. Prefect of the Vendée to the Minister of the Interior.

2 Arch. Nat., F7. 6740, 6741.

3 Arch. Nat., F7. 6767. Prefect of the Charente to the Minister of the Interior, 1829.

professors were accused of Liberalism and the two schools were temporarily closed. Guizot, Cousin, and Villemain had a great influence over the students who crowded their lecture halls. After 1824 this younger generation of Liberals read the *Globe* and the Saint-Simonian *Producteur* as well as the older Liberal journals. By 1830 Liberalism had come to be the dominant political force both in the Chambers and among the mass of Frenchmen of both the older and younger generations.

The electoral system, which supplied the membership of the Chamber of Deputies, was the only place in the whole system of government which permitted effective political expression for these conflicting principles and interests. This accounts for the lively interest in the electoral problem. Certainly no question, not even that of the censorship of the press, was more debated in the Chambers or more discussed in the newspapers and cafés. All seemed to agree on the necessity of a high property qualification for voting. Even so thoroughgoing a radical as Benjamin Constant says of this:

> Those whom poverty keeps in an eternal dependence and who are condemned to daily work are no more enlightened on public affairs than children, nor are they more interested than foreigners in our national prosperity, of which they do not understand the bases and whose advantages they enjoy only indirectly. Property alone, by giving sufficient leisure, renders a man capable of exercising his political rights.[1]

The excesses of the Revolution had completely discredited the idea of universal suffrage which had been

1 B. Constant, *Réflexions sur les constitutions* (1814), p. 106.

embodied in the Constitution of 1793. The question was never debated in the sessions of the Chambers during the Restoration.

The questions usually discussed, now that the principle of limitation had been admitted by all, were the conditions of age and income, and direct versus indirect elections. And though fine arguments a-plenty were used on both sides, each party was really less interested in creating an electoral law that would in itself be reasonable than in finding one that would assure a majority for itself in the Chamber of Deputies. Hence in the early years of the Restoration, when the current of Royalist reaction was strong, the Ultras worked to lower the qualifications for voting. Later, with the rapid growth of a Liberal opposition, the Ultras changed their tactics entirely and advocated a very strict limitation of the suffrage. The Liberals made much capital of this reversal of Ultra opinion, but they were themselves guilty of the same inconsistency.

The basis of the electoral system had been fixed by the Charter. To be eligible for election to the Chamber of Deputies a man must be forty years old and pay a direct tax of 1000 francs. If there could not be found in any department fifty persons of the required age and income, the number might be filled up from those nearest the 1000-franc limit. To possess the right to vote a man must be thirty years old and pay a direct tax of 300 francs. Half the deputies representing any given department must be chosen from eligibles resident in that department; the rest might be selected from eligibles residing anywhere in France. The Charter maintained the system of indirect election in two stages which had long been in use. The qualified voters were divided into two classes; the first class voted in the collège d'arrondissement, the second class voted in the department collège. The admission to this last was limited to the proportion of one elector to every 1000 inhabitants, and the members must be chosen from the 600 most heavily taxed individuals in the department.

The collège d'arrondissement, according to these elaborate arrangements, elected candidates equal to the total number of deputies to be sent up by the whole department. Eight days later the departmental collège met, and in this final election at least half of the deputies chosen must be from the lists sent up by the collèges d'arrondissement. One fifth of the membership of the Chamber was to be renewed each year. Louis XVIII, and later Charles X, kept the right, granted by an Imperial decree of 1806, to add to any electoral collège those who had "rendered special services to the state." Following this principle, an ordinance of 1815 authorized the prefects to add twenty members to the departmental collège and ten to each collège d'arrondissement. This, of course, greatly increased the government's influence in elections. In theory the persons so nominated had rendered "special service to the state," but in practice a reputation for holding "healthy opinions" far outweighed other considerations. It is easy to see from the correspondence of the Ministry of the Interior what great importance the government attached to this measure. In 1815 one of the prefects wrote to the Minister of the Interior:

> I have the honor to send Your Excellency a list of electors which I am authorized to add to the electoral collège. In the choice that I have made of these new electors I have followed the spirit rather than the letter of the ordinance, and I have thought it my duty to give preference to men who have always possessed healthy opinions both in morals and politics.[1]

This abuse was continuous through the whole period of the Restoration. An average electoral collège numbered about 200 electors, and the effect of introducing into such a body twenty electors pledged to vote for the ministerial candidate speaks for itself.

The next important electoral regulation after the Charter of 1814 was a law of February, 1817. This abolished the whole system of indirect elections, and conferred a direct vote on every male citizen of thirty years or older, who paid a direct tax of 300 francs. There was hereafter to be only one type of electoral collège, which was to meet at the chief town of the department. The Liberal framers of this law had had the fixed intention of devising a scheme whereby the ascendancy at future elections would be given to the middle class. The success of the Liberals in electing their candidates to the Chamber of Deputies — 25 were returned in 1817, 45 in 1818, and the same number in 1819 — pushed the Royalists to devise a new law which they succeeded in passing in the conservative reaction that followed the murder of the Duc de Berri in 1820. This law of 1820, called the "Law of the Double Vote," restored the collège d'arron-

1 Arch. Nat., F^{1c} Seine 5.

dissement, and allowed the members of the departmental collège to vote in both collèges. This last provision meant that about 10,000 voters could vote twice, once in each collège, and they were thus twice represented by the deputies chosen. The membership in the departmental collège was limited to a group of the most heavily taxed inhabitants, equal in number to one quarter of the whole body of electors in the department. The Ultras, who framed this law, hoped that it would keep the control of the Chamber in the hands of the large aristocratic landholders. They seem somehow to have forgotten that taxes on the rights of incorporation, unknown before the Revolution, were now counted as direct taxes and so allowed to large numbers of lawyers and manufacturers the right to vote. In 1824 the Ultras carried their program one step further by abolishing the annual renewal of the Chamber of Deputies by one fifth, and by providing for an entire renewal of the Chamber every seven years.

The practical working of this electoral system revealed its abuses. The presidents of the electoral collèges were appointed by the king, and, as a result, when a local magnate was not selected the president chosen was generally the candidate whom the ministry hoped would be elected. The secretary of the collège and the four tellers were named by the collège. Great importance was attached to these offices by the political parties. The presidents received 1500 to 3000 francs for their services, though sums as high as 47,000 francs were sometimes given to them. The government assumed that some of this money would be used to buy votes — not directly, but through lavish entertainment. A report of 1820 divides the electors into four groups, and tells in detail just how and when each group must be entertained, and what honors, awards, and decorations must be given out.[1] The ministry often sent to these presidents a list of the candidates whose election it favored, and usually with instructions to get as many of them elected as possible.

The collèges d'arrondissement always met about a week earlier than the departmental collèges. Each collège met for ten days, with one session a day. This practice of holding the polls open for ten days favored manœuvres at the last minute. On one occasion, Benjamin Constant, the Liberal candidate of the Department of the Seine, had, just before the closing of the polls, a thousand more votes than his nearest rival, Ternaux, a Royalist. Thereupon the Prefect of the Seine wrote at once to the mayors of the Paris arrondissements: "You know the result of yesterday's session. It is important that all good citizens come forth. I beg of you, then, to have all the electors of your commune go immediately to their assemblies and to vote for M. Ternaux, as the candidate who is the most approved."[2] After the balloting in the collèges d'arrondissement, a list was drawn up from those receiving the greatest number of votes. This list contained double the total number of deputies to be elected by the department. It was then forwarded

1 Arch. Nat. F^7. 4348, 1820.

2 G. D. Weil, *Les élections législatives depuis 1789* (1895), p. 130.

to the departmental collège. The collège d'arrondissement was usually divided into two or more sections, each of which was under a vice-president appointed by the president. Ostensibly this was done to save the elector the trouble and expense of a long journey to record his vote. The real reason, however, was that by a sub-division of the collège into small boards of this sort the voting could be more directly influenced by the president or his representative. The place of meeting was determined by the president, and was sometimes suddenly changed to a town where the prevailing sentiments were more favorable to the government's candidates, or where it would be more difficult for the Liberals to attend.

It was not customary for the candidate to declare himself openly or to do extensive campaigning. In referring to the elections of 1824, a pamphlet published that year in Bordeaux compares French conditions in this regard with those existing in England.

> In France campaigning is limited to intriguing in secret. One may wish to be nominated, but pride forbids that this be made known in public. Publicly question a man who in the bottom of his heart is ardently desirous of being elected to the Chamber of Deputies whether he aspires to this honor, and he will answer you that he has never dreamed of such a thing.[1]

The names of the candidates usually did not even appear in the newspapers, and until nearly the end of the Restoration an election was in many districts hardly more

1 *Du gouvernement représentatif et les élections de 1824* (Bordeaux, 1824).

than "une affaire du salon ou du café"— that is, merely a matter of personal relationships. The election of the successful candidate was looked upon as the bestowal of an honor from the ruling class. A deputy had not yet come to be regarded as the appointed mouthpiece of his constituency. Moreover, the deputies, as in the Revolutionary assemblies, prided themselves on their independence from party ties, and would have scorned the modern practice of voting at the bidding of a party.

After the organization of the Liberal party in 1817, through the "Comité directeur" under Laffitte, Manuel, and Constant, public political speeches became somewhat more common, at least in the larger towns. The custom arose, also, of sending out letters to the electors. This was not difficult, owing to the comparatively small number of electors. This epistolary form of campaigning became common, and was used by both Royalists and Liberals. The letters were usually printed, and numbers of them are still extant, folded into the reports of the prefects. The Liberals were more successful in the use of such letters, whereupon conservative opinion decided against them. "The demagogic effrontery with which at the last election in Paris," said the *Conservateur*, "a candidate appealed for the votes of a certain part of the electors — these printed letters scattered in profusion about the election hall, in game rooms, and goodness knows where else, with their appeals addressed in the name of the nation to all the 'friends of liberty,' asking them to vote for 'the friend of the people'! One recalls the election of Robespierre and other friends of the people."[1] The "Comité directeur" of the Liberal opposition announced through handbills that, "in order to aid the electors to surmount the difficulties which they meet, an office will be open every day at 22 Quai Pelletier, Paris, from 11 to 4. Here electors may receive advice for nothing."[2] The Liberal society, Aide-toi, le Ciel t'aidera, organized electoral committees all over France on a much greater scale. Speeches were made to large gatherings in the open air. This Liberal agitation was gradually arousing public interest in elections.

The electioneering often took the form of an attempt to force the prefects to revise the list of electors, and to enforce the proper posting of these lists. There was undoubtedly a great deal of dishonesty on the part of the prefects in the preparation of these lists. From a study of the police archives one may see what elaborate statistics were kept of nearly all the electors. The opinions of electors at various times during the Restoration, the amount of education of each, the books and newspapers they read, their habits and manner of life, and their supposed influence on others, were all carefully tabulated. The electors were even divided into categories based on the amount of influence each was supposed to have, and those in certain categories were more carefully watched or flattered, as the case might be. The police also advised government officials which electors to entertain at dinner, and for whom to procure titles

1 Weil, pp. 133–134.
2 Weil, p. 134.

and decorations. In all these matters the police and the prefects worked together.

Every time an election was held the Liberals protested that the electoral lists were falsified. Their exasperation is well displayed in an article in the *Constitutionnel* of February 26, 1824. "Innumerable protests are being made all over France against the manipulation of the electoral lists. Many electors are being deprived of their rights. Some with white hair and bent with age have been refused because they had no baptismal certificate at hand, even though they were born before 1794. Others are refused because they cannot show proper papers for possessing lands which have been in their families for years, others for having falsely represented their tax returns, and others, finally, because authorities claim that their first names are not exactly as in the government records." Printed appeals were sent out by the Liberal organizations urging the Liberal electors to see to it that these lists were honestly and correctly made out. Many of these circulars still exist. A typical one of 1830 emphasizes the dangers that threaten all Liberal thought and action, and urges the Liberals of the district to hunt for any names on the electoral list which should not be there, to see that all the electors have really paid the necessary tax and that they are old enough, and, finally, to see that none of the names that should appear are omitted.[1] And then even after the list was prepared the prefect would often refuse to post it until the morning of the election, when it was too late to

1 Arch. Nat., F^7. 6776, Isère.

THE ELECTION LIST

CARICATURE OF 1817

make any rectifications. Another trick was to print the names of the electors in a non-alphabetical list that made them hard to read. Sometimes the prefect had the list posted four or five feet above the heads of the readers. Again, posters eight feet high were put up, with divisions into five and six columns, with much extraneous matter strung along between the names. That these efforts of the Liberals did some good is attested by a report of the Prefect of the Sarthe on January 28, 1830. "The increase of electors in this department from 16 in 1827–8 to 59 in 1828–9 is almost entirely due to the agitation of the Liberals and the forced admission to the electoral lists of some whose rights had before been denied."[1]

In the elections themselves all sorts of means were used to intimidate the voters, and as the voting was not secret this was not hard to manage. The voters wrote out their ballots under the eye of the president. Pressure was freely used. In 1827 a prefect sent out the order: "All government officials must be informed that they must vote. They ought to vote for the president of the electoral collège, who is the government's candidate. Such is the King's intention."[2] The prefects of the Restoration were most of them old men who had won their positions by some service or other rendered to the Bourbon cause during the long years of exile, and they seem to have done everything in their power to please the King. The government itself was fairly

1 Arch. Nat., F[7]. 6776.

2 Duvergier de Hauranne, *Histoire du gouvernement parlementaire en France* (1857–72), IX, 415.

demandative. Peyronnet, the Garde des Sceaux, sent out the following circular letter in January, 1824:

> Whoever accepts employment from the government contracts at the same time the obligation of consecrating all his efforts, his talents, and his influence to the service of the government. It is a contract of which reciprocity forms the bond. If an employee refuses the government the services expected of him he betrays his trust and breaks deliberately the pact of which the position he holds is both the object and the condition. The government owes nothing to him who does not render it its due. Prescribe for your subordinates a prudent and uniform conduct. Condemn unqualifiedly all division of votes, whose surest effect would be to offer chances of success to the opposition.[1]

Ever since the earlier years of the Empire the number of officials in France had been very large, and it is estimated that during the Restoration, exclusive of military officers, half a million persons were in the employ of the state. And as a large portion of an electoral collège was often made up of public functionaries of some kind, the ease with which this type of pressure could be exercised is obvious. The police and prefectoral reports which give the list of candidates elected often say of the Liberal candidates chosen that they were elected "malgré tous nos efforts."

Even the king himself sometimes intervened in elections. In 1816 Louis XVIII issued the following proclamation: "The King expects that the electors will direct all their efforts to keep from the polls all the enemies of the throne and of legitimacy." The next year Louis XVIII explained to the Municipal Council of Paris his

1 Weil, p. 115.

hope that "his people would justify by their choice the confidence he had placed in their love and wisdom." A royal proclamation of 1820 called on all loyal voters "to keep from holding the noble office of deputy the fomenters of trouble, the creators of discord, the propagators of unjust accusations against the government of the King and his family." Finally, in June, 1830, Charles X issued the following: "Frenchmen, the last Chamber of Deputies misconceived my intentions. I must count on your coöperation to do good. O that a single sentiment might move you! It is your king who demands it. It is a father who calls on you."[1] Evidently neither Louis XVIII nor Charles X had any better conception of what parliamentary government really meant than had the majority of their subjects.

The Church was also used as a means of enforcing the choice of the government in elections. The bishops frequently issued orders to vote for the Royalist candidates, and certain bishops used their priests as electoral agents. Here, as elsewhere, methods were used which, to borrow an expression from the president of the royal court at Grenoble, were "très peu délicats." All these abuses became so notorious that in 1828 Martignac sent out a committee to investigate electoral methods and usages. The examination came to little. Eight prefects were, however, condemned on charges that are interesting to note: for having neglected to verify the tax qualifications of voters and eligibles in 1827, for registering other electors whose rights had not been investigated

1 Weil, pp. 110–111.

for three years, for being satisfied with inadequate documentation or with mere hearsay, for ignoring rules as to domicile of parliamentary candidates, and, finally, for having neglected to notify the electors of the formalities necessary to legalize their transactions.

But even had the electoral system been honestly handled, it was really not fitted to give any adequate expression of public opinion. According to the electoral law of 1820, there were in all France, even as late as 1829, only 88,275 electors in a population of about thirty-two million. Through the working of the electoral law of 1820, the selection of the quarter of the electors paying the highest taxes for the departmental collège made the right of being an elector therein depend on paying a direct tax of 1000 francs, which was as high as the tax of eligibility for a deputy. This was true of fifteen departments. The electors were distributed in a most unequal way. The Department of the Seine had 10,000, while Corsica had only 30. Moreover, between a third and a half of the electors never went to the polls. In 1815, out of 72,199 eligible to vote, only 48,478 voted; in 1816, 47,427. In 1819, out of 4800 voters of the Seine-Inférieure 2500 voted, and of 1700 voters of Eure-et-Loir only 938 voted; and these figures are typical. As it was often hard for the country voters to get to the polls, their abstentions from voting were always larger than those of the town dwellers, so that in practice most of the votes were cast by the wealthy bourgeoisie. This explains why, in spite of the government's manipulation of the elections, Liberal candidates were often returned to the Chamber of Deputies.

The majorities which decided elections were usually very small, often not more than ten votes. If, of 88,000 voters, a third abstained from voting, and a tenth of the remainder held the balance in elections, the Chamber of Deputies represented less than 6500 out of a population of thirty-two millions. Out of the 18,000 eligibles for a seat in the Chamber of Deputies, certain departments did not have more than ten men who paid the necessary tax of 1000 francs, and three fourths of the departments did not have more than a hundred eligibles apiece. The Charter had, it is true, foreseen this difficulty, and had provided that there should be at least fifty eligibles for each department, but as the deputies received no pay, and as the expense of living six months a year in Paris was very heavy, many men who were technically eligible would not allow their names to be presented. It was thus frequently the case that the choice of the electoral collège had to be made from two or three candidates. Hence, for all these reasons, the elections of the Restoration never reflected adequately the public opinion of France. Indeed, many departments which were notoriously Liberal returned Ultras to the Chamber of Deputies. Such was the case of Yonne, the Rhône, the Haut-Rhin, and a number of departments in the East of France. In turn, the Vendée, the most Royalist department in France, returned three Liberals, one of them the firebrand Manuel. There was, as a result, almost no relation between the regional distribution of public opinion and the electoral map in the France of the Restoration. The narrow limitations of the suffrage, the widespread abstention from voting, the extensive pressure and manipulation used by the government in all elections, together with the lack of experience and understanding of what a real electoral system or even free government itself is, meant that the Chamber of Deputies failed to represent anything more than a very small segment of public opinion.

IV. THE PRESS AND PUBLIC OPINION

Next to the electoral system, the regulation of the press was the subject most often debated in the Chambers. The Charter contained only the general provision that "Frenchmen had the right to publish their opinions in conformity with laws which should suppress all abuses of this liberty." This was so general that it left all practical interpretation to later ordinances and laws. As a result, the regulation of the press from 1815 to 1830 was in a constant state of change. At first there was no censorship at all, though attacks on public officials and institutions which were considered injurious sometimes brought publishers and editors into court. The first important press law of the Restoration was that of 1819, which provided that a newspaper or periodical containing any political news, and appearing more than once a month, should furnish a money deposit, varying according to the place and nature of the publication, and should submit a copy of everything published to the censorship of the prefect or sub-prefect. Anything not meeting all the conditions of this inspection would leave the publisher open to prosecution. The assassination of the Duc de Berri in 1820, and the fear of all Liberalism which followed, led to the passing of a new bill on the press (1820), the novel feature of which was its requirement of an examination by the censor of every issue of a journal prior to its publication. The punishments for breaking this law were heavy fines, and in some cases the entire suppression of the newspaper. Lest this should not be strong enough, the Ultras in 1822 carried through a still more drastic law. This specified certain new offences, among them "outrages on the religion of the state and on other recognized sects" and "attacks on the hereditary rights of the King." The chief feature, though, of this "Law of Tendency" was the right it gave the government to prosecute the proprietor of a newspaper merely for a general tendency to be unfavorable to the government. This law, for the time being, reduced the Liberal press almost to silence. In Paris all but two Liberal journals ceased to be published, and they continued to appear only after a number of lawsuits. The effect of all these laws depended on their enforcement. This was usually fitful, but after 1822 the existence of the Liberal journals was precarious. Some of the Ultra papers were also fined for the exaggeration of their statements. In 1828 Martignac carried through a more moderate press law which abolished the censorship but still made all periodicals subject to action for slander.

The Ultras, though they used the press, suspected and hated it. "The censorship," said Bonald, "is a sanitary institution established to preserve society from the contagion of false doctrines. In a government where seven or eight thousand landowners, selected from the highest levels of society, come together each year from every part of the kingdom, to meet under the eyes of the authorities, and to discuss their needs, what need is there of a political press?"[1] The prefects complained often of the evils of the press. "These local papers, useful when they can be controlled, have today the effect of fire and poison on everything that is sacred or powerful or honorable."[2] Another writes, "Of a hundred who read the papers, ninety-five at least are blinded by the influence of their patent lies."[3] In 1826 the Abbé Liautard, a priest prominent in Parisian society, petitioned the government to suppress all newspapers and periodicals and supplant them by a government paper, edited by the Minister of Police. This journal was to contain a summary of events of importance, a record of variations in the temperature, and the current prices of wheat, sugar, and other commodities. The government never acted on this, but there were many who shared the ideas of the Right who would have been glad to see it tried. In 1817, Benjamin Constant, Laffitte, Lafayette, and the Duc de Broglie organized a "Société des Amis de la Presse." This organization collected funds which were widely used in helping to pay the expenses of trial and the fines of Liberal journals.

1 Charléty, p. 260.

2 Arch. Nat., F^7. 6776. Prefect of the Corrèze to the Minister of the Interior, December, 1829.

3 Arch. Nat., F^7. 6772. Prefect of the Vendée to the Minister of the Interior, August, 1829.

The chief Royalist papers, beside the official *Moniteur*, were the *Quotidienne*, the *Drapeau Blanc* (1819–30), the *Journal des Débats* (until 1824), and the interesting but short-lived *Conservateur* (1817–20), to which Chateaubriand, Bonald, and Lamennais were the most distinguished contributors. All these papers were at various times subsidized by the ministry. Their stock in trade was ridicule of the pretensions of the middle class, and a violent attack on all ideas and institutions connected with the Revolution. With the withdrawal of the support of Chateaubriand in 1824, these Royalist papers, in spite of their violence, became exceedingly dull.

The most important Liberal papers were the *Minerve Française* (1818–20), the *Indépendant*, which changed its name to the *Constitutionnel*, the *Courrier Français*, and, after 1824, the *Journal des Débats*. In 1830, Thiers, Carrel, and Mignet founded the *National*. These journals were clever at flattering the tastes of the bourgeoisie, usually by glorifying their humble virtues of honesty and industry. The *Constitutionnel* loved to call itself the "journal des épiciers." They were all strongly anti-clerical, and one of the specialties of the *Constitutionnel* was a famous column called the "Gazette ecclésiastique," wherein all the worst possible stories about the ignorance and venality of the priests were set forth in a lively style. These Liberal papers annoyed the government by leaving blank spaces for the parts censored and inviting their readers to use their imaginations.

Both sides made some use of the foreign press. Especially in the English newspapers, under the heading of

"Private Correspondence," it became the custom to express views that could not be published in France. The ministry before 1824 used this method of combating the tactics of the Ultra-Royalists. In the time of the Decazes ministry Decazes himself attacked the Comte d'Artois in the London *Times*. The *Gazette d'Augsbourg* was open to the French Liberals, but it was little read except in Alsace. In Holland and Belgium, united from 1815 to 1830 in a single state, there were many French political refugees. They published numerous pamphlets and a number of journals,— such as *L'Observateur Allemand*, the *Gazette de Brème*, and the *Gazette du Rhin*,— many of which secretly found their way into the hands of French readers across the border.

The younger generation during the reign of Charles X expressed its views in the *Jeune France*, the *Producteur* of the Saint-Simonian group, the *Globe*, the *Tribune des Départements*, and the *National*. One of these, the *Globe*, stands out as the most interesting periodical of the period. Started in 1824 by Dubois, Jouffroy,— two teachers dismissed by Villèle,— and Pierre Leroux, it did not until 1828 have sufficient funds to pay the preliminary deposit to the government, and so was obliged to limit itself to literary and scientific news. Its attitude, as we have seen, was one of contempt for both the old Royalism and the old Liberalism. To these young men of the *Globe* both the older parties were still living in the ideas and philosophies of the eighteenth century. Their program was one of a moderate liberalism in all things, but above all they insisted on the necessity of a revision of all the old values. In the name of liberty, the editors championed Romanticism and demanded the abolition of the old rules in art and literature; in religion they stood for the absolute neutrality of the state; in politics, so far as these were touched upon, they defended the ideas of self-government and the liberty of the press. This brilliant journal soon had a circulation of ten thousand copies, and was read all over Europe. Manzoni in Italy and Goethe in Germany found it the herald of a new day. Like the Doctrinaires, whose views it came nearer to sharing than those of any other political group, the *Globe* was disliked both by the Ultras, who could see in it only another Liberal journal, and by the older Liberals, who were annoyed at its superior tone and at its contempt for many of the old Liberal tactics and shibboleths.

In the provinces, there was for each department a semi-official journal, published twice or three times a week, under the supervision and partially at the expense of the prefecture. It usually contained an article or two quoted from one of the Royalist papers of Paris, a brief chronicle of local news, and some market reports. In the larger cities, when the Liberals were able to support them, opposition papers were published. Chief among these were the *Précurseur* of Lyons, the *Ami de la Charte* of Nantes and another journal of the same name at Clermont-Ferrand, the *Indicateur* of Bordeaux, and the *Phocéen* of Marseilles. The Royalists likewise published a number of provincial papers that were read outside the local district, the most important of which were the

Gazette Universelle of Lyons and the *Echo du Midi* of Toulouse. These provincial newspapers were very simple affairs. Their chief article was usually quoted from one of the great Paris dailies, and the rest was news of purely local interest. At various periods the government forbade the departmental journals to copy articles from the Paris papers until they had passed the censorship a second time. Likewise the Paris journals were not allowed to reproduce articles printed in the departmental papers. On the whole, it was rather the newspapers of the capital that were sought after and read in the departments. In Paris as in the provinces, after 1824, it was only the extremist newspapers of both sides that interested the public.

The total circulation of all newspapers was not large. Single copies were not sold, and only annual subscriptions were accepted. These were comparatively expensive. In addition, a stamp tax of two cents on each copy and a postage charge of one cent increased the cost. Only those who were well-to-do could establish a newspaper, because of the large preliminary deposit required. In 1826 it was estimated that there was in France one newspaper subscription to every 427 persons. In 1823 the estimated subscription lists were as follows: the *Constitutionnel*, 16,250; the *Journal des Débats*, 13,000; the *Quotidienne*, 5800; the *Moniteur*, 2250; and the *Drapeau Blanc*, 1900.[1] The widely prevailing habit of passing newspapers about among friends, in a period

1 Ch. Dupin, *Forces productives et commerciales de la France* (2 vols., 1829), I, xxi; Ch. Simond, *Paris de 1800 à 1900* (3 vols., 1901), I, 306–307.

before books were common, must greatly have increased the number of readers. A German who visited Paris in 1830 was amazed at the number of people he saw reading newspapers. "Everybody reads — the cab-driver while waiting for his client, the fruit dealer in the market, the porter in his hallway. In the Palais Royal a thousand persons sit about in the morning reading newspapers."[1]

This rapid growth in the reading of newspapers and the discussions they aroused in the cafés attracted the attention of the prefects. "The cafés," writes one prefect, "are very much frequented here, as elsewhere. There the newspapers are read and the intentions of the government attacked. Everything that is sacred is made fun of, and the most sinister reports are circulated."[2] The café, even more than the salon, was the great center for political discussions and exchange of opinion. Cafés were common all over France, and in the larger towns both the Liberals and the Royalists had their favorite rendezvous where they met informally over their coffee or beer. Almost every café had at least one newspaper about for its patrons to read. Many who could never themselves have afforded to subscribe to a journal knew very well how things were moving in the political world by reading the papers in the cafés.

Almost as influential as the newspapers were the pamphlets of the Restoration. Chateaubriand, Constant, and Paul-Louis Courier were the most brilliant of many

1 Charléty, p. 125.

2 Arch. Nat., F7. 6767. Prefect of Ardeche to the Minister of the Interior, September, 1829.

who used the pamphlet as a form of political or religious discussion. Many of the poems of Béranger also circulated in this form. Cheaper than books, and more permanent than newspapers, these pamphlets were read and reread, arousing new layers of public opinion, and in the later years of the Restoration spreading further and further the doctrines of Liberalism.

In turning finally to the regional distribution of public opinion during the Restoration, one must say at once that not only has no satisfactory study of this ever been made, but it is doubtful if there is sufficient material to make such a study. Many of the prefectoral reports of the period, especially for the period 1820–30, were destroyed during the Second Empire. Charléty, in his volume on the Restoration in Lavisse's *Histoire de la France contemporaine*, has made some use of the extant reports in a study of public opinion in France in 1820. I have supplemented this survey by a study of the scattered reports for the years 1820 to 1830 in the Archives Nationales in Paris.[1]

All sorts of local conditions affected the movement of public opinion. The method of landholding, the type of crops raised, the presence or absence of large industrial centers, the means of communication, and the amount of foreign influence, were all important factors. On the sentimental side, the memories of the Revolution — Royalist, Republican, and Bonapartist — were still strong. The presence of certain local figures who had played an important rôle in the years 1789 to 1815 often

1 Series F^{1c}. III.

had a large influence on local political views. The degree to which the local party organization had ascendancy through the newspapers, the clergy, and the local notables also formed a significant element in the formation of local opinion. Public opinion, however, is in the last analysis hard to account for, and just why the West and South of France were Royalist and clerical, and why the East and North were rationalist and Liberal, escapes any complete explanation.

The extreme north of France, with its mines and industries, was largely occupied with its own commercial concerns and was not greatly interested in politics. In the large cities, like Lille, the situation was entirely in the hands of the Liberals. The Picards and the people of Laon and Soissons were famous for their attachment to the Revolution. At Saint-Quentin there were 8000 workers who discussed politics in their workshops. Through all this region the middle class was numerous and prosperous, and strongly equalitarian. The clergy found its influence on the wane. The bourgeoisie furnished almost no recruits for the priesthood, and many parishes had no priest.

Toward the east, in Alsace, Lorraine, and the Ardennes, the spirit of Liberalism was reinforced by patriotism and a strong dislike of the Bourbons for having signed the Treaties of Vienna. Education was more highly favored and more widespread than anywhere else outside of Paris. The old nobility had almost entirely disappeared, and the land was distributed in small holdings. The presence of many Protestants weakened the power of the Church, and nowhere did one encounter the pure type of Ultra-Royalism. Following the eastern frontier to the south, one found among the Burgundians a strong love of political discussion. The whole bourgeoisie was Liberal. One of the prefects publicly declared himself a follower of Rousseau at a time when the clergy were calling loudly for the burning of Rousseau's works. Dijon was considered a "foyer de jacobinisme." As elsewhere, the middle class — in this case lawyers, tradesmen, and wine merchants — despised the nobility. In the Department of Côte d'Or around Dijon, 80 communes out of 400 were without a priest, in Yonne the proportion was greater, and in the Saône-et-Loire there were only 252 priests for 605 communes. Schools, which were looked upon with favor, were more numerous than parsonages. In Franche-Comté Ultra-Royalism hardly existed. At Besançon, out of 49 cafés 31 took only the *Constitutionnel*. As in the case of Alsace and Burgundy, Franche-Comté was a region where the anti-clerical "enseignement mutuel" had been popular. Lyons, according to all Royalist accounts, was always cited as "the city faithful to her king," a reputation won in the insurrection of 1793. In reality, after 1815 this Royalism was confined to a small group of old families dispossessed now of all political power. In 1817 the Royalists had tried to organize a White Terror and had failed. The same year, the Liberal Camille Jordan was elected to the Chamber of Deputies. As in many urban centers, the shopkeepers and lawyers were Bonapartists. Lyons became famous for the seditious songs sung in her cafés and for the manufacture of seditious emblems and prints. The near-by district of Beaujolais, where the population had opposed the Civil Constitution of the Clergy, remained an island of ardent royalism. The two departments of the Hautes and Basses-Alpes were sparsely settled. Here the population was poor, and was strongly under the influence of the priests, who were mostly peasant in origin. Almost no newspapers circulated in this mountainous region, and the people knew little about politics. Thus the North and East of France, with these few exceptions, were largely anticlerical and Liberal.

Turning now to the South, we come to Provence, the first large section that was Royalist. Here occurred the worst outrages of the White Terror of 1815. The priests were numerous and schools were few. The Royalist party was well organized, especially at Marseilles and in the larger towns. After 1824, however, this Royalism waned. The *Phocéen* of Marseilles, a rabid Liberal journal, had a large circulation, and probably represented the views of the majority of the middle class during the reign of Charles X. Languedoc was still a battle ground between Catholics and Protestants. Both sides were extreme in their views, and the departments here were usually occupied with local squabbles. After 1824 the prefects noted the rapid growth in the circulation of Liberal papers even in towns that had earlier been considered purely Royalist. The valley of the Garonne, particularly toward its source, shared somewhat the Royalism of Provence. Toulouse, the home of Villèle, was still Royalist, though in a lukewarm way. The peasants of Languedoc were usually prosperous but ignorant. Schools were few, and the clergy fairly strong. As elsewhere, Liberalism had its centers in the towns, where the Liberal journals circulated in the cafés. Bordeaux, whose commerce had been ruined by the Continental Blockade, was strongly Royalist at the opening of the Restoration. This Royalism gradually waned, as it did in Languedoc and Provence. The extreme South-West of France, the departments of Dordogne and Charente, were agricultural districts with no marked political currents. The same is true of the departments of the Massif Central. The clergy recruited from the peasant class were usually ignorant, and fairly influential, though less so than in the country districts of Provence or Brittany. The nobles were very poor, and with little influence except in the most backward districts. The bourgeoisie were, as usual, Liberal, but they were very few in number. The peasants here, as in most other districts, were indifferent, though the least delay in the regular news from Paris caused uneasiness, and set going rumors about tithes and the confiscation of national lands.

Moving up the western side of France, we come to the rich valley of the Loire and its tributaries. Here the peasants were prosperous, but showed little interest in politics. The towns had strong Liberal organizations, especially after 1824, but the comparative indifference of the whole region to politics is striking in view of its prosperity and its easy accessibility to Paris. Nantes was, however, a strong Liberal center. Brittany was a curious mixture. Its country districts, like those of Provence and Languedoc, were strongly Royalist and Clerical. Rennes, Vannes, and Quimper were, on the contrary, decidedly Liberal. Brest was a center for the distribution of Liberal literature through the whole North-West of France. Morbihan, near by, had, however, fewer schools per capita than any department in France, and was Royalist and Clerical. Normandy and the valley of the Seine were divided. Cherbourg, like Brest, was regarded by the government as a "foyer dangereux." The peasants were prosperous, stubborn, and averse to change. Rouen was a strong center of Liberalism. The section about Paris was without an intense political life. From Beauvais to Orléans, and from Chartres to Rheims, there was no class strong enough to dominate. Paris, in the center of this region, was a hotbed of political controversy and the center of all political propaganda; and Paris grew steadily more Liberal from 1815 to 1830.

Thus, if one neglects a few isolated regions in Provence and Brittany which were Royalist, France divided itself politically into two regions: that of the North and East, the most industrialized region of France, which was definitely hostile by tradition and interest to the Restoration, and that of the West from the Pyrénées to the Seine, which accepted the government as a compromise, but paid little attention to politics except in the larger urban centers. Nowhere, except in Brittany and Provence, did the government of the restored Bourbons rest on a profound sentiment of loyalty. The peasants were never free from the fear of the seizure of their lands. The bourgeoisie disliked their exclusion from the highest positions in the army and the government, and they were displeased with the government for the power it gave to the Church. To the great mass of the population the Restoration seemed only to have profited the clergy and the nobility. One can only conclude that the majority of Frenchmen from 1815 to 30 were either hostile or indifferent to the political regime under which they lived.

V. CONCLUSION

From 1814 to 1830 the monarchy struggled with difficulties inherent in the conditions under which the Restoration had been effected. The Bourbons had come back, not because any large number of Frenchmen wanted them, but because no other government seemed possible to the Allies. It was galling to the national pride that the King should owe his crown to foreign intervention. As the popular expression went, "The Allies gave us the Bourbons, but it was Frenchmen who gave us the Bonapartes." The masses always believed that the loss of territory and prestige which France suffered in 1815 was the price the Bourbons had agreed to pay the Allies for their assistance. Indeed one of the first questions asked Louis Philippe in 1830 was, "What are your opinions about the Treaties of 1815?"

At the bidding of the Powers, Louis XVIII had been compelled to adopt an untried form of parliamentary government which fitted very ill with the centralized bureaucracy of the Empire. The Charter which he granted was hopelessly vague and confused on nearly every important aspect of free government. Moreover, the establishment of a party system, the essential complement of a parliamentary regime, in a country still without any real experience in self-government, and at the end of a terrible national upheaval, led to endless and bitter contention, and to that evil practice of splitting up into small parties which has since marked every parliamentary regime in France.[1]

The vast majority of the population was agricultural, and took only slight interest in politics. The people cared little whether the franchise was limited or extended, or whether the press was free or censored. They placed their faith in the Charter, not because it established a parliamentary government, of which they had no conception, but because it prevented a return to the economic and social abuses of the Ancien Régime. They wanted peace and a stable government that would assure prosperity, and though they had no enthusiasm for Louis XVIII, they accepted him.

So things drifted on; and it was not until the accession of Charles X, and the subsequent passage of the "Law of Indemnification" and the "Law of Sacrilege," that the government of the Restoration was brought seriously into question. Charles X surrounded himself

1 Ruggiero (p. 163), observes that, "in order to understand the positive value of political parties, the example of England is not enough; there is also required a religious experience which a Catholic people does not possess — the experience of religious sects."

with advisors who lived in a curious world of ideas utterly alien to the vast majority of the population. The clergy were particularly bitter against anything that savored of the Revolution, and Charles X leaned heavily on the clergy. "The great error of the Bourbons," wrote Cournot, the economist, "as well as of the Royalist party and the clergy during the Restoration, was to compromise both the monarchy and religion. Each communicated to the other, not its force, as it supposed, but its weaknesses. The French have loved and still love Catholicism and royalty, but that which they have never liked has been religion put to the service of politics, or politics put to the service of religion."[1] The hatred of Polignac and of the King in 1830 was due to their social and religious views and their reputation as "priest-ridden Emigrés," rather than to their attempted political tyranny. A year before Polignac had come into power, Metternich had observed that "France is lost. The institutions she possesses do not suit her, and they will fall to pieces. For France there is nothing but the Republic or the Empire. It is possible that France may have once again to pass through confusion to arrive at order."[2] By 1830 the Bourbon regime had alarmed the peasants and disgusted the middle class and the intellectuals. When the government was in distress the mass of the nation stood aloof and let the monarchy fall to pieces.

1 Cournot, *Souvenirs* (1913), p. 129.
2 *Cambridge Mod. His.*, X, 358.

CHAPTER II

THE CLERICAL QUESTION

WHILE France was struggling with the new political regime established by the Charter of 1814, a still more envenomed quarrel was going on over religious questions. Here, even more than in the political field, the old and the new were engaged in a bitter struggle, though politics and religion after 1815 were everywhere intertwined. Political absolutism implied a reactionary religious policy, while the advocates of political Liberalism inevitably joined forces with those who believed in some form of free thought. The Church made the mistake of trying to resurrect a dead political and social regime, and thus it aroused all the old animosities that in the eighteenth century had helped to bring on the Revolution. In no period of modern French history is it possible to understand the political situation without a full consideration of the clerical question.

No institution in France had undergone more vicissitudes of fortune in the momentous years between 1789 and 1815 than the Church. Powerful and wealthy under the Ancien Régime, with a tradition centuries older than that of the monarchy itself, the Church was suddenly deprived of its estates and of its independence by the Civil Constitution of the Clergy of 1791; and it fell even lower in the red days of 1793. During the Reign of

Terror priests married, the church bells were melted into cannon, and the altars were stripped. From the violence of this Robespierrian extremism a sharp reaction appeared at the close of the century with the return of peace and with the rise of Napoleon. Where else had the Revolution shown such violent contrasts?

The French Revolutionary period, taken as a whole, was, however, less anti-religious than it has sometimes been made to appear. Except for the followers of Hébert and of Robespierre, with their worship first of Reason and then of the Supreme Being, all the leaders of the Revolution wished to conserve Catholicism. They dreamed, it is true, of a profoundly modified Catholicism, a Catholicism reformed in its discipline according to Jansenist theories, in its relation to the state according to the Concordat of 1801, and in its spirit according to the ideas of Rousseau. It must be a settlement which gave to the state its full and independent lay existence, and one which would conform with the very radical land policy of the Revolution.

The Napoleonic Concordat shows that the Revolution had strengthened the lay state. The Revolution, too, had made very important contributions to the growth of nationalism. It had inculcated the doctrine that all citizens owed their first and paramount loyalty to the national state, and it had prescribed quasi-religious rites before altars of "la patrie" and over the remains of the dead fallen "pour la patrie." It had inaugurated such nationalist forms as the national flag, the national anthem, and national holidays. All this new political and social orientation meant a loss to the Church. This was merely a part of a general process that had been going on since the close of the Middle Ages. The state had for centuries been gradually taking over from the Church the care of vital statistics, the regulation of family relations, and many other matters that were formerly handled in the parishes or in the old ecclesiastical courts. Also the conduct of poor relief and other forms of charity, and finally the control of education, were made state affairs. The contrast between the Concordat of 1516 — between Leo X and Francis I — and the Concordat of 1801 shows strikingly this growth of the power of the lay state.

Napoleon's Concordat, however, represented some improvement in the status of the Church. The clergy were given state support and the moral backing of the government, though even before the Restoration in 1815 many of the priests were not satisfied with these arrangements. In spite of all that the Concordat did to repair the worst clerical losses of the Revolution, most of the clergy remained during the Empire in secret opposition to the government. Napoleon's regime failed to restore its old landed possessions to the Church. He appointed the bishops himself, and then went further and censored their sermons and pastoral letters. His ill-treatment of Pope Pius VII was displeasing to the faithful. So the majority of the clergy welcomed back the "Son of Saint Louis" in 1814, and again in 1815. They gladly united their cause — as they had in the years of exile — with that of the restored Bourbons and the returning Emigrés.

I. THE CATHOLIC REVIVAL

In 1815 the restored monarch and the nobles of France were no longer the care-free Voltairian gentlemen they had been in the years before 1789. Exile and privation had deprived clergyman and noble alike of their easy-going eighteenth-century skepticism, which they seem to have kept into the early years of the Revolution. Even as late as 1792 the Archbishop of Narbonne had said that the resistance of the upper clergy in 1791 was not due to their faith, but to their honor as gentlemen. By 1815, however, a fervent piety had largely replaced the fashionable skepticism that had dominated the salons up to the downfall of the old monarchy. The royal family and the old nobility owed a great deal to the clergy for the help given to the Royalist and aristocratic causes, both at home and abroad, in the trying years since 1789. For sentimental and for tactical reasons, a close "union between the throne and the altar" had naturally grown up, and by 1815 this had come to mean a common religious and political program of war against the principles of the French Revolution — a program which condemned liberty of conscience, equality of religious sects, and individualism in politics, religion, and philosophy.

The Constitutional Charter of 1814, though it assured freedom of worship in Article 5, spoke in the next article of Catholicism as the "religion of the state." This involved a fundamental contradiction, and, like other terms in this highly ambiguous document, was bound to cause difficulties. The mass of the French people were still Catholic, at least in name. Out of a population of about 32,000,000 there were not more than 680,000 Protestants and 60,000 Jews.[1] It is hard to generalize about the religious faith of the majority of the population. Certainly there had been a gradual decline in faith since the seventeenth century. On the other hand, the gospel of Voltaire, as the Parisian salons knew it, and the anti-clericalism of some of the Revolutionary governments had neither of them penetrated the masses. The majority of Frenchmen were pleased with the restoration of the Church by Napoleon, and, though there was much fear of the Jesuits and of a seizure of the old Church lands, during the Restoration the French people were still profoundly Catholic. The decline in faith was far more marked in the cities than in the country districts. If one may venture a generalization, it would seem that such dislike of the Church as was manifest among the great mass of the French people during the years 1815 to 1830 was due to political rather than to purely religious reasons. Hence after 1815 a moderate Catholic policy on the part of the Church and the state might very well have succeeded.

It was at once evident in 1815 that the return of the Bourbons was to be accompanied by a strong clerical agitation on the part of many churchmen and a reactionary policy on the part of the government. "The throne and the altar" would have their revenge on the Revolution. The most extreme group in this reactionary movement was a small number of bishops who had

1 A. Lods, *Traité de l'administration des cultes* (1896), Appendix.

refused to accept the Concordat of 1801, a group called the "Petite Eglise." Their program was in less degree shared by many of the clergy. It included the abolition of the Concordat of 1801 (above all, the abolition of the hated "Articles Organiques"), the reconstitution of the old dioceses abolished by the Revolution, the restoration of the Church's ancient sources of income, the destruction or sharp limitation of Napoleon's system of state education, the "Université," the prompt restoration of religious orders, especially the Jesuits, the protection of the clergy from attacks by the press, and the abolition of divorce and of civil marriage. It was, in a word, a declaration of war on the Concordat.

While it is true that many of the bishops and priests who had accepted the Concordat were far from being so hostile to the Revolution, in 1815 and 1816, and again in the reign of Charles X (1824–30), the more reactionary elements were in control of the situation. The leader, Talleyrand-Périgord, Archbishop of Rheims, was in 1814 head of the whole Church administration under the Minister of the Interior. This group was in some degree responsible for some of the excesses of the White Terror after the return of Louis XVIII in 1815. Twice the Pope, once in 1819 and again in 1828, tried to dampen this clerical ardor, but during the fifteen years between Waterloo and the July Days of 1830 it grew rather than diminished.

Behind all the political and social changes there existed among the intellectuals of the time a new attitude toward the Church and toward Christianity itself.

Even before the end of the eighteenth century a certain reaction against atheism and doctrinaire rationalism had appeared. Diderot, Voltaire, and Holbach had taught the generation that made the Revolution that historic Christianity was a vast imposture. But by 1800 this doctrine was no longer fashionable, nor was it even acceptable to Napoleon's government, which had now made its terms with the Church. Thus by 1801 both the philosophic and the popular emotional reaction toward historic Christianity which followed the downfall of Robespierre had found official recognition.

This new Christian apologetic is very interesting to trace. It paralleled the exaggerations of the French Revolution which had tried to put into legislation and into institutions the philosophy of Voltaire and Rousseau. These attempts had seemed absurd to many thinking men, and from such extravagances and violence a reaction was bound to come. In 1796 there appeared two works which clearly marked the turn of the tide.[1] One of these, *Considérations sur la France*, was the work of a subject of the King of Sardinia, Joseph de Maistre; the other, Bonald's *Théorie du pouvoir politique et religieux*, was written by an embittered French exile. Here was a new note. Along with a fierce hatred of the Revolution appeared an ardent devotion to the Catholic faith, all set forth with the keenest dialectic. De Mais-

1 Even before this, Mallet du Pan had published his *Correspondance Politique* in Germany, while Rivarol and others had collaborated on the *Spectateur du nord.* Both were interested in a new philosophic and religious orientation. Cf. Boas, *French Philosophers of the Romantic Period* (Baltimore, 1925), p. 70.

tre had been in correspondence with Louis XVIII, and at least in one instance had written under Louis XVIII's direction. Bonald, born in 1754, the same year as de Maistre, had suffered as an émigré. Both men attacked the whole modern political, social, and religious idea of individualism as it had existed since the Reformation. The world had gone mad because individuals had anchored their faith in human reason. There had disappeared from the moral order in the eighteenth century two fundamental sentiments: the sense of the supernatural and the sense of tradition. The "principles of 1789"— individualism, belief in science, and faith in human progress and perfectibility — were the very epitome of evil. "Liberty and equality," says Bonald, "are only the love of domination and the hatred of all authority that is not exercised by yourself."[1] Much of this argument may seem an offence to reason, but to them contrariety to reason is the sign and seal of truth. Authority, as first established by God and then tested through the centuries by experience,— not by reason alone,— is the only sure guide.[2] As has been seen in discussing the political aspects of the doctrines of Joseph de Maistre and Bonald, they abhorred Rousseau's idea that society is a thing established, for convenience' sake, by a social contract out of an original state of nature in which all men were free and virtuous. Men are not

1 Cited Desdevises du Dézert, *L'église et l'état en France* (*1908*), II, 31.

2 Boas (p. 74) points out the similarity in many of Hegel's and Bonald's political and social ideas, and concludes that the really basic difference between the two men is Hegel's Protestant and Bonald's Catholic background.

good by nature, but corrupt, was the answer of Bonald and de Maistre. It is the old ascetic tradition of Paul, Augustine, and Calvin. "Man exists only for society," says Bonald, "and society forms him only for herself."[1] Plato and Hegel hold the same view, though hardly in so extreme a form.

The Revolution and its calamities are quite as much the result of skepticism in religion as of radicalism in politics. Both arose from the evil ideas of the eighteenth century, "ce vilain siècle." It is as impossible to discover ultimate truth by reason as it is by reason alone to frame a good constitution for a state. Nothing is more vicious or inane than to believe in these things. Change exists, but it is evil. Over against reason they set divine revelation, embodied in the Pope and the Catholic Church, and in long-established institutions. Both, as we have seen, supported the theory of the divine right of kings, and both believed in political absolutism, but above the state, as a court of final appeal, they placed the Pope. The Pope is the source of Truth here below. The king is responsible to Truth. Hence the Pope may advise and admonish kings. Part of their theory brought them to the same conclusions that had been set forth by Bossuet in the seventeenth century, but they disagreed with Bossuet in being strongly anti-Gallican in their devotion to the Pope.

The works of Joseph de Maistre and Bonald did not have a wide circulation in France until after 1815. Bonald's influence during the Restoration was largely

1 Bonald, *Théorie du pouvoir politique et religieux*, Préface, p. 3.

exerted through his speeches in the Chamber of Peers. De Maistre continued to write, and his later books, especially *Du pape* (1819) and *Soirées de Saint Pétersbourg* (1821), had a large circulation. From his letters we know him to have been a man of extraordinary wit and personal charm, and a man of warm human feeling. Few of these qualities, however, did he allow to enter his cold and almost repellent books. Both men, though they were extraordinary dialectitians, were lacking in popular appeal.

Bonald and de Maistre furnished an excellent and perfectly reasoned defence for the Catholics of the Ancien Régime, but they had little to offer that would allure a young and restless generation. They did not desire so much to rescue souls as to rescue tradition. They craved religion as a panacea for lawlessness, and the persistency of their appeal to authority is due to their bankruptcy in everything except authority. Their writings, especially those of Bonald, were excessively dry, and their style was as coldly analytical as that of the most rationalistic of the eighteenth-century Philosophers whose doctrines they execrated but whose style and whose weaknesses they unwittingly shared. In Bonald, there is for every argument the same application of cause, means, and effect, the same grave, monotonous tempo. Indeed, Bonald is almost unreadable because of the very passionlessness on which he prided himself. Both Bonald and de Maistre found more readers than disciples. The younger generation was to be reached, not by dogma and dialectic, not by the Christianity of a reactionary government, nor by a Christianity with the personality of Jesus left out entirely, nor, finally, by a religion that was merely an engine of social repression. They could only be aroused by enthusiasm and sentiment. These qualities Chateaubriand possessed to an unusual degree.

In 1802, Chateaubriand published his *Génie du christianisme*, whose original title, significantly enough, was *Beautés de la religion chrétienne*. It was a rhetorical and rather shallow book which nevertheless had a tremendous vogue. No book was ever more opportune. On the day when a Te Deum was sung at Notre Dame in honor of the establishment of the Concordat, Napoleon ordered a long review of Chateaubriand's book to appear in the *Moniteur*. The *Génie du christianisme* was as much a part of the program of Napoleon's celebration of the Concordat as the décor at Notre Dame or the gorgeous liveries of his attendants. The argument was all founded on emotional conviction and the religion of the heart, borrowed largely from the confession of faith of Rousseau's Savoyard vicar. It appealed to the imagination and to sentiment, not to reason.

As a young man Chateaubriand's mind had been fed on history, on Montesquieu, on Voltaire and Bossuet, whose stylistic manner he sometimes imitated, and above all others on Rousseau, whose ideals he detested but whose type of imagination he adored. During the Revolution he had suffered privation and wretchedness in years of wandering exile. In his *Essais sur les révolutions* of 1797, Chateaubriand had criticized the faith of the philosophers in scientific progress and human perfectibility, the two great positive ideals of the eighteenth century — "a century," as he adds, "that doubted nothing except the existence of God." Chateaubriand's own conversion, which followed his mother's death and which he describes in the short phrase, "I wept and I believed," furnished the motive for the writing of the *Génie du christianisme*, and gives one also the essential character of his apologetic. "It was," says Brandes, "a parade religion, a tool for the politician, a lyre for the poet, a symbol for the philosopher, a fashion for the man of the world."[1] Brandes goes on to say that "in the seventeenth century men believed in Christianity, in the eighteenth they renounced it and expiated it, and now, in the nineteenth, they looked at it pathetically from the outside, as one looks at an object in a museum and says 'How poetic,' 'How touching.' Fragments from the ruins of monasteries were set up in gardens; a gold cross was thought a most becoming ornament for a fashionable lady; the audiences at sacred concerts melted into tears. . . . To make the antiquated principle of authority look young and attractive they painted it with the rouge of sentimental enthusiasm."[2]

In his plea for a Christian revival, Chateaubriand emphasized the long tradition of Christian service to the race, its monastic schools and hospitals, and its love of the downtrodden through the ages. Chateaubriand said he wrote his book "to prove that of all religions

1 G. Brandes, p. 79.
2 Brandes, p. 85.

that have ever existed the Christian religion is the most poetic, the most human, and the most favorable to liberty, art, and letters. The modern world owes it everything from agriculture to the abstract sciences, from humble hospices for the downtrodden to the churches built by Michelangelo and decorated by Raphael."[1] It was all written in a glowing and passionate style. "Chateaubriand was," says Sainte-Beuve, "an Epicurean who had a Catholic imagination." He calls attention to the beauty of the Gothic art, to the rich splendor of the Mass, to the poetry of bells, of mediæval ruins, and of Christian legends. Here is no cynicism, no raillery, and no frigid dialectic. His pages are rich with eloquence and perfumed with melancholy and reverie. His work is not great in thought, but in sentiment and oratory, and, above all else, in a certain opportuneness. It rambles on without plan, and the reasoned defence of Christianity is often most amazing. The Trinity is proved by the Three Graces, clerical celibacy is supported by the Malthusian theory, and the divine creation of animals is demonstrated by the statement that each animal is furnished at birth with just the amount of instinct necessary to provide it with food. Priam, Plato, and Diana are brought into the chapter on "Chastity." The Christian and the pagan are strangely mingled. Yet, with all its incoherence, no book had a greater effect on the religious life of France during the first three decades of the nineteenth century.

The same attitude, though less clearly formulated,

1 A. Cresson, *Les courants de la pensée philosophique française* (1927), II, 69.

may be found in the early work of Lamartine and Hugo. Lamartine was before 1830 an ardent Catholic and Royalist. He wrote an ode to Bonald in which he called him the "modern Moses, who derived from the rays of the new Sinai the divine light with which he illuminated human laws." Lamartine also wrote for Chateaubriand's *Conservateur*, and after that was given up he joined with Lamennais and Bonald in founding a new reactionary paper, the *Défenseur*. Louis XVIII was so pleased with the ardent royalism and Catholicism of Hugo's early poetry that in 1822 he gave him a pension of a thousand francs, which he increased in 1823 and again in 1826. The King had good reason for showing approval, for these early poems of Hugo contain the whole system of orthodox political and religious principles valid under the Restoration.

Certain it is that by 1815 France had achieved a new religious orientation. The old skepticism of the eighteenth century had waned, and even the official Catholicism of Napoleon now seemed inadequate.

II. THE LIFE OF THE CLERGY

While the struggle between Ultra-Royalists and freethinkers was raging in the press and in the Chamber of Deputies, the life of the parish clergy, especially outside of a few of the larger cities, went on very much as it had before the Revolution. In general, the parish priests were poorly educated. In the country districts the priests had won the reputation of being conscientious and hard-working, though they were insufficient in numbers. Before 1789 about 6000 priests had been ordained each year, but between 1801 and 1815, in a period of fourteen years, only the same number, 6000, had been ordained.[1] After 1814 each department was allowed a seminary for the training of priests; yet in 1820 there were 1500 positions vacant out of 50,000.[2]

The clergy of the Restoration were more ardent than they had been in the easy-going eighteenth century. The priests of the time of the Revolution were now many of them dead, and the parishes were supplied more and more after 1815 with young men who had grown up hating the Revolution. The priests in Balzac's novels show, however, that in many ways the life of the clergy had not changed in its essentials since the days of the Ancien Régime. In the *Curé de Campagne* Balzac presents a priest's life of humble devotion; in the *Curé de Tours* the priest's life is one of petty intrigues. In other novels Balzac pictures priests who are the tame pets of great families.

The Concordat of 1801 had given the bishops more power in the control of their dioceses. Before the Revolution the bishop had often had to tolerate opposition from his priests. Moreover, he had often to consult the monastic clergy, or even lay individuals, in the granting of a benefice. After 1801, and more so after 1815, the bishop became a pope in his own diocese. He appointed the local priests, who were then supposed to be irremovable. To get around this restriction the bishop some-

1 G. Goyau, *Histoire de la nation française: histoire religieuse* (1922), p. 553.
2 Charléty, p. 156.

times forced priests to keep their resignations on file in the diocesan offices. The bishop of the Restoration was as much in command of his clergy as the colonel of his regiment. He taught in the seminary of his diocese. He kept an eye on all local matters through frequent pastoral visits. The clergy had become in its administration, as the First Consul had wished it, a corps of closely regulated functionaries controlled by the bishops for the state and paid by the state. Many of the higher clergy after 1815 were rather old men who held their positions largely because of their devotion to the Royalist cause during the revolutionary upheaval. Especially was this true of the bishops appointed to the new dioceses created in 1821. Many were nobles. Brought up in the ideas of another age, they were often curious anomalies in the civilization of the nineteenth century. Among the clergy of all degrees were a few men of great learning, and others who were able administrators and controversialists, but the number of clerics with any general interest in the new currents of the time was very small.

The chief differences of clerical opinion, in the earlier years of the Restoration, arose over the continuance of the Napoleonic Concordat, and, after the accession of Charles X in 1824, over the old seventeenth-century problem of Gallicanism versus Ultramontanism. The opposition of a small group of priests — "La Petite Eglise"— to the Concordat never amounted to much, and by 1820 had practically died out — or, in other words, this controversy was gradually merged with the

Gallican and Ultramontane discussions of the reign of Charles X. The doctrine held by the majority of the clergy, a doctrine taught at the famous seminary of Saint-Sulpice in Paris, and officially set forth in Frayssinous' *Les vrais principes de l'église gallicane*, was the moderate and conciliatory view of the historic Gallicanism of Bossuet, which had been held by the majority of the clergy in the last century of the Ancien Régime. While believing strongly in the importance of the Church in civil society, and holding in bitter hatred the deism and rationalism of the eighteenth century and everything that was reminiscent of it in the nineteenth, they had no more exalted ideal than that of settling down to the quiet round of duties and offices that had marked the days of the old monarchy. This type of bishop and priest somewhat resembled the typical English "fox-hunting parson" against whom Newman and the leaders of the Oxford Movement were to raise a protest in the thirties.[1]

The two most interesting activities of the clergy, besides the daily round of parish and diocese, lay in the work of the Missionaries and in the Congrégation. The religious orders — the monastic clergy — had been abolished by the Revolution, and the Napoleonic government had been very slow in authorizing the establishment of new orders, though these had at least been

1 There is an interesting glimpse of the daily life of the clergy in a report of the Prefect of Corrèze: "Vertueux et zêlé, le clergé s'apperçoit à la tendance des esprits que l'autel et le trône s'appuyent et par son action les principes monarchiques non moins que les idées morales, s'entretiennent paisiblement dans les campagnes écartées des villes." (Arch. Nat., F^7. 6776.)

permitted by the Concordat. By 1815 several hundred convents for women had been authorized, but only a few monasteries for men had been allowed. After 1815 the same laws demanding governmental authorization were more leniently applied and a number of orders were allowed. Most of these were old religious orders that had existed before the Revolution. A few were new. In some cases the orders came in, opened schools, and carried on their work without government authorization. This was possible because the prefects were often willing officially to ignore their existence. The Jesuits had not been readmitted, at least under their old name, though it was generally recognized that the "Pères de la Foi" were the Jesuits under a new name, and that these men had a large place in the work of the Missionaries and of the Congrégation.

The "Société des Missions de France," founded in 1816, sent out, from its central house on Mont Valérien near Paris, bands of priests who went about the country, even to very remote districts, holding revivals and preaching. Their preaching, which was frequently in the open air, was in a simple, familiar, and often highly emotional form, very well suited to appeal to the great crowds that gathered to hear them. The organization of the enterprise followed the model of the old "Missions étrangères" which had been sent out earlier to convert the heathen of Asia and the Americas. These new "Missions de France" set up as their object the restoration of the religious and monarchical faith of France, which the Revolution had so profoundly disturbed.

A group of four or five Missionaries would go into a town, gather together a large mixed chorus which sang hymns to popular tunes of the day, preach during several weeks, and then finally organize a great "cérémonie de réparation." On this occasion a large cross, sometimes eighty feet high, was borne in solemn procession and planted in some prominent place, in the presence of the prefect, or the mayor, or some other important governmental official. Then, at the cross, public penance was made for the outrages of the Revolution and for the death of Louis XVI, of Louis XVII, and of "l'auguste Marie Antoinette et l'inimitable Elisabeth." The ceremony was closed with an oath to maintain religion and legitimate government. After 1817 there was added to this closing manifestation "la guerre aux mauvais livres," in which a great auto-da-fé was held and the works of Voltaire and Rousseau were consigned to the flames. Sometimes these Missionaries created something of a sensation with their preaching. Before quitting a town, there was a final distribution of medals and rosaries, and when they left it was the custom for a great crowd to follow them out of town. After the Missionaries departed — "ces pieuses caravanes," as one wit has called them — churches were more frequented and balls and parties were for a time given up. But skeptics saw in this only the hypocrisy of people trying to achieve social status or of public officials trying to get advancement by parading their piety.

Sometimes the violent attacks of the Missionaries on the great men of the Revolution or on those who had acquired national lands led to demonstrations so hostile that the police had to intervene. The Liberals also protested strongly against the frequent appearance of public officials in the ceremonies of the missions, especially when they came in such large numbers that they were suspected of obeying the government's orders. Others took part in these extravagant ceremonies to court favor. Certainly few public officials dared to show their disapproval of the methods of conversion used by the Missionaries. The missions seem to have had no permanent effect on manners and morals, and they did much to discredit the whole work of the Church.[1]

A branch of Church activity that gave rise to even more heated controversy was the famous "Congrégation de la Vierge." As in the case of the work of the Missionaries, no definitive study of the Congrégation has ever been made, and the available accounts are all somewhat biased. The Congrégation was a society partly ecclesiastical and partly lay, the members of which were bound to use for the general good of society any political or other useful information or influence which they might be able to command. It had been founded as far back as 1801, and, though suppressed by Napoleon in 1810, had continued to exist secretly until it dared again to come out into the open in 1814. From

1 Viel-Castel, whose judgments on the Restoration are usually sound, says of the missions, "Il faut reconnaître que la faveur réelle ou apparente des sentiments religieux était un titre puissant pour l'obtention des emplois, et que même dans les professions qui semblaient les plus étrangères à la politique, celles de notaire, d'avoué, d'huissier, les opinions religieuses des titulaires et des aspirants étaient trop souvent un motif d'admission ou d'exclusion." [Viel-Castel, *Histoire de la Restauration* (1860–78), XI, 96.]

1815 to 1828 it had its central offices of direction on the rue du Bac in Paris, but after that year, to divert public attention its main offices and assembly-room were moved to the Hôtel de Rohan. Branches of the mother society in Paris were scattered over the kingdom. While it is true, as the members claimed, that its fundamental statutes never urged anything except piety and charity, in practice its political and social influence was widespread.

The Liberals always insisted that the Congrégation was very closely connected with the Jesuits, whose headquarters at Montrouge, on the outskirts of Paris, were allowed to exist in spite of the laws against unauthorized religious orders. A Society for the Propagation of the Faith, founded at Lyons in 1822 under the patronage of Saint Francis Xavier, was directed by the Grand Aumônier de France, a government appointee. The public was, of course, convinced of the influence of the Jesuits in the government. In 1826, Frayssinous, then Minister of Ecclesiastical Affairs, publicly acknowledged the existence of the Jesuits, so that it was no longer possible to deny that this much-hated order was at work in France. According to public rumor, it was to Montrouge that Père Rousin, a well-known Jesuit and also a leader of the Congrégation, brought some of his most promising disciples, as well as various persons of high rank, to be admitted as "Jesuits of the short robe"—that is, as lay members of the order. The Jesuits have always denied this, holding that the rules of their order did not allow any such lay affiliation. Though there exists no positive proof of a connection, the prominence of the same persons in both organizations seem to indicate an affiliation between the Jesuits and the leaders of the Congrégation. Week after week the public saw the rue du Bac crowded with the carriages of the aristocracy and the higher officials of the civil administration. It was known that these meetings in the Convent of Foreign Missions were closed to all who were not members of the Congrégation, and no one believed that so many people would gather merely to listen to a Mass and a sermon which they could easily hear in the churches of Paris. The public saw in these mysterious meetings a great conspiracy against all the liberties for which the Revolution had stood, particularly since the Comte d'Artois and his circle of political reactionaries were among the most prominent members.

Subject to the direction of the Congrégation were a large number of auxiliary societies: La Société des Bonnes Œuvres, devoted to charity; La Maison de Refuge des Jeunes Condamnés; La Société de Saint Joseph, which did charitable work among the laboring classes; La Société des Bonnes Etudes, designed to work among students and young men in the middle classes about to enter the civil service or the professions; and La Société Catholique des Bons Livres and La Bibliothèque Catholique, which proposed to fight evil books, and in two years alone distributed over 800,000 volumes of Catholic literature.

Among the most prominent members of the Congrégation itself were a great many prominent Ultras: Mathieu de Montmorency, Minister of Foreign Affairs under Villèle; Franchet d'Espérey, Director of Police; Delavau, at one time Prefect of Police; the Duc de Doudeauville, Director of the Postal Service; and the Prince de Polignac. There are no authoritative statistics on the number of members enrolled in the Congrégation. The most reliable estimate gives 1400 as the number enrolled in the main organization and 48,000 as the number in all the affiliated societies.[1] It was not the numbers, however, but the high position of some of its members and the known violence of their religious and political pronouncements, that gave the Congrégation its great prominence in all political and religious discussions. It was only natural that a mysterious and considerable power should be attributed to it. At a time when the secret police were especially active, many were indignant to see the Prefect of Police one of the important members of the Congrégation. The learned world was aroused when the candidate of the Congrégation, Récamier, obtained the chair of medicine for which the Collège de France and Académie des Sciences had recommended Magendié. Scarcely a month passed without some scandal of this sort coming to the attention of the public. The exaggerated insistence of certain members of the Congrégation that they had no aims save "piety and charity" and had never meddled in the affairs of the government did not allay suspicions. Some members of the Congrégation finally acknowledged that a group of its members, among them Mathieu de Montmorency, Alexis de Noailles, Delavau, and Franchet

1 G. de Grandmaison, *La Congrégation* (1889), pp. 313–314.

d'Espérey, had worked hard to place certain men in government offices.[1] The best witness on the whole subject of the Congrégation is Viel-Castel. He was a strong Royalist and a nobleman who had in his youth served the government of the Restoration. His final comment on the Congrégation is interesting and fair: "Among the members of the Congrégation, some, especially at the beginning, joined from purely religious motives, in others these motives were mixed with political considerations, while still others joined only to advance their fortunes."[2]

While the partisans and the adversaries of the Catholic Church stirred France with their discussions, the Protestant Church continued a modest but steady religious work. Without legal existence for a hundred years before the Revolution, Protestantism had been barely kept alive in France. Its ministers were trained in Switzerland, Germany, and England, and its work had to be carried on in secret. The Protestant Church in France was legalized by Napoleon, and in 1806 there were 479,312 Calvinists and 201,408 Lutherans in France.[3] The Charter of 1814 confirmed the revolutionary principle of freedom of worship as well as the Napoleonic agreement that the clergy be paid by the state. The Protestants during the Restoration, though

1 Frayssinous' official defence of the Congrégation and of the Jesuits — a defence made for the government in which he was a minister — was made in the Chambers in 1826. It is summarized in Debidour, *Histoire des rapports de l'église et de l'état* (2d ed., 1911), I, 394–395.

2 Viel-Castel, IV, 478.

3 Lods, Appendix.

denounced by certain Catholic writers and by the Missionaries in their sermons, were — except in the White Terror of 1815 — left unmolested.

In 1818 the French Protestant Bible Society was founded, to provide Bibles for Protestant children. In 1822 the Protestant Société des Missions began its work. In 1829 Guizot and a group of Protestants founded La Société pour l'Encouragement de l'Instruction primaire parmi les Protestants de France. The new toleration after 1801 was renewing the forces of French Protestantism. Among the most prominent Protestants of the Restoration were Guizot, the statesman, Cuvier, the scientist, and his friend, a remarkable Alsatian pastor and social reformer, Jean Frédéric Oberlin. It was a group of Protestant manufacturers of the department of the Haut-Rhin who saw first in France the social obligations of the capitalist to the workers. Within the Protestant churches, both Calvinist and Lutheran, there were sharp differences in religious opinion between the liberals and the orthodox. The orthodox said it was impossible to maintain the Church without discipline and a common dogma, and they found these in the decisions of the Protestant theologians of the sixteenth century. The liberals maintained that the root idea of Protestantism was free inquiry and the right of the individual to interpret the Bible. The center of orthodoxy after 1815 was Geneva, where a conservation revival called "Le Réveil" was started. The two chief figures of the Réveil in France were the Monod brothers, one of whom, Adolph, gained the reputation under the July Monarchy of being the most powerful Protestant preacher in France. An important manifesto of French liberal Protestantism appeared in 1829 — *Les vues sur le protestantisme*, by Vincent, the Protestant pastor of Nîmes. It was a clear and able defence of Protestant liberalism. The greatest of all liberal French Protestant thinkers, Alexandre Vinet, was a Swiss citizen. From his position at Basel, however, he exercised an important influence on French thought. His first two important works, *Mémoires en faveur de la liberté des cultes* (1826) and *Essai sur la conscience* (1829), belong to the period of the Restoration. His emphasis was on conscience and on the value of a personal religion, and he believed in the complete separation of church and state. He was a man of great intellect and persuasiveness, and his influence, which belongs rather to the history of the July Monarchy, was great.

There were about 60,000 Jews in France during the period of the Restoration. Judaism had been emancipated in 1791, and had received official recognition in 1808, though the Jewish rabbis in France were not paid by the state until 1831. Napoleon had, however, suspended for ten years the rights of the Jews in Alsace, in order to encourage them to become more thoroughly French in their culture. This ban was lifted in 1818. Most of the Jews in France were at this time to be found near Avignon, in the old papal Comtat Venaissin, about Bordeaux, where they were mostly Portuguese, and in Alsace.

A survey of the religious situation in Franee should at least mention the Freemasons. Freemasonry had been introduced into France from Scotland early in the eighteenth century, with the object of helping the cause of the Stuarts. Thus by a strange irony of fate the association the members of which the Pope has since excommunicated, and which has been regarded as the worst enemy of hereditary kingship, was originally brought into France for the purpose of upholding the legitimist rights of the Stuarts, who in turn were using their influence to extend the power of the Catholic Church. In 1772 the Grand Orient de France was reorganized under the Grand Mastership of the Duc de Chartres, the famous Philippe Egalité. Many nobles joined, and these Freemason lodges before the Revolution were often anti-clerical and anti-monarchical. Napoleon favored the Masonic lodges, regarding them as a necessary outlet for the repressed political energies of the people. Under the Empire the order grew rapidly, in spite of the fact that it had split into two organizations. One of these was directed by the Grand Orient de France, the other by the Scotch Supreme Council. The Grand Orient, which after 1818 had as its head Marshal Macdonald, was much more democratic than the Supreme Council under the direction first of the Duc Decazes, then of the Duc de Choiseul. The Freemasons always declared they did not meddle in politics and respected any government in power. They were, however, greatly suspected by all conservatives, who openly accused them of being the main cause of the French

Revolution. During the Restoration some of the Freemasons were well-known radicals, and there was probably some relationship between some of the Masonic organizations and the Carbonari.

III. CHURCH AND STATE UNDER LOUIS XVIII

Politics and religion in the France of the Restoration were so inextricably mixed there is no understanding of the one without a full consideration of the other. Indeed, as we shall see, many of the political questions of the day were more religious than they were political. The political Liberals usually centered their attack on the influence of the Church in politics and in education. They were convinced that many of the clergy wanted to restore that combination of divine-right monarchy, landed aristocracy, and established church that had dominated the society and the culture of the Ancien Régime.

In the earlier years of the Restoration the government found itself in a very trying situation in regard to the Church. The mass of the population wanted peace, but there were groups of ardent Catholics on the one hand and protesting freethinkers on the other who were dissatisfied with any compromise that might be proposed. A middle course of "healing the wounds of the Revolution" was even more difficult than in the field of politics. The fanatical Catholics were responsible for some of the worst excesses of the White Terror, especially for the attack on the Protestants at Nîmes and on the Jews in Alsace. The King, Louis XVIII, was inclined to be tolerant, but he depended on the clergy for support, and the extreme Catholics hoped they would be able to use him. In 1814 Louis XVIII had said that "The restoration of the altar ought to follow the restoration of the throne." Earlier, in the dark days of his exile during the Empire, he had written that "the bishop should persuade his subjects of the intimate connection between the throne and the altar, and he should show them that, as they cannot count on any happiness in the life to come without religion, they cannot hope for any in this life without the monarchy."[1] Still, in comparison with his brother, the Comte d'Artois, Louis XVIII seems rather an admirer of Voltaire than of Loyola. He tried, at least before 1820, to restrain the more insistent clericals. For this his brother denounced him to the Czar, Alexander I, as a Jacobin. Louis XVIII was really a churchman of the point of view of Louis XIV and of the Gallicans of the seventeenth and eighteenth centuries. The Catholic Church seemed to him one of the most useful agents for the reconstruction of France, and both for religious and for political reasons he was obliged to lean on the Church. His dislike of the Concordat, however, seems to have been due chiefly to thc fact that it was the work of a usurper. In the end he proved too easy-going to stem the tide of clerical reaction led by his brother the Comte d'Artois, who in 1824 became Charles X.

During the first Restoration, in 1814, the King issued a series of royal ordinances, forbidding work on Sun-

1 Lucas Dubreton, *Louis XVIII* (New York, 1927), p. 108.

day, under penalty of a heavy fine, ordering the closing of the shops during religious services, forbidding dancing and merrymaking on certain occasions, and com manding the decoration of all houses for the religious processions on Corpus Christi Day. These ordinances lasted until they ceased to be enforced after the Revolution of 1830. They were widely disliked, and were bitterly ridiculed in the poetry of Béranger and in the brilliant anti-clerical pamphlets of Paul-Louis Courier, especially in *La pétition pour des villageois qu'on empêche de danser*. A counter-revolution in religion had already begun.

In 1814 the most bitter attack of the clericals was on the Université, Napoleon's system of public education. The Université de France was one of the great achievements of the Revolutionary period. Planned in the earlier stages of the Revolution, the system was organized and put into working order by Napoleon. It was the first general scheme of national education which was to be state-supported and state-directed, compulsory and universal, and in which national patriotism and national duty were to be taught equally with the three R's. Because this system of education was to be handled by the state independently of the Church, it was anathema to the clericals.[1]

1 The Université was characterized in 1814 as "un mélange impur de clercs et de laïques, de prêtres mariés, d'apostats, de déistes, d'incrédules, de banqueroutiers et de divorcés." "Mémoire anonyme sur l'université," 1814. At the same time Lamennais spoke of the Université as "la conception de toutes les conceptions de Bonaparte la plus effrayante et la plus anti-sociale," . . . "monument de la haine du tyran contre les générations futures." [Lamennais, *De l'Université Impériale*, (1814).]

Early in 1814 a royal ordinance abolished the Université and in its place established seventeen regional departments of education, each under the local prefect and the local bishop. Alongside the regular government schools, there were to be established secondary ecclesiastical schools, "les petits séminaires," under the entire control of the clergy. These schools, which were intended for the earlier training of priests, before they entered "les grands séminaires," were not supposed to take any lay students. This provision was ignored in practice, and, as was very soon evident, the Church intended to turn the "petits séminaires" into a system of illegal but tolerated secondary education. The return from Elba came before the seventeen regional departments of education had been established. The Université had for the time being weathered the storm, though it had from this time on to meet the serious competition of the authorized "petits séminaires."

In the Chambre Introuvable of 1815 the militant Catholics called for the passing of a series of extreme measures: that men be outlawed if they professed no religion, that the Université be abolished or placed entirely under the control of the Church, that divorce be abolished, and that the clergy be given an income independent of annual grants of the Chambers. After long debates, the extreme clericals made only two gains: laws were passed abolishing the pensions of married priests and denying the right of divorce. The abolition of divorce was a pure piece of clerical reaction. Divorce had been made too easy by the law of 1793, but the Civil

Code of Napoleon had remedied this and had provided a reasonable regulation of divorce. Failing to gain more through the Chambers, the extremists persuaded Louis XVIII to draw up a number of royal ordinances. These were directed chiefly against the Université, where, according to Chateaubriand, "children became irreligious and debauched and contemptuous of all virtues." The Institut de France, a creation of Napoleon, was dissolved. The Université, though it was declared to be only temporary, was not so severely handled. Louis XVIII, who usually had much better judgment than most of his followers, realized that the abolition of Napoleon's form of state education was impossible. The position of the Grand Maître of the Université was, however, abolished, and the school system was placed under a Commission of Public Instruction which was to form part of the Ministry of the Interior.[1] Royer-Collard was made head of this Commission. Gradually and with a genuine spirit of compromise the Université was somewhat "royalized and Christianized," largely through changes made in the teaching staff, many priests being introduced. Royer-Collard's policy was one of moderation, though he always maintained his belief in state-controlled education.[2]

1 The name Commission de l'Instruction Publique was changed in 1820 to Commission Royale de l'Instruction Publique, and several minor changes were made.

2 Royer-Collard said of the Université: "L'université n'est autre chose que le gouvernement appliqué à la direction universelle de l'instruction publique; elle a été élevée sur cette base fondamentale que l'instruction et l'éducation publiques appartiennent à l'état." [*Archives parlementaires* (2e série), XIX, 58.]

The elections of 1816 modified the Chamber of Deputies, introducing more Liberals into the membership, and for the next few years, under the ministries of the Duc de Richelieu and the Duc Decazes, the clericals found themselves checked. If a law of 1817 allowed religious orders to receive legacies, provided a royal authorization were given, it carefully specified that this was only to apply to religious orders recognized by the law; new orders had, as before, to be approved by the Chambers. This was, of course, aimed directly at the Jesuits, who, unauthorized by the government, had returned after 1815 and in a number of cases had been allowed by the bishops to take over the teaching in the diocesan seminaries. What the Jesuits could not do as a teaching organization they were in many cases able to accomplish as agents of the bishops.

The clericals failed to stop the sale of the remaining church lands by the government. All that was obtained was the reservation for the Church of enough land to add four million francs to its income. In 1817 the King himself and the Church met a sharp and dramatic rebuff in the failure of the negotiations to form a new Concordat with the Pope. After a Concordat had been drawn up by Blacas, the French Ambassador at Rome, and Cardinal Consalvi, Louis XVIII refused to accept it unless a clause were added restating the principle of the Gallican Liberties. New negotiations were opened and a Concordat satisfactory to both the Pope and Louis XVIII was framed. When the completed document was presented to the ministry they rejected it, and the matter was dropped. The whole affair was popularly considered a great victory for the Napoleonic Concordat of 1801.

The religious question had largely subsided by 1817, and remained more or less in abeyance until the assassination of the Duc de Berri in 1820. During this period, 1816–7 to 1820, the orators of the Right confined themselves to defending the traditional Gallican position, avoiding the excessive views of the Extreme Right. Neither the Ultra-Royalists of the Extreme Right nor the radical freethinkers of the Extreme Left were powerful enough to affect the situation.

During the years of moderation — the ministries of Richelieu and Decazes — the prevailing attitude toward the Church was represented in the Chamber of Deputies by Royer-Collard and Camille Jordan, and in the Chamber of Peers by the Comte de Serre. These men were devoted to the Church, but they believed in freedom of worship and in a lay state independent of clerical interference.[1] The liberty of the state demanded by these statesmen was of a different sort from that now called for by Lamennais. These men were neither atheists nor religious indifferentists, but they wished to conserve some of the political results of the French Revolution.

1 In a speech in the Chamber of Deputies in 1819 Jordan asserted the independence of the state as a long-established fact in the French tradition. He concluded his argument as follows: "Voilà notre véritable droit public, Messieurs; voilà ce qu'eussent professé les Pithou, les d'Aguesseau, les Talons, l'illustre Chancelier l'Hôpital, s'ils avaient pu faire entendre leurs voix dans cette grande délibération." [G. Weill, *Histoire de l'idée laïque en France au XIXe siècle* (1925), p. 16.]

They were bent upon finding a middle course between the doctrines of Voltaire and those of Joseph de Maistre.

This same attitude of compromise was common among the clergy, the majority of whom took little part in the controversies of the time. Their point of view was well represented in the government by the well-known bishop, Frayssinous. He had first attracted attention, in the days of the Empire, by a series of public lectures at Saint-Sulpice. These lectures had been well attended and popularly acclaimed, though there was nothing startling or original about either their substance or their style. "Let us equally reject," he writes, "those authors who dare to say that the Christianity of Bossuet is not the true faith [he refers here to the small group of Ultramontanes who wanted to raise the Church above the state] and those writers who in the name of 'our liberties' would push us into license."[1] This was perfectly safe and perfectly innocuous. It represented the point of view of the average cleric and the average laymen, to whom the Ultramontanism of Bonald, of Joseph de Maistre, and, later, of Lamennais was as extreme as were the Gallicanism of Montlosier and the freethinking anti-clericalism of Jouffroy and of the new *Globe*.

The last four years of the reign of Louis XVIII, following the assassination of the Duc de Berri in 1820 and the fall of the Decazes ministry, showed a definite revival of clerical reaction that in some ways resembled the situation in 1815 and 1816. The King was growing

1 Frayssinous, *Les vrais principes de l'église gallicane*, (3d ed., 1826), avertissement.

weary. The extreme Clericals had an agent very close to him in the person of Madame de Cayla, who now practically dominated the King. In 1822 the Chambers passed a law creating thirty-two new bishoprics. Great changes came in the Université, which was being more bitterly attacked. Lamennais and Chateaubriand denounced it because it was despotic in its organization and democratic and freethinking in its teaching. Liberals like Benjamin Constant and Voyer d'Argenson attacked it because it interfered with the freedom of thought and gave the government too large a control in the formation of public opinion. In 1822 the headship of the Université was given to Frayssinous, who was also made Ministre des Affaires Ecclésiastiques.[1] Changes now came rapidly in the ranks of the teachers. Many laymen of doubtful orthodoxy were expelled and their places taken by priests. Some of these changes were due to the fact that in 1821 an ordinance had been issued which gave the President of the Royal Council and the Grand Maître de l'Université, Frayssinous, an almost absolute authority in appointments to teaching positions. The bishops were henceforth given the right to inspect the schools of their dioceses. Gold medals were to be given to teachers who were "distinguished for their moral and religious conduct."

The Ecole Normale was closed and then reëstablished under the name of Ecole Préparatoire. The Ecole de

1 Cournot says of him, Frayssinous "n'était pas jésuite, mais sulpicien, c'est à dire qu'il représentait cette nuance extrême et affaiblie du gallicanisme qui touche au parti jésuite et ultramontain, et qui tient pourtant à s'en distinguer." (Cournot, p. 74.)

Médecine was closed in 1822 and then reorganized after the expulsion of twelve professors. The name Lycée was dropped and the name Collège Royal substituted. No one could teach in one of these schools who, in the words of Frayssinous, had the "misfortune to live without religion or to be without devotion to the royal family." Tissot, who was accused of showing in his teaching too much sympathy with the Revolution, was put out of the Collège de France. Victor Cousin's lectures at the Sorbonne, and later Guizot's, were stopped. The teaching of reading in the state elementary schools by an inexpensive method borrowed from England, and known as *l'enseignement mutuel*, in which the older students taught the younger, was abolished. All these changes were simply made by royal ordinances, since the Université had been originally sanctioned in 1815 by a royal decree.

These reactionary measures, especially in the higher schools, aroused strong opposition among the students. "Young France" was in these years stirred by new ideas. The philosophy of Cousin, the history of Guizot, the development of physics and chemistry, and the new studies of Egyptology and oriental languages were all attracting students in the secondary schools and the universities. Outside the schools were Romanticism in poetry and painting and various new doctrines of social and economic reform. The government's educational policy ran counter to all these new forces. Students were frequently expelled from the collèges royaux and from the universities for objecting to the repressive measures of the government. The students objected to being forbidden the right to read certain books, and they protested even small changes such as the replacement of the drum by a bell to announce classes.[1] These repressive measures of the government from 1820 to 1824 did not, however, prevent Lamennais from declaring that the schools of France were nothing but "séminaires d'athéisme" and "the vestibule to hell."

IV. THE EDUCATIONAL REGIME

The internal condition of the national school system of France during the Restoration was very bad. The incessant meddling of the government, which has just been discussed, and the continual use of the schools for propaganda prevented the development of a professional attitude on the part of the instructing force. "Youth needs a religious and monarchical direction," read the ordinance of 1821. It added that "the teacher should take as the basis of his instruction religion, monarchy, and the Charter." Napoleon had said, "the Catholic religion, the Napoleonic dynasty, and liberal ideas." At bottom the formula was the same, and in both cases education was a form of propaganda.

The highest institutions of the Université de France were the various universities. These were small. In 1814 there were in all 1210 students in the faculties of letters of the French universities.[2] The number seems to

1 There is much interesting material in the French Archives Nationales on the suppression of freedom of thought among students. (Arch. Nat., F7. 174.985, 174.649.)

2 Arch. Nat., F174.649, 174.657, 175.653, 174.657, 174.727.

have diminished slightly during the Restoration. The teaching in the provincial universities was poor. A number of special professional schools date from the Restoration. In 1820 the Ecole Supérieure de Commerce de Paris, a private foundation, was opened. In 1824 the Ecole des Arts et Manufactures was founded. Both schools gave courses in banking and bookkeeping. In 1821 the government opened the Ecole des Chartes to train archivists and librarians. It soon became a great force in the revival of mediæval studies in France. The Ecole des Beaux Arts, the greatest art school of modern Europe, dates from 1830, as does also the Academy of Médicine.

In the field of primary and secondary education the state provided a certain number of schools. Other schools were in private hands, while a large number of a third group were in the control of the Frères des Ecoles Chrétiennes. This last was an order founded in the seventeenth century, ruined by the Revolution, and then revived in 1803. After 1818 they were licensed by the government to conduct primary schools. In 1830 they had 87,000 pupils in their schools. Theoretically all public and private schools were under local inspection, though the government officials of the Restoration seem in practice to have found it expedient to pay almost no attention to church schools. In the country districts the primary education provided by the government of the Restoration was poor in quality and very limited in extent. The central government appropriated only about 50,000 francs a year toward primary instruction. This left the matter primarily to the local authorities. The money appropriated by the central government was chiefly expended on printing textbooks and pamphlets. The pay of the schoolmaster was very small. Each household paid a small tax to support the primary school, and had in addition to pay a small fee for each child that attended. One of the reasons always urged by the Church to prove the advantage of sending children to church schools, especially to the petits séminaires, was that it would cost the parents less, as the church schools were for the most part free. In most small villages the schoolmaster, if there was one, acted as secretary to the mayor, for which service he received a small addition to his meager income. He wrote out the minutes of the town meetings, kept the town records, and wrote the mayor's letters, as well as such letters as were written by the villagers. He was likewise often called on to aid the priest, to carry holy water, and to ring the church bells. The village schoolmaster, though often ignorant enough, was usually considered a veritable "oracle du village."

The standards of primary education were low. Comparatively few children went to school. In the country districts, where the majority of the population still lived, the parents who did send their children to school allowed them to attend only a few months in the winter. Textbooks were poor. The teachers were ignorant, too few in number, and often badly overworked. Much waste of effort resulted from having the boys and girls taught separately, either in separate rooms or on different days of the week. Too much time was spent on learning the catechism. Guizot's famous report of 1833 showed a deplorable state of ignorance both in the teachers and in the mass of the population. In spite of an ordinance of 1816 which said that every commune in France must support a school, there were only 28,000 primary schools in 1821, and 30,000 in 1829. In the whole of France at the end of the Restoration only ten million out of twenty-five million adults were literate, and only 24,000 out of 39,000 communes had schools. Out of every hundred conscripts in the army only forty-two could read. Yet in the field of education, in spite of the poor quality of her schools, France was still one of the first countries in Europe. A second royal ordinance of February, 1830, completing the one of 1816, ordered every commune to bestir itself to found a school, and made the Conseil Général of the department responsible. It was not, however, until after the law of 1833 that primary education became common throughout France.

After 1824 primary and secondary education was more closely supervised by the bishop and by a local committee in each canton. These cantonal committees had existed since 1816, and had made reports through letters to the departmental prefect. Little notice seems to have been taken of these reports by the prefect or by the authorities of the Université until the ascendancy of clericalism in the government, after the accession of Charles X, changed the working relationship of the educational regime to the state. Early and late, however, the Church did all it could to discredit the state schools and to draw as many students as possible from them into church primary and secondary schools.

The lycées, or collèges royaux, as they were called during the Restoration, stood between the ecclesiastical and state primary schools and the universities. These collèges were few in number, and were confined to the larger towns. As reading, writing, and arithmetic were the principal subjects in the primary school, Latin and mathematics were the basis of the curriculum in the collège. In 1820, at the Collège Henri IV in Paris one lesson of history a week was added to the usual routine of Latin and mathematics. This represents the very beginning of the break-up of the old classical curriculum that had prevailed in French secondary schools since the Renaissance. The teachers in these state secondary schools were better trained and better paid than the primary school teachers. Too few children, however, attended these secondary schools, and during the Restoration the state, though it made many and varied regulations in regard to them, did very little to extend or improve their teaching. Nevertheless, the impetus given by the Revolution to the cause of free public education had been so strong that even the hostility and the indifference of the governments of the Restoration were powerless to destroy it.

V. NEW SCHOOLS OF THOUGHT

Before discussing the final struggle of the Restoration between the Church and the growing forces of Liberalism in the press and in the Chambers, let us turn to several new schools of thought — Eclecticism, Liberal Catholicism, and Positivism. These represented, at least among the leaders of the time, a new religious and philosophic outlook which marks the later years of the Restoration, as the Catholic Revival had characterized its earlier years. After 1815 philosophy again came to have the place that it had lost during the Napoleonic regime. At the time of the Revolution philosophy had passed from the salon to the tribune; under Napoleon it had been forced into almost complete silence. After 1815 it reappeared in the Sorbonne and in the Collège de France. This revived interest in philosophic studies dates largely from the lectures of Royer-Collard on the history of philosophy at the Sorbonne in the years 1812–4.

The scholarship of Royer-Collard was only moderate; his point of view was a traditionalism derived from his legal training and his own temper of compromise. He was always, in the classroom as later in the Chamber of Deputies, a man of poise, dignity, and intelligence, but he was never a profoundly original scholar. His philosophic system, which derived much from the Scotchman Thomas Reid, represented the beginning in France of a middle course between the skepticism of Condillac, who held that all knowledge was mere sensation, and the orthodox metaphysics of Catholic theology. It differed from most of the French thought of the eighteenth century in being positive, and this marks it as belonging to the great current of positive and constructive thought of nineteenth-century France. Madame de Staël expressed the note of the new age when she declared: "I do not know exactly what we must believe, but I believe that we must believe. The eighteenth century did nothing but deny. The human spirit lives by its beliefs. Be certain, through Christianity, or through German philosophy, or through enthusiasm, but believe in something."[1]

There were still some thinkers who followed the older currents of the eighteenth century. These Ideologues still cherished the faith of Condorcet and Helvétius in reason and progress; and their general faith in humanity was, in the work of Auguste Comte, to give birth to Positivism and the new Religion of Humanity. This current of the eighteenth-century thought was not so purely negative as Madame de Staël believed. It still had life in it and the power of creating new schools of thought. "We who no longer have religious faith," writes one of the younger men of this philosophic group, "must use our enthusiasm for the profit of humanity." Comte's first book was published in 1822. His philosophy is indicative of the tendency of the thought of the period to turn from a negative and destructive attitude, which either defended or attacked the ideas and institutions of the Ancien Régime, to some new and more positive faith. Comte's thinking in its earlier stages was first influenced by Condorcet, from whom he derived the theory that the development of the race follows the plan of the development of the individual. He

1 Faguet, *Politiques et moralistes du XIXe siècle* (2e série), p. 232.

was likewise influenced in his youth by the writing of Joseph de Maistre, whose sense of social solidarity and whose criticism of the eighteenth-century insistence on individualism he admired. This individualism, Comte was early convinced, had produced unlimited anarchy. Society now needed a new unifying force based on wider knowledge, "une physique sociale."

The greatest influence in Comte's thinking, however, came from Saint-Simon, one of the founders of modern Socialism.[1] From Saint-Simon Comte acquired his great conviction that religion, ethics, and faith must rest on scientific investigation, and that society was to be improved primarily through the application of science. Like most of the other thinkers of the day, Comte's system starts with a reinterpretation of history. The writing of the Restoration abounds with these new interpretations of the past. According to Comte, the history of the race shows three stages — first a theological stage, in which a supernatural origin is sought for all phenomena, then a metaphysical stage (the seventeenth and eighteenth centuries), in which an effort is made to demonstrate the existence of abstract forces, and finally the present, a positive age, in which all vain search after the causes and essences of things is abandoned and man restricts himself to the observation and classification of phenomena and to the study of their laws. Comte believed absolutely that all political and social phenomena are capable of being grouped under laws, and that the

1 Cf. on this matter W. Pauck, *Journal of Mod. His.*, I, 245–252, and Dumas, *Rev. philosophique*, LVII, 136, 263.

true object of such a thinker as himself must be the reorganization of the whole moral, religious, and political system. This was all first set forth in his *Plan des travaux scientifiques nécessaires pour réorganiser la société* of 1822 and in his *Cours de philosophie positive* of 1825, two of the most impressive and least read books of the Restoration. The period of his great influence belongs to the latter part of the nineteenth century.

Science, although maintaining an independent development, had many interesting relationships to the philosophic movements of the Restoration. At a time when Bonald and de Maistre conceived of the individual only as a part of a great social organism, and when Saint-Simon and Comte wanted to found a "science of mankind" as a branch of natural history, a group of French scientists were developing the conception of the unity of the forces of nature and the idea of the common origin of all living creatures. These new scientific concepts go back to the work of Lavoisier, Laplace, and Lamarck in the eighteenth century, but new methods of research and demonstration were now giving their concepts a surer foundation and a wider application. The movement began in the field of optics with the work of Fresnel. Before Fresnel, light was considered the result of the impression on the retina of particles emitted by the luminous object. In 1818 Fresnel published his *Mémoire sur la diffraction*, which showed that light was a vibration, and thus founded the later science of optics. In the field of electricity, Ampère and Arago were making interesting discoveries. Before Ampère, Galvani had studied the electric current, and Volta had constructed a battery. In 1820 Orsted had found that an electric current would deflect a magnetized needle. Ampère, following Orsted's experiments, worked out tables of the relationship of different electric currents and these deflections, and established the laws of the mechanical action of electric currents on each other. Arago discovered that an electric current drew iron filings as would a magnet. In these experiments of Ampère and Arago modern electro-dynamics had their origin.

At the same time, Fourier and Sadi-Carnot, in works published in 1822 and 1824, arrived at the conclusion that "heat was motive power, or rather movement that had changed form." This was to be the fundamental principle of modern thermo-dynamics. Here, as in the work of Ampère and Arago, experimental science was moving toward the doctrine of the conservation of energy, and toward the ideas of the unity of forces of physical nature and of the fundamental identity of all matter. On the practical side, this preluded a great economic and social transformation through increased production and easier transportation; and on the philosophic side, if applied to living creatures, it implied the unity of all species and a new conception of the whole nature of life. Soon the idea of the separate creation of all species as described in the Bible, and generally believed until now, was called into question by Geoffroy Saint-Hilaire. He held that man was no longer to be considered a type of being specially created by God, but part of a great unity. This meant, as the nineteenth century soon realized, that the foundations of the old beliefs would have to be reëxamined. One might remain indifferent to the question of whether light was an emission or a vibration, but when Saint-Hilaire and Cuvier began to debate the unity of all species men were not slow to see some of the social and religious implications.

The reading public of the Restoration took a lively interest in this famous dispute between Cuvier and Geoffroy Saint-Hilaire. Cuvier, taking the orthodox side, maintained that the idea of the unity of species was a limitation of the absolute liberty of God, who might create independently of any law of nature. In March, 1830, this controversy came to a climax in a famous session of the Academy of Sciences. Cuvier was the better tactician in the argument. Saint-Hilaire set forth his views through exaggerated analogies that weakened his position. When Eckermann told Goethe the news of the July Revolution in Paris, Goethe remarked that he cared little about the Revolution but that he was deeply interested in the discussion that was going on in Paris over the theories of Saint-Hilaire. The great question involved was the place of man in nature. Cuvier, in defending the Biblical doctrine, was much praised and quoted by the theologians of the time. The future, however, belonged to Saint-Hilaire, though not until twenty years later was his hypothesis taken up by Darwin and given an adequate inductive basis.

In the field of purely religious thinking, our chief concern here, the greatest new force in the later part of the Restoration was Victor Cousin. He was first known as the most promising of all the young men who flocked to the lectures of Royer-Collard. In 1815 Cousin began to teach at the Ecole Normale and at the Sorbonne. He went to Germany in 1817, and he brought back to France much enthusiasm for, and some knowledge of, German Idealism, especially of the thought of Kant, Schelling, and Hegel. After the government forced him to retire from his teaching position in 1822, he again spent some time in Germany. Here, at the instance of the French police, he was imprisoned for four months by the Prussian government. In 1826 his first important work, *Fragmens philosophiques*, was published. The next year his *Cours de l'histoire de la philosophie* appeared. In 1828 he was restored to his position at the Sorbonne, and in 1829 he published his *Philosophie de Locke*. The last years of the Restoration were the period of Cousin's greatest triumph as a lecturer. The hall of the Sorbonne was crowded as the hall of no teacher of philosophy in Paris had been since the days of Abélard. He had in his lectures on the history of philosophy a singular power of identifying himself with the system he expounded. Clear and comprehensive in the grasp of the outlines of his subject, his exposition exhibited in a striking manner the generalizing abilities of the French genius. His influence was enormous, and the taste of philosophy — especially its history — was revived in France to an extent unknown before this time. Cousin is today remembered as an effective teacher, but hardly as a significant philosopher. His Eclecticism, wherein religion and philosophy harmonize, has long since lost its interest. Yet his name was almost a household word in France in the first half of the nineteenth century.

Cousin seems to have seen his goal from the very start. It was no more a purely philosophic goal than that of the Idéologues of the eighteenth century or of the Traditionalists of the school of Bonald. It was fundamentally a political and social goal. His task was to found a philosophy that would be non-Catholic and non-atheist, which would provide for constitutional liberalism but not for republicanism. It was to be the philosophy of the "juste milieu," neither extreme Right nor extreme Left. He declared himself a believer in the principles of the French Revolution, yet he thought that they could be best safeguarded in a constitutional monarchy. He believed in rationalism, yet, following Maine de Brian and Royer-Collard, he emphasized the importance of human purposes and the fact of free will, condemning both the obscurantism of the Church and the rationalistic skepticism of the eighteenth century, which made man the victim of a mechanism. "We finally choose the eighteenth century," he said, "because, while recognizing what there was of true and noble even in the desires and tendencies of the century from which we are emerging, we propose firmly to combat and break the tradition of materialism and atheism, of the blind hatred of Christianity, of revolutionary violence and servility, which it handed on to us, and which at the beginning of the Restoration still weighed upon our minds and souls in a deadly weight, and was an obstacle both to the establishment of liberty and to true philosophy."[1] He

1 Cousin, *La philosophie sensualiste,* Preface to edition of 1855.

wrote later that his philosophy was called "Spiritualism" because "its character is to subordinate the senses to the spirit, and to tend — by all the means which the reason admits — to elevate and ennoble mankind. It teaches the spirituality of the soul, the freedom and responsibility of human actions, moral obligation, disinterested virtue, the dignity of justice, the beauty of charity; and beyond the limits of the world it shows a God, author and pattern of humanity, who, after having made man for an excellent end, will not abandon him to the mysterious unfolding of destiny. This philosophy is the natural ally of all good causes."[1] This, as Cousin said himself, was "not blind syncretism," but a fitting together of fragments into a whole. But it was a whole which the pattern-maker determined beforehand and made up of fragments selected with deliberation and intent. One might imagine that this philosophy of compromise would have done very well after the excesses of the Revolution. But the Restoration was not yet ready for compromises. Hence Cousin was more appreciated in the reign of Louis Philippe.

Much the same point of view as that of Cousin was set forth in the teaching of Guizot in history and of Villemain in literature. In the years 1820 to 1822 Guizot had given the lectures published in 1822 as *Histoire des origines du gouvernement représentatif en Europe.* After an enforced retirement from the Sorbonne, he returned in 1828 — and began his famous course, *Histoire de la civilisation.* In both series of lectures it was the free-

1 *Lettres inédites de Cousin à Bersot* (Versailles, 1897).

thinking bourgeoisie who were eulogized. Civilization was the result of an equilibrium of democratic, aristocratic, theocratic, and monarchical elements. Civilization is at its best when the middle class is strong, the middle class representing the "juste milieu" between liberty and authority. Guizot was the prophet of the bourgeoisie as Rousseau was of democracy, Bonald of theocracy, and Bossuet of absolute monarchy. Cousin and Guizot agreed that philosophy and religion have the same end, religion being the result of inspiration, philosophy of reflection. All hoped for a new alliance of faith and reason in a via media. All spoke of religion with sympathy and respect, at the same time vindicating the rights of reason, and defending the secular state against the encroachments of the Church. It was, in spite of its lack of clarity or originality, a doctrine of wide comprehensiveness and of toleration far above ecclesiastical bigotry or philistine narrowness. In these respects it formed a marked contrast to the arrogance and dogmatism both of the Church and of the most of the eighteenth-century Philosophers. As in the case of Cousin, the period of the great influence of Guizot lies after 1830 rather than before.

The eighteenth century had hoped for the greatest results from the action of the legislator and the philosopher. The new generation of the eighteen-twenties expected less from reason, and looked vaguely but enthusiastically for progress from a spontaneous evolution within the souls of men. This philosophy of compromise was just coming into great vogue in the third decade of the nineteenth century. In 1824 a group of Cousin's more radical pupils led by Dubois and Pierre Leroux founded a new journal, the *Globe*. They were soon joined by another remarkable young man, one of the most able of his generation — Jouffroy. The new journal, whose political aspect has already been discussed, appealed strongly to a group of young intellectuals. These "jeunes gens" were bored with the stock phrases of Voltairianism and the older bourgeois liberalism. They disliked Bonapartism because it represented tyranny, and at the same time they found the new Ultramontanism and religious emotionalism of Lamennais reactionary. The young Romanticists of the time liked to paint the agonies of the soul of a young man deprived of his faith. French society after 1824 was full of these young Adolphes, Renés, and Werthers. They were weary of the old formulas, and many were not very clear about what they did believe. The result was frequently an incongruous mixture of anti-clericalism and religiosity, together with an ardent interest in any new cult — Romanticism, Positivism, or Socialism. The Chambers were closed to this group because of their youth. They were to play their great rôle in the days of the July Monarchy. Now they were to be seen at the lectures given at the Athénée, a privately endowed Liberal teaching association in Paris largely under the influence of Benjamin Constant.

The *Globe* became the organ of this group, which grew rapidly in the later years of the Restoration. This new journal prided itself on its range of interests. It specialized in foreign news and in information about scientific and literary works and industrial changes. It was Liberal in politics, Eclectic in philosophy and religion, and in favor of Romanticism against Classicism. The editorial policy was largely opportunist, and the editors were forced by the journal's franchise to avoid political discussions except by indirection. On any question, however, that involved religious toleration or the freedom of thought the editors became eloquent and quite definite. The aged Goethe found the *Globe* the most interesting journal in Europe. In 1825 there appeared in its pages one of the most significant utterances of the decade, Jouffroy's famous article, *Comment les dogmes finissent*. Here was a brilliant defence of religious indifference. A doctrine, he argues, when it is near the end of its life, is believed only by force of habit. Some men of critical temper examine the old doctrine and announce its absurdity. In course of time, in spite of inertia, and often in spite of official disapproval, the old doctrine is gradually replaced by a new one. But the champions of new ideas have already pushed ahead and are already disagreeing among themselves. By this time the adherents, then, of all the old doctrines, who see cleavages appearing on entirely new lines, consolidate all their forces and raise a great hue and cry about the downfall of morality, religion, and order. A counter-revolution begins, and the old doctrine seems to be returning to power. Then there comes a new generation which adheres to neither side, and, leaving the old partisans to decide the battle among themselves, it turns to new ideas and to new causes. This article was the manifesto of a new generation which looked with contempt on their elders, who were living in what seemed past controversies. They scorned both the old revolutionary Liberalism, with its sentimental memories and its Bonapartism, and the doctrines of Bonald and Chateaubriand. Their journal set forth what was to become one of the root ideas of the nineteenth century — namely, that all values are relative. "Traversed by every kind of doubt," as an editorial put it, "face to face with a thousand different religions, a thousand contradictory systems, seeking without tutor or priest the solution of the great problem of God, of nature, and of man, individual minds have proclaimed themselves sovereign. Whether this anarchy of intelligence be conducive to happiness or the reverse does not affect the issue; it is an anarchy that is now our chief desire, our chief good, our life."[1] They represented a small but significant group, full of promise, but full of conceit and a false notion of their own originality. Their journal the *Globe* was, however, intelligent and refreshing, and in its thinking it outdistanced all of the older and more reputed prophets of the time.

Among the younger Catholics, the leader in the last decade of the Restoration was Lamennais. The greatest chapter in the spiritual Æneid of this ardent soul belongs to the July Monarchy. His influence, however, was already widespread before the Revolution of 1830. Born in Brittany in 1782, he had been a sickly and sensitive

1 Dickinson, p. 80.

child and had had no regular education. In those years when other boys were in school he had done a great deal of desultory reading, especially in Rousseau and Pascal. He had also devoted much time to music and mathematics. He had various love affairs, wrote poetry, and fought a duel. He was so little inclined to accept the dogmas of Christianity that he did not take his first Communion until he was twenty-two, and he was so filled with horror at the idea of a vow that he did not become a priest until he was thirty-five. Having a strong character and a narrow mind, it was his nature to take a side obstinately, and to defend what he for the moment regarded as absolute truth with eloquent love and passionate hate.

His first book, *Réflexions sur l'état de l'église en France*, appeared in 1808. It was promptly suppressed by Napoleon for its ultramontane tone. In 1811, after some theological training, he went to teach mathematics in a church school at Saint-Malo. In 1814 he published an attack on Gallicanism which was praised by Bonald and Joseph de Maistre. His reputation dates from the publication in 1817 of his *Essai sur l'indifférence en matière de religion.* This, according to Lacordaire, "cast a spell on many readers and invested a humble priest with all the authority once enjoyed by Bossuet." It was its extraordinarily vivid and poetic literary style, even more than the novelty or force of its doctrines, that made Lamennais famous throughout ecclesiastical France almost in a single day. "The tendency and even the title of the book," says Brandes, "suggest comparison with the work which inaugurated the religious revival in Germany in the beginning of the nineteenth century, Schleiermacher's *Lectures on Religion to Those Who Despise It.* Both works aim at counteracting the same thing, the indifference toward religion and the positive contempt for it prevailing amongst the educated classes. Both make an attempt, now that faith has become weak, to rebuild the edifice of piety upon a new foundation."[1]

In this work Lamennais denounced the whole idea of toleration, following in most cases the arguments of Bonald and Joseph de Maistre. The right of private judgment introduced by Descartes and Leibnitz into philosophy and science, by Luther into religion, and by Rousseau and the Encyclopedists into politics, had ended in atheism and anarchy. Ecclesiastical authority founded on the absolute revelation delivered to the Jewish people and since supported by the universal tradition of the nations — the same idea that obsessed the mind of Newman, carrying him into the Catholic Church in 1845 — here was, indeed, the sole basis for the regeneration of human society. Three more volumes of this *Essai* appeared between 1818 and 1824. These took up the same arguments for the value of the experience of the human race and the insufficiency of human reason to which Burke in eighteenth-century England had given such eloquent expression in his *Reflections on the French Revolution.* Here the new Romantic doctrines which glorified the mediæval romances and epics, the cathedrals, and the folk song as the collective creation

1 Brandes, p. 255.

of the folk soul squared with a philosophy which put its faith in the general reason, in common consent, and in historical continuity. Lamennais also called attention to the human need of divine guidance through the Church, and to the historical rôle of the Church and its Pope as the repository of revealed truth and as the judge of the governments and institutions of the world. "There is," he declares, "no peace for the intellect except when it is certain of possessing the truth, and there is no peace for the nations except when they are under the rule of order. Society is so agitated and uneasy because everything is uncertain — religion, morality, and government. The world is the prey of opinions. Reëstablish authority, and order will reappear."[1] These arguments, as we have seen, were already familiar to many through the writings of Bonald and Joseph de Maistre. The eloquent manner in which they now were set forth was, however, new. These volumes of Lamennais met with a mixed reception from the Gallican bishops and from the older monarchists, but they fired the ardor of many of the younger clergy. The work, now complete, was examined by three Roman theologians, and received the approval of Leo XII. Lamennais went to Rome, where the Pope apparently offered him the cardinalate, which he refused.

On his return from Rome Lamennais contributed to the journal of Villèle and Chateaubriand, *Le Conservateur*. Later he withdrew from this and aided in the founding of *Le Mémorial Catholique*. In 1825 and 1826

1 Cresson, II, 72.

appeared his two-volume work, *De la religion considérée dans ses rapports avec l'ordre civil et politique.* At the same time he was forced to pay a fine of thirty-five francs for calling the government atheistic. He now retired to La Chênaie and gathered about him a brilliant group including Montalembert, Lacordaire, and Maurice de Guérin. It was this group that founded *Le Correspondant* in 1829. In 1828 Lamennais published his *Progrès de la Révolution et de la guerre contre l'église.* This marks his complete renunciation of Gallicanism and of royalist principles. Here he proclaims the advent of a theocratic democracy. The Church had made a grave mistake in attaching its cause to the cause of kings. The submission of the Church to the state since the age of Louis XIV had ruined the Church. Inertia had seized the clergy. The state was really an atheist institution, and yet it controlled the Church. The Chambers voted the income of the Church, thus giving it each year its "permis de séjour." The Church can do nothing. It cannot register the birth of a child, found a school, or open a monastery, except at the whim of the state. The law is atheist, since it tolerates all sects. The Church is impotent, since it is a slave to the state. The decline of faith is due to the stupidity of the Church in attaching its cause to the dying cause of kings. The state is killing the Church. The hatred of the masses for the monarchy is spreading very rapidly to the Church. Thus the cause of the Church must be made independent of the cause of the monarchy. "Au lieu de trembler devant le libéralisme il fallait le catholiciser."

These opinions were now vehemently supported by two journals, *Le Mémorial Catholique* and *Le Catholique*, the latter founded by a curious Danish Jew, Baron d'Eckstein, who had been converted to Catholicism. The prophet of the movement was, however, Lamennais. There was a natural magic about his spoken and written words that made his ardent group of followers hang on his every utterance. In 1829 appeared another volume of his *Progrès de la Révolution*, which was largely an attack on the state control of education. This book was to become after 1830 the charter of French Liberal Catholicism in the nineteenth century.

VI. CHARLES X: REACTION AND REVOLUTION

With the accession of Charles X in 1824 the "union of the throne and the altar" seemed complete, though already, in the last years of Louis XVIII, the monarchy had fallen more under clerical influence. Just a few days before he died Louis XVIII had issued a number of reactionary ordinances. He created, as we have seen, a special Minister of Ecclesiastical Affairs and of Public Instruction, to be independent of the Ministry of the Interior. He had also brought into the Council of the State the Archbishops of Rheims and Besançon, and into his private Council the Cardinal de la Fare. The accession of Charles X brought more dramatic changes. His elaborate coronation at Rheims in 1825, where the ritual seemed to belong to the age of Saint Louis, was indication enough of the reactionary character of his religious views. On the morning after the coronation

1824

the King mounted a white horse and rode in the midst of a brilliant retinue to the Hospital of Saint-Mark. There the chief physician of the royal household awaited him at the head of a band of 121 persons afflicted with scrofula. The King, after a short prayer, set boldly to the task of curing them by the royal touch.

Before the Coronation an Ultra-Royalist deputy had set forth the immediate ecclesiastical program of his group. The program called for a law against sacrilege, a crime that had never been punished by the state in France. It also demanded laws abolishing all the ecclesiastical legislation of the French Revolution. As one of the Liberal deputies remarked, this program would "restore all of the old regime, with the addition of the Jesuits!" While waiting for the meeting of the new parliament the Ultras proceeded to exploit the King's known sympathy for reaction. A wave of clerical obscurantism swept over the country. Burial was refused by some priests to those suspected of Jansenism, as it had been in 1815–6. State aid was refused to poor people who could not produce certificates of confession. Others were refused marriage or burial because of their liberal views. Civil marriage was referred to by the clergy as "concubinage." All marriages made during the Revolution were declared void in the eyes of God. The Bishop of Rouen ordered his priests to post on the doors of all churches the names of any who were not in good standing with the ecclesiastical powers. The Jesuits opened eight new colleges within a few months. The police forbade performances of Molière's *Tartuffe* and of Voltaire's *Mahomet.* Even Racine's *Athalie* had to be expurgated before it could be performed. The Missionaries became more active. It was rumored that the King had been ordained and said Mass privately. A former army colonel who kept a book shop was condemned to nine months in prison for having published the Gospels without the miracles. The King bestowed the Ordre du Saint-Esprit on the most rabid of all French churchmen, the Cardinal de Clermont-Tonnere, who had in a pastoral letter of 1823 used very denunciatory language in speaking of the secular state, demanding at the same time the abolition of the Concordat. The whole country was in an uproar. As one of the Liberal papers of the time declared: "The present period will be hard to explain to our descendants. One talks now of nothing but bishops, priests, monks, Jesuits, convents, and seminaries."[1]

The King, it was known, saw much of a well-known Jesuit, the Abbé Liautard, one of the founders of the Missionaries, who urged him in his *Le Trône et l'Autel* to adopt a number of measures, among them the establishment of a censorship of the press so close that it would allow only what was approved by the government to circulate. In 1826 the King made a great show of participating in the Papal Jubilee, and in a number of important religious processions the whole royal family walked behind the clergy carrying candles. "Had Charles X flaunted a mistress in public, the people would have forgiven him," says Thureau-Dangin,

1 P. Thureau-Dangin, p. 319.

"but they were indignant at this open subservience to the Church."[1] The papal bull authorizing the celebration in France of the jubilee of 1826 called on the French clergy to combat with new ardor all books and ideas which might sap the foundations of faith. The Archbishop of Paris took this occasion to fulminate against those "pestilential doctrines which circulate in all the veins of the social body." The Bishop of Strasbourg denounced "those infamous writers, those journalists, philosophers of lies, artificers of revolution." This language was officially rewarded when the same bishop was made preceptor to the young grandson of the King, the Duc de Bordeaux.

A veritable war broke out in the Chambers over a series of religious laws. In 1825 a law was passed allowing the king to authorize the giving of money to religious orders for women if the gift were agreed to by the bishop of the diocese and the Council of State. New religious orders for men and women might still be founded and endowed by private persons on the permission of the king, if the king cared to take the risk of arousing popular disapproval or of provoking new legislation by the Chambers. Even Charles X, as time proved, did not care to take this risk. Only in the case of religious orders for women were gifts of money or property permissible. Lamennais wrote with characteristic bitterness and insight that this law made of French nuns "une classe de parias."[2] It was the debate on the Law of Sacrilege of

1 Thureau-Dangin, pp. 353–354.
2 Charléty, p. 247.

1825 that raised the greatest clerical furor of the period both in the newspapers and in the Chambers. The Clericals wished to pass a law making sacrilege — that is, the attempt to steal anything from a church — a crime punishable with death. Bonald, as we have seen, stated the case for the clericals by declaring such a law perfectly reasonable, in that "it sent the criminal before his natural judge." The case for the Liberals was taken up vigorously in both the Chambers and in the press. Camille Jordan, Benjamin Constant, the Duc de Broglie, and above all Royer-Collard, pointed out that sacrilege was a crime that had never been recognized by the French state, and it could only be punishable by a complete theocracy like the Mediæval Empire or Calvin's Consistory at Geneva. The law was finally passed by a small majority and under the personal pressure of Charles X. Though it remained a dead letter and was never enforced, it gave a tremendous impetus to the growth of Liberal bitterness toward the government of Charles X. It seemed that the work of the Revolution was undone and that the Charter of 1814 had been torn up.

The debate over the law raised the most fundamental questions, and both sides grew more acrimonious. It is in this period that the beginnings of anti-clericalism, at least in some of the forms it was to take in nineteenth-century France, are first clearly marked. The idea of a "free church in a free state," of which so much was to be heard in the second half of the nineteenth century, was first proposed in the Chamber of Deputies in 1828 by

Courcelles, a friend of Lafayette. The bitterness of rationalistic and democratic critics was not, however, the sort of attack that the clericals found it hardest to combat. Much more did they fear attacks from individuals who, though they were not avowed enemies of religion, and believed that religion should have a large place in society, were nevertheless strongly opposed to the influence of the Church in politics. Of this type of moderate anti-clericalism the first clear statement had been made by Madame de Staël in her *Considérations sur la Révolution française* (1818) and by Benjamin Constant in a more elaborate work, *De la religion considérée dans sa source, ses formes et ses développements* (1824). Alexander Vinet and Guizot supported the same principles. Both were members, as were also the Duc de Broglie and Constant, of a Société de la Morale Chrétienne, founded in 1821, whose object, while religious, was also the separation of Church and state. These ideas of greater religious liberalism had been popularized by Paul-Louis Courier and by Béranger. They attacked the bigotry of the Missionaries and the Jesuits while they liked to celebrate, rather in the spirit of Chaucer, the good-natured and unselfish parish priests, true shepherds of their flocks, "serviteurs du Dieu des bons gens." " 'Go and teach all the nations,' said the Master," so Courier writes, "but it is not written, 'Go with the police and teach.' " In 1824 Thiers published the first part of his *History of the French Revolution*, which produced much the same effect as the songs of Béranger and the pamphlets of Courier. When the

Constitutionnel and the *Courier* defended such ideas and leveled fierce attacks against the *Drapeau Blanc* and other of the Ultra-Royalist papers, the editors were haled into court. The state's case against them failed and both were acquitted. In the public mind, now more aroused than at any time since the Restoration began, it seemed that there was a secret conspiracy of the Jesuits and the Ultra-Royalists to undo the results of the French Revolution. The Missionaries were attacked and in some places driven out of the town. The many new editions of Voltaire and Rousseau are further indications of the growth of anti-clerical sentiment. From 1817 to 1829 there were twelve new editions of Voltaire and thirteen of Rousseau. Helvétius, Diderot, Holbach, Dupuis, and *Lcs Ruines* of Volney were all resurrected and reprinted. It is estimated that during the Restoration, one publisher, Touquet, printed a million and a half copies of Voltaire and nearly a million of Rousseau.

The most telling blows against the Ultras and the King came from a sturdy and somewhat cantankerous nobleman, the Comte de Montlosier, a former Emigré and a man known for his conservatism and for his devotion to the monarchy. In 1826 he published his famous *Mémoire à consulter sur un système religieux et politique tendant à renverser la religion, la société et le trône.* This book is a discursive but forceful attack on the Congrégation and the Jesuits — on a regime in the Church that threatened to overpower the state. As early as 1816 Montlosier had written: "Some priests consider themselves God. They will ruin the Church, and they will bring down the monarchy with themselves."[1] He now saw in the influence of the clerical party in education and in the government a great revival of the Ultramontanism that had led to the declaration of the Gallican Liberties in the seventeenth century. According to Montlosier, the Congrégation and the Jesuits dominated the ministries; they could count in 1826 on 105 deputies; they were spreading their propaganda everywhere, even among the workers. Moreover, the Jesuits had never rendered any real service to religion. D'Alembert, Helvétius, and Voltaire were all educated in Jesuit schools. The Jesuits had only succeeded in discrediting all religion. By clerical meddling in politics all respect for the clergy was rapidly disappearing. It is not by talking of hell, and of the police, and by double-dealing, that men are to be saved. The Ultras and the Clericals were ruining religion and working to upset the throne and to break up the monarchy.

The work was widely read. Eight editions of it appeared in a few weeks. It expressed the fears of a large part of the French people who never read Lamennais, or Cousin, or the *Globe*, and, coming as it did from a sincere Royalist and a devout Catholic, it had great weight. Frayssinous made several characteristically weak and equivocal rejoinders to Montlosier's attacks, one of them a speech in the Chamber of Deputies in which before he had finished he acknowledged the existence of the Jesuits in France. Frayssinous' official defence of the government was his *Vrais principes de l'église gal-*

1 Charléty, p. 249.

licane of the same year. Simultaneously in 1826 appeared the second volume of Lamennais' *Religion considérée dans ses rapports avec l'ordre politique et civil*, a thoroughly unqualified attack on Gallicanism and a eulogy of the Jesuits and Ultramontanism.

Such was the religious situation in the closing years of the Restoration. Alongside the traditional antagonism between the old forces of the Revolutionary period, represented now by Charles X, by most of the nobility, and by the older clergy, and the traditional freethinking Liberalism of the schools of Royer-Collard and of Benjamin Constant there was now growing up a new set of controversies between the adherents of the *Globe* and the school of Lamennais. A new generation was coming into maturity. The majority of the men living in France in 1824 had been born since 1789. It was, however, the older generation which controlled the Chambers, the newspapers, and the higher positions in the Church and in the government. It was this older generation which fought the struggle through in 1829–30 and the traditional divisions made by the French Revolution furnish, to the end of the Restoration, the framework of the practical situation.

The law of Sacrilege, the permission given to the king to authorize the religious orders for women, and the Papal Jubilee of 1826 had shown the French people that the most reactionary elements in Church and state were in control. Many further projects to strengthen the hold of the Church on the state were discussed in these closing years of the reign of Charles X. Some of the clergy were loud in their demand that the government grant the Church a large endowment, preferably in land, which would assure the Church of an income independent of the grants voted by the Chambers. The fall of Villèle in 1828, and the attempt of the King to try a more Liberal government under the ministry of Martignac, mark a lull in the attacks and counter-attacks. Martignac restored Guizot, Cousin, and Villemain to their positions in the Sorbonne.

The most striking event in this short ministry, so far as the Church was concerned, was a law in regard to education. It arose over the old problem of the petits séminaires taking students not destined for the priesthood. Large numbers of these lay students, sent by devout parents, had been taken into the petits séminaires. In 1828 there were nearly as many students in the petits séminaires as in the state schools of the same grade of instruction. To prevent this in the future, a royal ordinance, framed by Feutier, Frayssinous' successor as Minister of Ecclesiastical Affairs, limited very sharply the number of students that might attend the petits séminaires, and refused the schools the right to grant diplomas until after their students had entered the priesthood. At the same time Martignac's government forced eight schools run by the Jesuits to close their doors. The meetings of the Congrégation on the rue du Bac were temporarily suspended. Ironically enough, the militant Catholics were of the same mind as the Liberal associations—La Société pour l'Instruction Elémentaire, La Société de la Morale Chrétienne, La

Société des Méthodes d'Enseignement — in favoring an educational regime unrestricted by the state. Both Ultramontanes and radicals demanded an educational regime largely free from government control, though, of course, for widely different reasons.

The fury of many of the clericals at these radical measures of the Martignac ministry knew no limits. After a year's trial of a semi-Liberal ministry, the Ultras and their clerical friends apparently found little difficulty in urging the King to give up the Martignac experiment. An Association pour la Défense de la Religion Catholique was formed under the leadership of Bonald. The Ultramontane journals announced that the Age of Persecution had begun. They spoke of Julian the Apostate and of Diocletian in the same breath with Martignac. Feutier was compared to Marat. A group of sixty-three bishops drew up a protest and sent it to the King. Their violence was so great that the Pope ordered them to moderate their attitude. It was the religious issue more than anything else which brought about the dismissal of the short-lived Martignac ministry (1828–9) and the formation of the cabinet under the Prince de Polignac, who was a prominent member of the Congrégation.

The Polignac ministry (1829–30) was not in power long enough to carry through the reactionary program it had in view. Most of its clerical efforts were directed to trying to get judgments against newspapers which in some manner or other attacked the Church or the ministry's attitude in ecclesiastical matters. However, the hatred and distrust of Polignac, which caused the downfall of the Restoration government in 1830, was due more to his religious than to his political views. In addition to his prominence in all the work of the Congrégation, Polignac was notorious for his refusal in 1814 to take an oath of allegiance to the Charter because of his religious scruples. No Frenchman was more distrusted and hated by all shades of Liberalism than Polignac.

In the last elections of the Restoration in 1830 many of the clergy took a very prominent place. Bishop vied with bishop in denouncing the Liberals and in calling on the faithful to vote for candidates approved by the Church. The most rabid element in the Church had come to the front. The terms used in some of these pastoral letters and sermons quite outdo any other clerical utterances of France in the nineteenth century. The outcome was the Revolution of 1830.

VI. CONCLUSION[1]

The failure of the Church during the Restoration was due largely to the bad judgment of some of the upper clergy and to their unreasoning bitterness against the

1 In the light of this failure it is interesting to recall a letter written to the Pope by Madame de Roland in 1792. "High priest of the Roman Church, sovereign of a state which is slipping out of your hands, know that the only possible way in which you can preserve state and Church is by making a disinterested confession and proclamation of those Gospel principles which breathe a spirit of the purest democracy, the tenderest humanity, and the most perfect equality — principles with which Christ's representatives have adorned themselves only for the purpose of supporting and increasing a sovereign power which is now falling to pieces. The age of ignorance is past." (Brandes, p. 15.)

Revolution and all it stood for. The Church had unusual advantages after 1815. It had great influence in the government, and it was carrying on its work in the midst of a period of genuine religious reaction against the deism and cynicism of the eighteenth century. As an organization the French Church, in the years 1815 to 1830, lacked neither power nor intelligence nor devotion. It failed, however, because it tried to resurrect a dead political and social regime. The French nation as a whole was Catholic still, but it believed that in spite of its excesses the period of the Revolution was one of the greatest ages in French history. It wearied of hearing some of the clergy insult its glorious memories, of being told that the leaders of the Revolution were monsters, of hearing Napoleon called the ogre of Corsica whose soldiers were drinkers of the blood of children murdered in their cradles. The Church, as Lamennais pointed out, had made the fatal mistake of making its cause the cause of a selfish nobility and a blind and bigoted monarchy. The best thought of the Restoration, though anti-clerical, was not anti-religious. All the able leaders — men as divergent in their outlook as Lamennais, Constant, Cousin, and Béranger — were seeking a religious basis for society. They all agreed that eighteenth-century rationalism was impoverished and even bankrupt. The French Church was too blinded by bitterness, selfishness, and the desire for revenge to use these forces, and by 1830 it had alienated many of the ablest minds in France, who might have supported it had they been given even slight encouragement. The

Restoration seems to have been more hated on the religious than on the political side. In 1815, when Napoleon entered Grenoble after his return from Elba he was greeted with cries of "Down with the priests!" and in the Revolution of 1830 the only destruction of property was by an infuriated mob that sacked the Archbishop's palace in Paris and the Jesuit establishment at Montrouge. The failure of the Restoration was thus even more a religious than a political failure.

CHAPTER III

THE RISE OF A NEW ECONOMIC ORDER

WHILE those who frequented the salons and cafés of Paris and the larger towns read the newspapers and pamphlets of the day and discussed in fiery phrases every aspect of Church and state, France was quietly undergoing a gradual but profound economic transformation. The advocates and adversaries of church schools, and those who debated eloquently the extension of the franchise or the liberty of the press, little realized that these less spectacular changes were creating a new society. Today we are so accustomed to thinking in economic terms that it is hard to realize that in 1815 there were very few thinkers in France who really grasped the meaning of the French Revolution. Still fewer understood the social and political consequences of the Industrial Revolution, which was only beginning to affect France. Yet the land settlement that came out of the Revolution and the steady penetration of French industry by the new industrialism did more to modify the structure of society than any number of constitutions, coups d'état, concordats, or military campaigns.

Between the years 1815 and 1830 machine processes were extended, agriculture was improved, credit facilities were developed, and the means of transportation reorganized. None of these changes, however, yielded their fullest fruits until after the middle of the century. The Restoration in itself is not a self-contained period in the economic development of France. It stands midway in a gradual transformation which took place, roughly, between 1750 and 1850. The Industrial Revolution in England, which in a short period quite revolutionized English industry and English agriculture, has no exact parallel in France. France was primarily an agricultural country, and her agriculture during the Ancien Régime developed steadily along with her industry and commerce. This condition did not fail to produce a number of critical periods, but none of these periods in itself created a wholly new situation. In the years from 1750 to 1850 the change consisted in the increasing introduction of industry and commerce into a society that was and continued to be predominantly agricultural. This development is fairly continuous from the Ancien Régime, through the Revolution, the Empire, the Restoration, and the July Monarchy.

I. AGRICULTURE

Among the sources of national wealth, agriculture still held first place. In 1826 landed property represented 66 per cent of the national wealth.[1] The vast majority of the French people — about two thirds, in fact — lived in the country districts.[2] The agricultural classes have remained the largest and most unchanged

1 H. Sée, *La vie économique de la France sous la monarchie censitaire* (1927), p. 12.

2 Statistics given in Charléty, p. 315.

group in French society. It is easy to forget their presence by turning one's attention too exclusively to the more varied, and in many cases more interesting, changes in modern French town life. Through all these changes the peasant has remained as a profoundly conservative element. The greatest of modern French mediævalists, Léopold Delisle, wrote soon after 1850 that "a thirteenth-century peasant would visit many of our farms today without much astonishment." The Revolution wrought many changes in French agricultural economics, but the changes were so gradual that in contrast with the industrial changes of the first half of the nineteenth century they must have seemed to contemporaries slight and unimportant.

The Revolution modified some of the machinery of land ownership. We now know that there were many freeholding farmers before 1789, especially in the outer regions of the old French monarchy, in Flanders, Artois, Béarn, and Alsace. Many of the French peasants before 1789, however, were still either "censiers," holding their land by a quit rent or cens, which might or might not be fixed, or serfs bound to the soil. The cens was so small that most censiers were virtually freeholders. However, both the serf and the censier disappeared with the Revolution. The serfs were freed. The censiers were relieved from the payment of quit rents and gained unrestricted possession of their lands. There were other ancient methods of land tenure, widely used before the Revolution, which survived it and which were later extended and applied in modified forms. The two most significant of these forms of land tenure after 1815, besides freeholding, were métayage and tenant farming.

Métayage was a form of farming on shares. The tools were supplied by the owner of the land, and the work was done by the peasant, who in turn owed his landlord from a third to two thirds of the produce of the land, depending on the agreement made. This form of landholding was the common one throughout the central highlands of France and in the adjacent lands in the period after 1815, as it had been before 1789. It was considered quite worthy of a free Frenchman, and it was, as administered after the Revolution, a fair enough arrangement, in that it made demands on the proprietor for furnishing material and tools and for paying part of the taxes. It was in marked contrast with the old serfage in two respects; first, the peasant was free to move about, and, second, the landlord could not collect his part of the produce without doing a corresponding part in keeping up his share of the working capital. Métayage. however, seems to have encouraged shiftlessness among the peasants, since they knew that the lord, rather than let his land lie idle, or become unproductive, would take care of them.

Tenant farming was common before the Revolution. It prevailed in the country between the Loire and Flanders, a vast plain that included much of the richest agricultural land in France. The tenant farmer merely paid a fixed rent. Renters usually took leases for three, six, or nine years. It was customary to pay the rent twice a year. The landlord did not furnish the renter with seed, cattle, and tools, nor did he share the taxes, which fell entirely on the farmer himself. Often a freeholder, who found his own lands too restricted, held small pieces of land from some great proprietor as a métayer or tenant farmer. Such men sometimes worked for wages by the day, because their own land was insufficient for the support of their families. Thus the conditions of landholding for any given peasant might vary on the different parts of the land he worked.

The class of small freeholding farmers was not, as was formerly believed, created by the Revolution. Throughout the seventeenth and eighteenth centuries impoverished noblemen had been obliged to sell pieces of land to their tenants, who often managed to save enough to purchase small tracts. Under the Ancien Régime these small freeholders also increased their holdings by reclaiming waste land. This freeholding class, though not so large as the class of métayers and tenant farmers, had come through the Revolution with increased holdings and with some increase in numbers. It formed a kind of rural bourgeoisie in contrast with the great mass of the peasants who constituted a rural proletariat below the level of this small group of freeholders. The contrasting interests of these two sections of the rural population was the chief reason why no united peasant movement had appeared in the Revolution. No reliable statistics are available for the extent of these various types of landholding after 1815.

At the time of the Revolution some of the great estates in France — those belonging to the Church and the Emigrés — had become national property and were put up for sale. It is interesting to note that the state seized and sold only those noble lands that belonged to the Emigrés. Wholesale seizure and distribution of all the noble lands would have upset too many renters, and such a program had had few partisans among the Revolutionary leaders. Little of the land seized outright from the Church and the Emigrés seems to have gone to the peasantry; it passed, rather, to a new class of bourgeois land speculators and to the returning nobles, who after 1800 gradually bought back a large portion of their former holdings. By 1820 it was estimated that the old nobility had regained a half of their lands. Some of these holdings had been reacquired during the Consulate and the Empire. The indemnification of the nobles in 1825 helped others to repurchase their old estates. In the Department of Cher, for example, the large noble landholdings during the latter part of the Restoration were about as they had been before 1789. Much the same situation existed in the old districts of Maine, Anjou, and the Vendée. In Normandy, however, especially in that part which was included in the rich department of the Seine-Inférieure, a great transformation in property holding had taken place by 1815. It is thus difficult to make generalizations.

Of the rest of the noble and church lands, the majority went during the period of 1789 to 1815 into bourgeois hands,— merchants, officials, deputies, and lawyers,— or into the hands of the new Napoleonic aristocracy, who let out their recently acquired lands to tenant farmers. This was particularly the case near the larger towns and cities. These new landowners merely stepped into the places of the old. After 1815 the large proprietors seem to have had a marked preference for tenant farming over métayage, which gradually disappeared. "This fresh influx of bourgeois landowners," says Clapham, "is the most significant outcome of the Revolutionary land settlement."[1]

After 1815 many of the great holdings were gradually broken up. The smaller freeholders bought pieces of land from the great estates, as the economic status of these freeholders slowly improved. No statistics for this land division for the period from 1815 to 1830 are available, but Lavergne estimated that at the close of the Second Empire the land holdings in France were twice as evenly distributed among the population as they had been in 1789.[2] Many of these holdings were very small. About 1870, out of five million rural proprietors, three million possessed but one hectare apiece.[3] The French law of succession in the Code Napoléon, which limits the parental power of the disposition of property to a part equal only to one child's share, and divides the remainder equally among the children has been one cause for these further subdivisions. Another cause is to be found in the continual purchases on the part of the peasants of small pieces of land — a practice, as we have seen, that goes back to the period before

1 G. H. Clapham, *The Economic Development of France and Germany* 1815–1914 (3d ed., Cambridge, 1928), p. 21.

2 Lavergne, *Economie rurale de la France* (4th ed., 1877), p. 49.

3 A Hectare is equal to 2.471 acres.

1789.[1] In the period 1815 to 1830 much land was added to small landholdings through extensive reclamation of swamp and waste land. In Picardy, from 1792 to 1821 there were cleared 1463 hectares, and from 1821 to 1833, 1862. This resulted in increased crops. In the one department of Ille-et-Villaine the amount of wheat raised rose from 49,830 hectolitres in 1820 to 59,720 in 1830.[2] The old common lands had been cut up among the peasants and sold, mostly during the period from 1792 to 1803. About one tenth of France still was in common ownership in 1815, but this was largely confined to backward districts in the Alps, the Pyrénées, the Vosges, and the Jura. In the more populous districts the common lands had practically disappeared by 1815.[3] Many of the farms were still so small that even as late as 1860, for which year there exist the first reliable statistics, only about a sixth of those who gained their livelihood from the soil could support themselves entirely from their own property.[4] In France, property had become a national possession as in no other country in Western Europe. In 1815 few had any voice in the government, but many had a stake in the country. For this reason many of the peasants who might have been Conservatives in politics because of their religious views were

1 Cf. T. Leslie, "Land System of France," in Cobden Club *Systems of Land Tenure in Various Countries* (2d ed., London, 1870), pp. 340, 343, for easy methods of exchanging property in France, and also for law of transfer and method of registering transfers.

2 Sée, pp. 21–22.

3 Clapham, p. 12.

4 Sée, p. 15.

Liberals because of their economic interest. In this process of land subdivision, the seventeenth and eighteenth centuries and the period since 1815 are quite as important as the period of the Revolution.

The Revolution had wrought many improvements in the peasant's life. The abolition of the tithe, the complete reform of the much-hated game laws, the redistribution of the whole system of taxation, the free right of cultivation, which corrected abuses existing before 1789, when the government regulated not only the rotation of crops and the amount to be planted, but also the marketing of everything, the disappearance of the old provincial customs boundaries that had made it possible for famine to exist in one province alongside plenty in another, and the great increase in the value of agricultural products caused by the Napoleonic wars — all these meant decided improvements in the lot of the agriculturalist. Those peasants who did not acquire land by the Revolution gained nevertheless a relative economic improvement which was to enable them to buy land whenever and however it came on the market.

In methods of farming the period was again one of gradual and steady amelioration. The period from 1815 to 1847 was a time of great agricultural prosperity, superior in this respect to both the period that preceded 1815 and the period that followed 1847. The old open-field system — winter wheat, spring wheat or some other cereal, and fallow — still prevailed in the North of France. In Flanders, the most highly cultivated region of France, an elaborate rotation system covering an eleven-year cycle was commonly used, according to Arthur Young: "Wheat, and after it turnips the same year, oats, clover, wheat, hemp, wheat, flax, coleseed, wheat, beans, wheat."[1] The peasants lived in villages, and about each village lay its three great fields, in which were scattered the holdings of the cultivators. About Paris and the larger cities many of the fields had been broken up into market gardens. Here patient hand labor raised mushrooms, asparagus, flowers, strawberries, and a variety of choice vegetables. In the South, this system of rotation was modified by the prevalence of fixed crops, olives, fruit, and vines, as well as by the growing use of artificial meadows of clover and lucerne to restore the soil. The ancient common grazing rights over arable land were still a hindrance to cultivation. Under the old open-field routine, where everyone grew the same crops, all the stubble was thrown open to animals on the same day; but as peasant proprietors were introducing variations in the course of cropping, this was no longer practicable. For this reason, "vaine pâture," as it was called, died out in the nineteenth century. It remained an annoyance wherever the majority of the peasants still used the three-field system, as was the case in many districts as late as 1845.

The best agricultural land was in the North and West of France, though the basins of the upper Rhine in the East, and the Garonne and the Rhone in the South, also had excellent soils and good rainfall. For variety of climate and soil France is the most favored country in

1 Clapham, p. 10.

Europe. She is capable of producing all the chief agricultural products except cotton, and only about one tenth of the soil is unfit for cultivation. Wheat and grapes are the staples, but there has always been a large output of rye and barley, as well as of silk and wool. A number of these crops, especially the vine and mulberry, are particularly well fitted for cultivation on the small holdings which have become characteristic of modern French agriculture.

Methods of farming improved slowly. The movement to better French agriculture goes back to the Physiocrats and the Philosophers of the eighteenth century. "About 1750," says Voltaire, "the nation, surfeited with verse, tragedies, comedies, operas, and romances, turned to reasoning on wheat."[1] The courts of the benevolent despots of Europe, Catharine of Russia, Frederick of Prussia, and Joseph II of Austria, as well as the salons of Versailles and Paris, had followed the writings of the Physiocrats in agricultural economics with an interest that was quite new in the history of European thought. "Everyone read their books," says Voltaire, "except the farmers."[2] This new interest had begun to bring practical results before the Revolution. The cultivation of the potato and the breeding of merino sheep were introduced, and some interesting experimental farms were opened before 1789.

The introduction of the potato was slow. Potatoes

1 G. Renard et A. Dulac, *L'évolution industrielle et agricole depuis cent cinquante ans* (1912), p. 259.

2 Renard et Dulac, p. 260.

were first used extensively for the feeding of animals in the North and East of France, the most advanced sections agriculturally. The peasants did not care for them, preferring bread and other vegetables, bread forming the basis of their diet. One government official in 1814 speaks of the potato as a fair substitute for rye and wheat, "at least for the poor and unfortunate."[1] In spite of this attitude, the production had risen from only five million bushels in 1789 to fifty-five million bushels in 1815.[2] Potatoes were usually grown on newly ploughed pasture land or on the fallow land between crops, so that in either case they represented a genuine addition to the supply of foodstuffs.

The prefects, who interested themselves in agricultural improvements, had better success in introducing the sugar beet. The blockade of the Napoleonic period had made it profitable to raise sugar beets, first in Flanders, then in the basin of the Seine. In his contemporary economic survey of 1819 Chaptal writes enthusiastically of the advantages of beet culture, pointing out that even the refuse after the sugar is extracted is an excellent food for live stock.[3] The increase in sugar beet production was only gradual, partly owing to the reluctance of the public to use beet sugar, but it became, especially in the second half of the nineteenth century, one of the great crops of Northern France. Silk culture

1 Comité des Travaux Historiques, *La statistique agricole de 1814* (1914), p. 523.

2 H. Gibbons, *Economic and Industrial Progress of the Nineteenth Century* (Toronto, 1903), p. 190.

3 Chaptal, *De l'industrie française* (1819), I, 159.

was another source of agricultural wealth in which advances were made. Remaining practically stationary between 1789 and 1815, it quadrupled between 1815 and 1850, paralleling in its development the growth of foreign markets for French silk fabrics. Various attempts were made during this period by experimental farms and seed companies to improve the type of seed used, especially of wheat. There was still much to be done along these lines.

Rather striking improvements were made in live stock. Again these changes go back to the Ancien Régime. Spanish merino sheep had been introduced in the reign of Louis XVI, and by 1830 there were great flocks of these merinos scattered all over France. They furnished the finest quality of wool. About 1825, pure-bred Durham shorthorns were introduced. More careful breeding methods for cattle and for horses — especially Percheron horses — improved the native strains. Writing in 1819, Chaptal emphasizes the dearth of live stock in France. They are insufficient, he points out, to do the necessary work on the farms. They are likewise insufficient in numbers to furnish the necessary fertilizer for the soil.[1] One of the reasons for this shortage of animals was the old habit of the peasants of eating very little meat. Poultry was common on the farms, but the cultivators ate almost no other meat except such as was salted down for the winter.

One of the most obvious ways of increasing the number and quality of the live stock lay in increasing the

1 Chaptal, I, 145–146, 153–154.

fodder for them. The extension of potato and beet culture aided in this. Even more useful was the increasing use of artificial meadows. Gradually the old three-field system was replaced through the use of clover, sainfoin, and lucerne. Chemical fertilizers were not used in the first half of the century. In these matters, as in horse raising and in methods of cultivation, England was more advanced, and many of the changes in French agriculture in the first half of the nineteenth century represented the adaptation of English agricultural methods to French conditions. French agriculture, however, lagged behind that of England because in France it was the small proprietor who determined the methods of cultivation, whereas in England (as in Prussia) the standard was set by large landowners who could afford to experiment with new methods.

Farming tools improved very slowly. Cooper, the American novelist, who visited an industrial exhibition in Paris in 1827, was amazed to see the excellence of the workmanship in French carpets, porcelains, tapestry, and wall paper, and the clumsiness and crudity of practical articles like ploughs, hammers, and hoes — a contrast that still surprises the foreigner. The peasant depended on his hand hoe, though the horse cultivator was being introduced from England. This was an important improvement and one fitted to increase the yield. Harvesting was usually done with scythes, and the grain was threshed out with flails. After 1820 simple types of threshing machinery were introduced, especially, as might be expected, in the more progressive

North of France. Ploughs, harrows, drills, and carts were gradually improved by making them stronger and heavier, metal parts replacing wood. Small holdings, however, hindered rather than encouraged experiments with larger and more efficient tools.

The government and certain private individuals made some efforts to improve agricultural conditions. In 1825 the budget for agriculture was 1,818,000 francs.[1] But the government's activity was confined largely to distributing pamphlets and to keeping statistics. After the general agricultural survey of 1814 nothing of so comprehensive a nature was undertaken. Most prefectoral reports, however, contain observations on agricultural conditions made on the basis of information collected in the department. The Ministry of the Interior seems to have paid little attention to these matters. The individual prefects did what they could by distributing a few pamphlets, and by writing articles for the departmental journals. The Liberal political papers show a great interest in agriculture and in industrial improvements and inventions — one of the many connections which the period shows between new economic interests and new political views. The era of agricultural exhibitions and prizes had not begun. Dupin, writing in 1829, urges strongly the value of introducing, under governmental auspices, agricultural meetings, exhibitions of agricultural products and machines, and the granting of awards for the improvement of live stock and crops.[2]

1 Sée, p. 20.

2 Ch. Dupin, *Forces productives et commerciales de la France* (1829), I, 129, 130.

Private societies and individuals did something to disseminate information. The Société Nationale d'Agriculture en France, which has counted among its members the ablest agriculturalists of each generation, was founded before the Revolution. In 1801 there had been founded in Paris La Société d'Encouragement à l'Industrie Nationale. Several of the members of these societies, which were really scientific academies, developed interesting experimental farms. The Duc de la Rochefoucauld-Liancourt was a pioneer in this. The most interesting and the most influential of these experimental farms was one at Roville in Lorraine. Here was tried out the first threshing machine that came from Scotland. The owner of the farm, Mathieu de Dombasle, published each year a much sought-after summary of the experiments and activities of the farm. Many agricultural societies of a semi-scientific nature were founded. By 1843 there were fifty-seven of these societies. Their influence, however, was not great until after the middle of the century.

The chief aid given by the government to the agriculturalist was through the establishment of a high tariff on most agricultural products. All parties in the government after 1815 agreed on the necessity of a high tariff to protect French agriculture — the chief economic interest of the aristocratic Right — and to protect the young commercial and industrial enterprises of the incoming Industrial Revolution — the great economic interest of the Left. The Right had as a part of its program the reëstablishment of an agricultural feudalism founded on a monopoly created by high tariffs against foreign cereals and live stock. The mass of small farmers was also desirous of continuing the monopoly of the days of the Napoleonic Blockade. Hence the protective tariffs on agricultural products mounted steadily from about 1819 to 1830.

In the case of cereals, a law of November, 1814, slightly modified by a law of April, 1816, allowed the free exportation of all cereals — forbidden since 1810 — except wheat, which was not to be exported if it went above a certain price in the frontier departments. Then it must be sold in France. Not until 1819 was a tariff set up against the importation of foreign cereals. The famine of 1817 had caused the government to encourage the importation of Russian wheat. The next year's wheat crop in France being a very good one, the price of French wheat fell sharply. Hence in 1819 a high tariff on all cereals was passed. This resulted in a great decrease in the sale of foreign cereals in French markets. The immediate result was an overplanting of wheat in France, and this brought on a decline in French prices for wheat during a period extending from 1819 through 1821. The agriculturalists now demanded a law that almost completely forbade the importation of cereals. Such a law was passed in 1821. It provided a sliding scale which allowed the importation of foreign grain only in very rare cases, when the French prices remained above a certain amount. The price of cereals, in spite of this law, continued to go down, and during only one month, February, 1828, did the government allow the importation of foreign cereals. Thus the French agriculturalists, at least after 1821, held the monopoly of the cereal market.

Other agricultural products were likewise protected. Wool was allowed to enter free of duty until 1820. Then, as the result of an agitation on the part of the wool growers, a tariff on wool was established. The wool growers had begun to complain in 1815 that the free importation of cotton into France was reducing the consumption of woolen materials. In 1816 an import duty on cotton was established, and at the same time the cotton manufacturers were allowed subsidies. In 1820 this same regime of subsidies was established for wool and the woolen manufacturers. In 1822, and again in 1826, the tariff on wool was increased, while at the same time subsidies to woolen manufacturers were raised. In 1822 a tariff on flax and hemp was established. French hops, vegetable oils, tallow, and rice were also protected. In 1822 a high tariff on live stock, and in 1826 tariffs on imported meats, were set up. Even the importation of tea was heavily taxed, lest tea should ruin the French wine industry! Thus by including all products of the soil in a system of practically prohibitive tariffs the government aided the peasant as well as the large landowner.

The government after 1820 passed some excellent laws for the protection of the forests. The forests in the North had suffered badly in the campaigns of 1814 and 1815, and laws of September, 1814, and March, 1817, had allowed large sales from the public forest lands to private individuals. Many protests against these sales, and against the government's neglect of the forests, were made by learned societies and by the prefects. Gradually the government was aroused to the danger of deforestation. Between 1820 and 1824 a special administration of forests was organized. A few years later a forestry school was opened at Nancy, and in 1827 a comprehensive forestry code was passed.

The government, to some degree, still regulated the markets. The laws of the Ancien Régime obliging the farmer to bring his grain to market were gone, but the government kept a check on the wholesale grain merchants to prevent the purchase of too much grain by any one merchant; likewise markets were by law obliged to close at noon. Many other minor police regulations were still enforced — such, for example, as that obliging bakers to keep a certain amount of flour in their bins, and those controlling the sale of meat. These regulations were survivals of the eighteenth century, and the majority of them disappeared during the July Monarchy.

The peasants were themselves doing something to improve their condition. A coöperative association for cheese manufacture had existed in the Jura since the Middle Ages. The wine growers of Touraine and the cattle raisers of Landes had organized early in the nineteenth century under the name of "cotises" or "concorses." Associations of this type were, however, still fairly unusual in 1815. These societies made provision for the use in common of agricultural implements and for the making of common purchases of seeds and small implements. In some cases, local parish organizations of farmers and tenants known as "comices agricoles" were formed to stimulate the improvement of methods of cultivation. None of these various organizations held a large place in the life of the country until after 1860.

In general there was a great gap between what was known scientifically about agricultural methods and about agricultural marketing and the ways and methods followed by the peasant in his regular activities. The peasant changed his ways slowly. Travel was still difficult, in spite of the extensive improvement of the roads under the Napoleonic regime. Products were usually sold in the local market, and overproduction for this local market in any given year was common. The peasant remained isolated. He held by habit to wheat raising and to following the three-field system. He had too few animals and his land was insufficiently fertilized. Agricultural credit and banking facilities were not yet developed. The peasant bought little in the towns. Laffitte complained in 1826 that "we still have an agricultural country of the fourteenth century to consume the products of an industrialized state of the nineteenth century."[1] The desire of the agricultural classes was to be stable and contented, while the new industrialists were possessed with the desire to be progressive and rich. Through all, however, there was a steady agricultural development that comes out of the eighteenth century into the nineteenth. The Revolutionary period did not cause these changes; it merely accelerated them; and if

1 Charléty, p. 305.

by 1830 one found more of the old agricultural order than of the new, there was still a clearly marked advance.

II. INDUSTRY AND THE INDUSTRIAL REVOLUTION

In the two decades following the downfall of Napoleon the progress of industry was more rapid and certainly more striking than that of agriculture. The Revolutionary upheaval and the Napoleonic Wars had prevented France from passing through the same Industrial Revolution that was transforming England. In both countries there had been a great commercial development throughout the eighteenth century. A prosperous town-dwelling class — in spite of certain hampering government regulations which were very much more severe in France — had grown rich, largely through colonial commerce. Capitalistic organization in the eighteenth century had for the first time developed on a large scale. Industry was being mechanized, and the steam engine was used for the first time. Though the Physiocrats were chiefly interested in agricultural development, some of the Philosophers waxed enthusiastic over the services to the state rendered by her citizens in trade and manufacture. Voltaire makes one of the characters in his *Philosophe sans le savoir* proclaim, "It is not a single people whom the commerçant serves; he serves men everywhere, and is served by them. He is a man of the universe."[1] It was not until the time of Guizot and Macaulay, in the middle of the nineteenth century, that the great bourgeois epics were written, but

1 Renard et Dulac, p. 20.

the glorification of the middle-class commerçant is already evident before 1789, and is an interesting indication of the economic movement of the later eighteenth century.

The loss to France of her colonial empire in 1763, and the hampering guild and trade regulations of the mercantilist code of the Ancien Régime, retarded this development in the years just before the Revolution. But in spite of these setbacks, French commerce toward the close of the eighteenth century surpassed in volume that of England. Industrially, though, if not commercially, the advantages before the French Revolution lay with England. She had a larger available capital, a better system of taxation, a better coal supply, and much more industrial and commercial liberty. The richness of French soil was also a hindrance to her industrial and commercial growth. The slowly increasing agricultural population was contented and fairly prosperous. In contrast with England, with its enclosure system and its agricultural misery, the peasants in France had no great desire to change a country for a town life.

The French governments between 1789 and 1815 all showed a strong bourgeois bias. All of them believed in the sacredness of private property. Though they agreed that the state must not fetter industry, as it had before 1789 through the old mercantilist regulations, no one of the Revolutionary governments accepted fully the laissez-faire doctrine of the Physiocrats, which advocated the complete removal of all government aid and control of industry and commerce. In fact, the Revolutionary governments, by regulations and subsidies, did a great deal to help commercial enterprises of all sorts. Much was also gained through the Revolutionary governments which abolished over two hundred conflicting law codes, suppressed most of the internal tariffs, and extended the metric system of weights and measures. The proposals of the Physiocrats to abolish the old guild regulations had been tried by Turgot in 1774–6. They were restored after Turgot's dismissal only to be wiped out again by the Revolution. It is true that during the eighteenth century the guild monopolies and regulations and the other trade regulations of the government had been frequently evaded, but they still remained up to the Revolution a serious hindrance to invention and free enterprise. The Constituent Assembly in 1791 had swept away most of these monopolies and privileges and had allowed everyone to follow any occupation, and in such place and manner as he chose. Hereafter trade and commerce were virtually free. To practise a craft, the individual had now only to procure a license from the public authorities and to comply with simple police regulations, one of which practically prohibited all combinations of workingmen. Everywhere the legislation of the Revolution showed that this great upheaval was a bourgeois enterprise.

Even during the Reign of Terror in 1793 industrial museums and exhibitions were projected, though the first exhibition was not held until 1798. Schools of civil engineering and mining were developed, in which France was ahead of the rest of Europe. Later the Napoleonic

Blockade had made the government willing to subsidize many industries, among them manufactories of chemicals, of coffee substitutes, of cloth, and of beet sugar. There was at least no lack of desire to help commerce and industry by government means during the years 1789 to 1815.

It was civil and foreign war that prevented this government aid to industry from achieving any large or important results, for in spite of all the various governments could do to free industry and commerce and then move intelligently to aid them, the years 1789 to 1815 proved disruptive to the immediate interests of French commerce and manufacture. France's loss of man power, the great depreciation of and then the fluctuation in the currency, and the exhaustion that followed years of civil and foreign wars, could not be offset even by the amazing energy of the various Revolutionary governments.[1] Industries were short of capital, short of skilled labor, and unable to get raw materials. Supplies sold by shippers and manufacturers for the Revolutionary and Napoleonic armies were often not paid for. This slow paralysis of commerce and industry, espe-

1 The general effect of the Revolution is well summed up in a government report of 1794. "Entravée par les circonstances, gênée dans ses moyens, extrêmement limitée dans les sommes qu'elle avait à sa disposition pour les encouragements privée même souvent de la faculté d'en diriger l'emploi, elle n'a jamais pu suivre aucun plan, ni combiner aucun système; sa marche perpétuellement interrompue et croisée par des directions partielles contraires à ses vues, des décrets opposés à ses principes, a toujours été incertaine et timide, ella pu opérer quelques biens dans ses détails, mais elle n'a pu conserver l'ensemble, ni asseoir aucune base fixe d'économie politique." (Arch. Nat., F[12]. 1556.)

cially after 1810, raised up more enemies against Napoleon than did his political tyranny, and his downfall in 1815 was accepted by the commercial classes even though it involved humiliation and defeat.

If now we go on into the period after 1815, we find that the industrial transformation of France in the years 1815 to 1830 was, unlike the transformation in England, so gradual that it can hardly be called an Industrial Revolution. Though France remained, until well past the middle of the nineteenth century, the most highly industrialized large state on the continent, it was only here and there in a few districts, where one industry developed very rapidly, that the great economic transformation seen all over England after 1815 could be paralleled in France.

To the men who lived through the period, with its government at peace with other countries, and with an improved system of taxation and public finance, the Restoration seemed a veritable economic millennium. Yet, as Levasseur points out, it was not until 1827 that commerce was as good as it had been in 1789.[1] If one turns from the volume of trade to the growth of towns as an index of the slow progress of the economic transformation of France after 1815, it is discovered that in comparison with England, in the period 1815 to 1830, changes in France were not of a very revolutionary character. Between 1821 and 1831 Sheffield, Birmingham, Manchester, Liverpool, and Leeds grew more than 40 per

1 E. Levasseur, *Histoire des classes ouvrières et de l'industrie en France après 1789* (2d ed., 1903–4), I, 624.

cent. There was almost nothing in France to compare with this, except in the case of Saint-Etienne, the great metallurgic center near Lyons, and in that of Roubaix, the textile center near Lille. It took fifty years, from 1801 to 1850, for cities like Paris, Lyons, Bordeaux, and Lille to double their population.[1] In comparison with the Revolutionary period (1789–1815), the years 1815 to 1830 were fairly prosperous ones, but had Frenchmen then been able to remember the great commercial activities of the Ancien Régime as well as they could recall the depressing economic situation under the later years of the Empire, their optimism would have been less marked.

If the French industrial situation is considered over a long range of years — for the period 1750 to 1850 — it is evident that the backwardness of France in comparison with England was not due merely to the evils of the French mercantilist control and regulation, nor to the losses of the French colonial empire, nor, finally, to the disturbances of the Revolution and the Napoleonic Wars. It was due quite as much to the bad quality and the poor distribution of the French coal supply. France is still inadequately supplied with coal, but at the opening of the nineteenth century the French did not even utilize the coal they had, owing to the inaccessibility of the deposits and to their backward methods of mining. All the French coal fields, except two, are quite small, and the better of these two larger fields, in the Department of Pas-de-Calais, was not tapped to any extent

1 Clapham, pp. 53–54.

before 1850. The two chief sources of supply used in the early nineteenth century were near Valenciennes along the Belgian frontier, and in the region about Lyons.

The most important coal-mining company, that of Anzin, was in the North. It had been founded in 1717. In 1825 the company had a canal dug to connect its mines with the Scheldt. There was no corporation in the Lyons district so enterprising. In a report of 1807 we find that nineteen different small collieries were worked in the country about Lyons, while much more coal was mined about Valenciennes from only six collieries. In 1830 there were about 15,000 coal miners in France.[1] The yield of coal for French use increased during the Empire because of the occupation of Belgium, which possessed very rich and accessible mines whose yield was much larger than that of all of France. These were lost to France in 1815. After the Congress of Vienna, France had an output of between 800,000 and 900,000 metric tons, compared with a yield of 700,000 tons in 1789. Thus some progress had been made within the old limits of France. By 1828 the yield had risen to 1,774,000 tons. France was nevertheless seriously handicapped in her industrial development by this lack of an adequate coal supply, and by the distances that separated the best coal and iron deposits.[2]

1 G. Martin, Histoire de la nation française, *Histoire économique et financière* (1927), p. 331.

2 Gibbins notes that the average output of a French coal miner has always been less than that of an English miner, often as much as one half less. This has been due partly to differences in machinery, but more to the poor quality of the French coal deposits themselves. (Gibbins, pp. 195–196.)

The lack of coal and difficulties in shipping it were severe handicaps to the development of the metallurgic industries, though coal had not yet come to be used extensively in smelting. In 1826, 78,000 tons of iron were smelted with charcoal, as against 40,000 smelted with coal.[1] This, however, marked a great advance, for in 1806 only one smelter used coke. In 1783 Henry Cort and Peter Onions, two Englishmen, had discovered the process of puddling, by which carbon could be burnt out of pig iron and a material similar to the old-fashioned malleable iron produced. This process was soon prevalent in France. Puddled iron became the characteristic structural material of industry. The upper valleys of the Marne, the Saône, and the Loire, and the Ardennes, held first place in this production. The output of iron, which was on an average of 79,000 tons for the years 1818 to 1820, rose to nearly 134,000 tons in the period 1831 to 1833. The most remarkable feature of this development of the iron industry was in the increase in steel production, which came up from practically nothing in 1806 to 5000 tons in 1827. In 1826 there were steel mills in twenty-one departments.[2] English steel was better in quality, and German steel was cheaper, so that only the high tariff kept the French steel industry alive. The importation of English workers and the imi-

1 Levasseur, I, 603. France had abundant forests, many of which belonged to national and local governments, and wood was very cheap — in contrast with England, where the high cost of wood stimulated the use of coal in smelting. High tariffs in France, also, made it possible to produce iron products by costly and old-fashioned methods.

2 Sée, p. 53.

tation of English methods of production (especially at some of the great French centers like Le Creuzot, and at Fourchambault near Nevers, which employed as many as 2400 workers) helped to improve the quality of the French output. The French iron industry was, however, very backward in comparison with that of England. Even as late as 1846 approximately three fifths of the pig iron in France came from hundreds of small charcoal furnaces scattered all over the country.

In the development of iron machinery France was behind England and Belgium. All the early textile machinery, which played so large a part in the Industrial Revolution everywhere, was made largely of wood, with only a few parts in metal. These first textile machines — the spinning jenny and the flying shuttle loom — were driven by water power when they were not operated by hand. Through its early stages the mechanization of industry does not imply a modern situation in which heavy metal machines in great factories turn out products on a large scale. Only gradually did metal machines come on the French markets, and still more gradually did steam power replace the common hand or water power.

In an extraordinary study of the mechanization of French industry published in 1923, Ballot summarizes the situation as follows:

> By 1815 the mechanization of French industry had been thoroughly established, thanks to the efforts of successive governments since about 1780, as well as to the efforts of many private individuals. All industries were not, of course, equally mechanized, but the change between the old and the new, in

> this matter at least, had already come about. One of the chief causes for the slowness of the mechanization of French industry and for the extreme differences in different industries was the fact that French industries were already so thoroughly well organized on other lines. Mechanization had to make its way against fixed habits, routine, and established interests.[1]

He proves, first that mechanization in France preceded the steam engine, and second that mechanization in the end profited by, though it did not create, capitalistically organized industry.

The steam engine, though it came later, was probably the most revolutionary invention in modern industry, and the extent of its use furnishes one of the best indications of the advent of a new economic order. Watt's steam engine was first introduced in 1782, but by 1815 there were only about 15 industrial plants in France which used steam engines, and these were mostly employed in pumping for mines. By 1820 there were 65 installations in French mines; by 1830 the total number of steam engines used in all industries had risen to 625.[2] Many of the earlier steam installations were used only in the summer, when water power failed. In 1820 Cave of Paris introduced an improved engine with a horizontal cylinder. Very slowly the use of steam engines spread to the textile and then to other industries. The 625 steam engines reported in 1830 may have had an average horse power of ten, which would make 6000 horse power

1 Ch. Ballot, *L'introduction du mécanisme dans l'industrie française* (1923), p. 40. I have summarized a passage in Ballot rather than translated him in detail. The work is dense with new material.

2 Levasseur, I, 627.

derived from steam in the whole country at the end of the Restoration.[1] Even as late as 1840, in the textile industries France had only 243 steam installations, as against 462 plants run by water power.

Turning now to the textile industries, it is evident that the transformation was slow compared with that which was taking place in England. In the eighteenth century textile weaving had come to be handled largely by manufacturers who managed the industry, though most of the work itself was done by workers who had their machines at home. A few large workshops for silk weaving, for printing on cotton, and for tapestry weaving, had been opened. Water power was extensively used, especially in silk manufacture, which was more concentrated and more modern in organization. Before 1815 English textile machines had been, in some cases, dismantled and smuggled over to France in parts and there reconstructed. After 1815 this practice continued, in spite of the efforts of the English government to keep English inventions secret. The prohibition on exporting machines from England was removed in 1825, and thereafter more English machines came in. These English machines were copied and adapted to French usage. English workmen and mechanics, who came over to France even before 1815, had also helped to develop French industry. After the peace in 1815 they came in greater numbers, though they seem never to have played a very important rôle in French industrial development.

After 1815 the greatest change was seen in the cotton

1 Sée, p. 66.

industry. This industry had shown a great development in the later eighteenth century, especially in the field of calico printing —"indiennes," as these prints were usually called in the trade. In 1786 chlorine had been applied to bleaching, and the eight-month process of hand bleaching of cotton was reduced to two days. The industry was also gradually mechanized before the Revolution. The chief centers of manufacture were in Northern France, at Lille, Abbéville, Rouen, Saint-Quentin, and about Mulhouse in Alsace. The spinning jenny and the water frame had been brought from England, and were widely used by 1800. The power loom was slowly introduced. Both water power and, after about 1812, steam power worked the greatest changes in the industries of the North of France and in Alsace.[1] By 1820 hand spinning had nearly disappeared in Alsace. The first factories in France, "ateliers communs," as they were called, belonged to this industry. They were simple weaving sheds built by men with sufficient capital to buy and run the new machines. The number of workers in any one of these "ateliers communs" was small, usually less than a hundred. The total number employed in the industry in 1829 was about 800,000. This indicates that most of the work was still done on a small scale. Here, as elsewhere in French industry, high tariffs retarded improvements.

The increase in the output of the cotton industry is another useful index to the growth of industrialization in France. Between the years 1815 and 1840 it increased

1 Some establishments used horse power, and even ox power.

threefold, in spite of the handicap of relatively poor machinery. The use of machinery increased steadily from 60 mechanical installations in 1806 to 291 in 1823. The use of steam power in the cotton industry came in much more slowly. At Saint-Quentin in 1827 only 14 out of 29 factories used steam power.[1] The amount of raw cotton imported rose from ten and a half million kilograms in 1812 to thirty million in 1830. The value of cotton exportations rose correspondingly from about fifteen million francs in 1822 to thirty-five million in 1826. Like other industries, the French cotton industry suffered badly from the financial panic of 1826. In spite of this rapid growth, in 1829 it was still only about a third as large as the cotton industry in England. Houdoy lays the blame for this on the poor machines in France and on the comparative incompetence of French workers.[2] A greater cause of backwardness was the lack of foreign markets such as England possessed. The existence of industrial capitalists like Ternaux and Richard-Lenoir, who owned whole strings of small factories, is proof that capitalistic organization was well understood and that there was no want of enterprise to exploit industries when they paid.

In the woolen industry, the greatest changes were in the improvement of raw materials. The rapid increase in the number and quality of sheep raised furnished plentiful and excellent material for cloth manufacture. Up to 1835 almost no wool was imported. French wool

1 Sée, p. 65.

2 Houdoy, *La filature de coton dans le Nord de la France* (1903), p. 53.

was plentiful in quantity and excellent in quality. The chief centers of manufacture were again in the northern half of France — Rheims, Sedan, Louviers, Bourges, Tours, Chateauroux, Paris, which did much of the dyeing and finishing, and finally Normandy and Flanders. After 1820 a process of making wool cloth with cotton warp was introduced from England and the manufacture of shoddy cloth, made of unraveled wool that had already been used once, was also extended. Spinning machinery came more quickly into the woolen than into the worsted (combed wool) industry — a reversal of the development in England.[1] The steady growth in the industry is seen in the increase in the value of wool exports, which rose from twenty-four million francs in 1788 to eighty millions in 1838. The great popularity of French woolen goods in foreign markets was due to their fine quality, especially to the way in which they were dyed. The industry was more primitively organized than the cotton industry. Wool requires more working than cotton, and is harder to spin and weave, and power machinery was not extensively used before 1850. Most of the new carding and spinning machinery, when introduced, was hand-worked. This part of the industry was still handled in the main by workers in the countryside about the town where the weaving and finishing were done, these last processes being usually mechanized after 1815. The final control of the industry was, in the larger centers, in the hands of organizing entrepreneurs,

1 Sée, p. 73. Clapham, in a review of Sée in *Eng. Hist. Review*, April, 1928, doubts this.

the "maîtres fabricants," who furnished the patterns, distributed the materials, and marketed the finished product. A large proportion of the actual manufacture remained in the hands of masters working at home or employing out-workers on a small scale. At Rheims, for example, there were at the close of the Restoration in the woolen-weaving industry only four or five real factories and over three hundred small home manufactories.

Except in a few districts, the silk industry in 1815 was backward, but it grew rapidly during the Restoration, though its methods of production were not greatly modified. The Lyons silk industry, the most highly developed, used large machines and water power in spinning and weaving. The most remarkable invention in the industry had been Jacquard's loom, a very successful mechanical loom for weaving figured silk fabrics. It had been greatly improved about 1815 by Breton. In 1825 ninety-six silk establishments at Lyons founded a "Réunion des Fabricants" to join with the Chamber of Commerce to give subventions to inventors and to devise means for the further improvement of the industry. The value of the silk products of Lyons rose from fifty-three million francs in 1810 to one hundred million in 1829. The development in the silk industry was paralleled by a great increase in the production of raw silk. The harvest of silk cocoons rose from five million kilograms in 1823 to eleven million in 1830. The industry, depending as it did primarily on the richer classes, had fluctuated greatly during the changes of the period 1789 to 1815. It prospered under the Restoration, at least until the panic of 1826–7. The silk industry had financially the most capitalistic organization of any of the textile industries. The chief risks and most of the profits belonged, much more than in the cotton or wool industry, to the "maître fabricant."

Linen manufacture was the most primitive of all the textile industries. Linen is more difficult to weave mechanically than cotton or wool. The village weaver still made up into cloth his customer's thread which had been spun at home. Most of the peasants did not even do this, continuing, as they had for generations, to raise their own flax and make their linen thread and cloth entirely at home. In many districts a "maître fabricant" went about collecting cloth made in the cottages by the peasants. Some small manufactories where linen thread was spun and cloth woven were scattered about France, most of them in the North. These were considered an innovation. The larger manufactories were commonest in Flanders. Valenciennes, and several other towns near the Belgian frontier, were famous for their lace made of linen thread, though very little of this was made mechanically.

A great number of other industries, some of them new, were gradually transformed. Chemical industries made considerable progress in the fields of dye stuffs, soap manufacture, soda, alum, and white and red lead. The introduction of acetic acid in 1819, of cheap artificial indigo in 1826, and of the stearine candle in 1827, brought in new chemical industries. The manufacture of beet sugar, which had been practically created by the Napoleonic blockade, was ruined by the peace in 1815 through the competition of cane sugar. The growth of a system of protective tariffs about 1820 revived the industry, especially in the departments of the Pas-de-Calais and the Somme. In 1828 there were fifty sugar beet factories in France, producing six and a half million kilograms of beet sugar a year.[1]

France has long been famous for her extensive manufacture of articles de luxe of all sorts, in which, since the seventeenth century, she has surpassed all other countries. French watches and clocks, jewelry, lace, perfumery and cosmetics, china, bric-à-brac, furniture, and musical instruments commanded the market throughout Europe, and to some extent in the Americas. The work in these industries, which were widely scattered, was done almost entirely by hand and by old methods which were not greatly modified until after the middle of the nineteenth century.

One of the most interesting results of this industrial development was the decline in the prices of certain manufactured articles in the period from 1815 to 1830. This was, for example, 60 per cent in the case of porcelain, and 25 per cent in the case of cloth. Despite this evidence, the industrial change from 1815 to 1830 had not been radical. Although large-scale production was beginning, small industries still predominated. The mechanization of industry and its concentration were in progress, though the changes effected by this process

1 Sée, p. 55.

were not nearly so marked as they were in England. Even as late as the census of 1851, 124,000 "grands entrepreneurs" in all industries in France employed on an average only ten workers, and the average number employed by 1,672,000 employers (including these 124,000 "grands entrepreneurs") was below five.[1] The Industrial Revolution in France was slow indeed. Among the large countries of the Continent, France was, however, the leader.[2]

III. PUBLIC FINANCE AND BANKING

French finance recovered rapidly after 1815. This was due not only to peaceful conditions and to the gradual improvement in industry, but also to the excellent handling of public finance. French public finance had gone through disastrous years from 1789 to 1815, yet the reorganization of her currency in 1803, and the establishment of a strong national bank in 1808, as well as Napoleon's consistent policy of making his wars pay for themselves by confiscation of foreign resources, had enabled France to emerge from the war in 1815 less burdened with debt than England. According to Dupin, writing in 1827, the six million francs borrowed for Napoleon's wars between 1803 and 1813, the billion

1 Sée, p. 87.

2 It is, moreover, interesting to notice that it was in the larger manufacturing centers of the North and East of France that political Liberalism grew most rapidly during the years 1815 to 1830. A study of the regional distribution of public opinion during the Restoration shows, as we have seen earlier, that both the growth of anti-clericalism and of parliamentarianism closely parallels the progress of the Industrial Revolution in France.

and a half's worth of public property destroyed by the invasions of 1814 and 1815, the billion and a half paid for indemnity and for the support of the army of occupation from 1815 to 1818, the heavy indemnification of the nobles in 1825, had all been paid off by 1827, and still the country had a large surplus in the treasury. In 1828 no continental state possessed so large an amount of specie. The financial achievement of the government of the Restoration is perhaps its principal title to honor.

In 1814 Baron Louis, the first Restoration Minister of Finance, rejecting the advice of the returning Emigrés, had decided that the new government must assume the financial obligations of the Empire. This had, at the beginning of the new regime, inspired in the nation at large a confidence in the financial soundness of the government — a confidence which had existed neither under the old monarchy nor under any of the various Revolutionary governments. The ever-increasing prices offered by the banks for government bonds show the steady growth of confidence in the financial soundness of the government. The 5 per cent bonds were sold successively at 52 fr. 80, 67 fr. 50, 89 fr. 55.[1] A system of careful budgeting was introduced. All the Ministers of Finance — Louis, Corvette, Roy, and, above all, Villèle — observed such strict economy in all the public services that the budget was always kept low. The various budgets were much fought over in the Chamber of Deputies, but they were never seriously modified.

1 G. Weill, *La France sous la monarchie constitutionnelle* (1912), pp. 204–210.

Villèle rendered a great service in establishing a uniform system of accounting in all the ministries. The great financial report of Chabrol, the last Minister of Finance of the Restoration, shows the French government in 1830 in a more stable and prosperous financial condition than it has ever been since that time.

A law of 1803 had established bimetallism for France. This prevailed after 1815 all over Western Europe, except in England. Gold and silver were interchangeable for monetary purposes at a ratio of 15½ of silver to one of gold. The Bank of France usually cashed its notes in silver, and the two metals circulated side by side. As there were no important discoveries of either gold or silver in the years 1815 to 1830, the bimetallic ratio remained practically stationary. There was, too, during this period, very little change in the purchasing power of money. Local prices varied somewhat owing to local disturbances, but metropolitan prices maintained a fairly stable mean level. Prices of a few manufactured articles, as we have seen, went down, but this was because of unusual improvements in methods of manufacture. It was a period of steady but low output of gold and silver and of some increase in consumable goods. A larger decline in prices might have been expected, but the increase of credit facilities offset approximately the increase of goods and helped to maintain a comparatively uniform price level.

Banking was supervised by the government. The central Bank of France was a Napoleonic creation of 1808. It was endowed with the exclusive right of note issue, and was forced to discount even the smallest bills when such discounts were expected to be for the good of French trade. The Bank administration was very conservative in issuing currency, and even in 1814 and 1815 it did not have to suspend cash payments. In 1817 branch banks with the right of issuing notes were opened in Rouen, Nantes, and Bordeaux. Bank statistics kept by the government show clearly the steady growth of French industry and commerce in the years of the Restoration. Deposits in the Bank of France rose from 46 million francs in 1814 to 145 million in 1830. The gold reserve in the same period grew from 93 to 172 millions.[1]

The expansion of credit transactions was a great aid to business, though many thought the Bank of France was still too hedged about with restrictions. It held commercial bills for 393 millions in 1816 and for 828 millions in 1830. It discounted bills for 206 millions in 1815 and for 617 millions in 1830. The cost of discounting to the commerçant fell in 1819 from 5 per cent to 4 per cent, where it remained until 1830. The Bank of France had to go through several severe financial panics. Nations were beginning to be so closely interrelated commercially that pressure in any of the great banking centers — London, Amsterdam, Paris, or New York — was felt in all the others. In 1815–6 the inability of the continental peoples to buy as freely as England had anticipated brought on the ruin of English merchants and English banks. By 1817 the effects of this were felt

1 P. Louis, *Histoire de la classe ouvrière en France depuis la Révolution* (1927), p. 49.

in France. A similar crisis in England in 1825, caused by wild speculation and over-investments, especially in South American enterprises, brought on a severe panic in France in 1826–7. It is interesting to note that, in spite of difficulties at home, the Bank of France was able in this crisis to lend nearly ten million dollars to the Bank of England — an indication of interdependence unknown before 1815. There were a great number of legalized private banks in the period, the most notable being that of the house of Rothschild.

The government sanctioned joint-stock companies. The French commercial code of 1807 distinguished between a true joint-stock company (société anonyme), which according to its constitution might or might not have limited liability, and any form of the traditional sleeping partnership (société en commandite). The capital of the silent partner had since the eighteenth century been split up into shares. Joint-stock companies of various types became one of the striking new features of the period. Before the Revolution they had been used only by a few banks and great trading concerns. Now they were extended to cover every form of commercial exploitation. Their increase was especially marked in the years after 1820. Ninety-eight new companies were formed between 1815 and 1830, among the rest — a great novelty — eight insurance companies selling insurance against death, fire, and the risks of sea shipping. Fire insurance had been known before the Revolution, but had practically disappeared after 1789. Life insurance was new to France. Most of the new companies, however, were formed in the mining and textile industries.

These joint-stock companies mark an interesting growth in the investment habit. Law's Mississippi Scheme, the English South Sea Bubble, and the three repudiations of fiscal obligations by the French government in the eighteenth century, had made Frenchmen afraid to put their savings into anything but land, a hidden strong-box, or a business directly controlled by the owner. Gradually during the nineteenth century these savings began to be invested partly in joint-stock companies and partly in government loans. The desire of the government to float loans developed somewhat more rapidly than the capacity or willingness of French buyers to take these loans. In 1817 the government had been forced to float a loan through the Hopes of Amsterdam and the Barings of London. Except in Belgium, foreign investments on the part of the French were very rare before 1830. Small private industries often found credit facilities inadequate.

Industrial capitalists, to whom the banks were rather slow to lend, acquired money partly by marriage portions, but chiefly by returning surplus into the industry. New entrepreneurs stinted themselves to the limit to save for reinvestment. The question of the sources of the increased capital invested in French industry after 1815 is an interesting one. Some of this capital came from the contraband gathered in by the officials and army officers of the Empire; a lesser amount came into France after 1815 with some of the returning Emigrés who had either married or made money in exile; some came from large foreign investments, especially English investments; but most of it was probably derived from money carefully saved from current industries. The lack of willingness on the part of the French to invest their money in commercial enterprises is well characterized by Cooper. "The French," he writes, "imagine a thousand grand projects, but hardly ever convert any of them to much practical good. The opinions of the people are formed on habits of great saving, and it requires greater familiarity with risks and more liberal notions of industry to induce the people to encounter the extra cost of improvements when they can have recourse to what in their eyes are simpler and safer means of making money."[1] Banks seemed most willing to lend on building operations. By small and moderate-sized loans to private individuals and to small companies, the section of Paris between the Seine and the Champs Elysées was developed after 1820. Most of the money in this case was lent by Laffitte and by James de Rothschild.

The period shows an interesting development in the Paris stock exchange, the Bourse. Some of the stocks of joint-stock companies were quoted, but most of the transactions were in the securities of the Bank of France, in the Mortgage Bank (La Caisse hypothécaire), and in government bonds of various sorts, especially those of the national government and of the two city governments of Paris and of Bordeaux. The bonds of foreign

1 J. F. Cooper, *Gleanings in Europe: France* (new ed., Oxford, 1928), p. 69.

governments, forbidden in 1785, were not again quoted until 1823. Most of the transactions of the Bourse were in the hands of a small group of Parisian capitalists. The government made repeated efforts to interest small investors in government bonds, but apparently without much success.

IV. THE TARIFF REGIME AND COMMERCE

The government maintained only a partial laissez-faire attitude toward industry. In 1817, and again in 1821, the Conseil des Manufactures strongly denounced a proposal to restore the old guild system which had gone out in the Revolution. At the same time they made a vigorous pronouncement against all government regulation of industry along the lines of eighteenth-century mercantilism. In one matter, however, all were in favor of government action — namely, in the matter of tariff. We have already seen the protection given by the government to agricultural products. A small group of large landowners and wealthy capitalists controlled the Chambers, and the same tariff policy for manufactures as for agriculture was elaborated. The ruling classes in the city and in the country were agreed in their demand for a high tariff regime. The fall of the Empire in 1815 had produced a commercial crisis. The economic policy of Napoleon, with its practically prohibitive tariff regime, had brought great profits to French manufacturers, who were bent, after 1815, on maintaining their monopoly of French markets. In 1814 the Restoration government reduced the tariff on foreign goods. German and English goods at once flooded the French markets. Temporary provisions were thereupon made in 1815 by royal ordinances, establishing very moderate duties on foreign sugar, coffee, and textiles brought into France. These measures, however, were not considered sufficient for the protection of French industries. A financial panic, a bad wheat crop in 1816, and a poor vintage in 1816 and 1817 that had thrust the country into a famine, together with the general economic maladjustment that follows war, were really much more responsible for the difficulties in which French industry found itself after 1815 than was the dumping of cheap English goods on to the French markets. The cotton manufacturers, nevertheless, besieged the Chamber of Deputies to raise the tariff on cotton goods. Other industries soon joined in these demands. The Minister of Finance, Baron Louis, and others told these manufacturers that the future economic progress of France could be rendered secure only by allowing foreign competition, insisting that high tariffs would retard improvement of French methods of production. This reasonable view did not, of course, prevail among the industrial leaders, who finally forced through a set of tariffs that practically excluded foreign competition.

By 1820 high tariffs had been placed on all iron and steel products. These were mainly directed against English, Swedish, and Russian manufactures. The ministry intended this to be merely a temporary measure to offset the immediate disadvantages of French manufacturers and to allow them time to improve their methods.

This did not satisfy the French manufacturers. In 1821 and 1822 duties were raised to such an extent — the duty on English iron, for example, was 120 per cent — that foreign metallurgic products practically disappeared from the French markets. Almost exactly the same tariff history is to be found in the case of cotton, woolen, and silk manufactures.

Toward the close of the Restoration a reaction in favor of free trade began to appear. High tariffs, it was discovered, were damaging to French commerce. They led to reprisals on French goods by foreign governments, especially by England, Spain, and the United States. In 1820 the United States put an extra tax of $10 a ton on all French cargoes entering her ports. High tariffs also led to smuggling on a very large scale. Certain French industries suffered from the high-tariff regime. This was especially true of the cotton industry. This industry needed steam engines, and yet in 1822 a prominent cotton weaver of Saint-Etienne had to pay duty amounting to 7000 francs on a small engine imported from England. The cotton-weaving industry, moreover, wanted English thread, which was far superior to French thread, and there grew up a great contraband business in English thread. The government officials connived at smuggling. After the English financial crisis of 1826 had begun to affect French industry, many blamed the high tariffs for the difficulties that the French found in selling their goods abroad. In 1827 Dupin published a kind of manifesto of free trade. During Martignac's ministry in 1828 a special Ministry of

Commerce and Manufactures was created. It conducted an extensive investigation, interviewing representatives of all points of view in the fields of commerce and industry. Various local chambers of commerce also made investigations and published reports. As a result, the ministry proposed a scheme of modified protection so as to prevent the aid given by the tariff to one industry from damaging another. These proposals were never passed. The agitation did result, however, in the formation after 1827 of a small free trade party in France, a party which was to play a very important rôle later on. The chief theorist of this group was the economist J.-B. Say, who set forth the principles of free trade in his famous *Cours d'économie politique* of 1828–30.

The French tariff policy from 1815 to 1830, so far as industries were concerned, was bad, owing largely to its exaggerations. These were the result of the agitation of a small group of private interests which, owing to the very restricted franchise, were the only ones represented in the government. Protection of a rather extreme sort was and had been for nearly two hundred years the policy of every country in Europe. England alone had begun to change, though not to any extent until after 1815. France was still mercantilist in outlook, indifferent or timid in undertaking foreign trade ventures of any sort, and strongly protectionist.

The governments of the Restoration can hardly be said to have pursued any colonial policy. In 1815 France had only a small colonial empire. This consisted of a few small islands in the West Indies, chief of which were

Martinique and Guadeloupe, French Guiana, an undeveloped region in South America, and a few trading posts in Africa and India. Napoleon had lost interest in colonial projects when he found himself so beset by enemies at home. His colonial governments, moreover, were notoriously bad, and led to the loss of San Domingo to France. Napoleon's schemes and achievements in Europe so occupied the French people that the nation at large seemed by 1815 to have lost all interest in colonies. In the meantime colonial trade fell from 165 million francs in 1789 to only 37 million in 1818. The parliamentary debates of the Restoration show a surprising indifference to colonial affairs, an indifference which is in contrast with the enthusiasm that had prevailed among the governing classes in the seventeenth and eighteenth centuries. Repeated objections were made in the Chambers between 1815 and 1830 to even the small amounts spent on colonial administration. Hence the colonies were left undeveloped, as was also the navy. The whole attitude of the period toward colonial enterprises is well summarized in a speech of the great Liberal orator, General Foy. "Just see the enormous expense of our navy, kept up to protect our colonies and our external commerce. Would it not be far better to use this in improving our agriculture and in developing our internal commerce and our industry?"

The chief product of the colonies was sugar. In 1819 they furnished 34 million out of 39 million kilograms imported. French colonial sugar was admitted into France with very small duties. In addition, French products might be shipped to the colonies without paying an export tax. This even included certain articles whose export from France was otherwise forbidden. Each colony and each colonial or French product had special legislation, so that generalizations are difficult.

Foreign merchandise of all sorts was still excluded from French colonies, except in emergencies, when a special order from the local governor might suspend the law. Many colonial products could be sold only in France. The government's commercial policy included the establishment of a merchant marine. A law of December, 1814, and other later laws placed an extra tax on certain classes of goods brought in foreign ships to French ports. In 1822 these regulations were modified by treaty in the case of the United States, and in 1826 in so far as they affected English shipping. The French merchant marine was small. In 1824 the government instituted an investigation into the causes of the relatively high cost of French shipping, but it came to nothing.

Industry and commerce were likewise aided by the government through the collection of statistics and through industrial exhibitions and technical schools. Three industrial exhibitions were held in Paris, in 1819, 1823, and 1827, of which the first was the most successful. They were larger than any held under the Empire. In each department the prefect appointed a "jury" to send representative products to Paris. The public took a great interest in these industrial exhibitions, and the attendance was large.

The Ecole Spéciale de Commerce et de l'Industrie, founded by private individuals in 1820, gave for the first time in France the special instruction necessary to the commerçant. This school, founded under the patronage of Casimir-Périer, Laffitte, and Chaptal, offered courses in modern foreign languages, in commercial and industrial legislation, and in technical methods used in various industries. It had seventy students in 1825. The Conservatoire des Arts et Métiers, the French patent office, was opened in 1820. Courses of lectures, of a very general nature, were given there by J.-B. Say and by Dupin. The Ecole Centrale des Arts et Manufactures dates from 1824. It offered courses in civil engineering, factory management, and applied science. There was complaint in industrial circles that there were no industrial schools offering more elementary training. After 1820 some of the French cities established such schools. The best ones were at Angers and Châlons. In 1826 a private legacy made it possible to open a school for the training of workingmen at Lyons.

In 1819 Decazes created a Conseil Général du Commerce and a Conseil Général des Manufactures. The first of these was composed of twenty members named by the Minister of the Interior, some of them selected from a list of names presented by the various local chambers of commerce. The second council was made up of sixty manufacturers. Statistics were kept and filed, and recommendations made to the ministry and to the Chambers. Most of the industrial and commercial legislation of the Restoration after 1819 either originated in these councils or passed through them. Below these central organizations there existed in most of the larger towns chambers of commerce and tribunals of commerce. The chambers of commerce were private organizations made up of capitalists who came together to discuss measures to improve manufacturing and commerce and to propose laws to the city and to the national Conseil Général des Manufactures. They were permitted by the government, whereas labor unions were forbidden. The tribunals of commerce were each made up of five judges selected from the manufacturing group in the larger cities. These tribunals handled special commercial cases. Thus the capitalistic group had developed an excellent apparatus for the control of the government in all business concerns, while at the same time the workers were forbidden to organize.

The Revolution and the Empire had been very abnormal periods for French commerce. Civil war and then wars of conquest had diverted commerce from its former channels, had ruined hundreds of merchants, and had made new fortunes for others. The Restoration brought peace, and as a result commerce tended to resume its former ways. As soon as the sea was opened in 1815, much of France's old trade came back to her. French wines, French silks, and French articles de luxe were in as great demand as ever. There was no competition to speak of for these products, so superior were the French in these lines. They had been smuggled out of France and smuggled into foreign countries during the days of the Continental Blockade. Now they were marketed openly. The essential conditions of commerce changed much less after 1815 than did the conditions of industry. Trade had been greatly upset, but after 1815 the old commercial methods and many of the old commercial relations of the eighteenth century were resumed. Commerce before 1789 had a more capitalistic and thus a more modern organization than industry. This was especially true of maritime commerce. Only after 1850 did commerce develop much beyond the conditions that prevailed before the Revolution.

The volume of French foreign commerce during the whole period from 1800 to 1830 was much less than that of England, though in commerce France led the continent. The greatest development in shipping appeared, not in the older ports of Bordeaux and Marseilles, where conditions remained nearly stationary, but at Havre, which profited by the growth of the textile industries in the basin of the Seine and in the North of France. The high tariffs set up by other countries after 1815, largely to keep out cheap English goods, often made it difficult to market abroad some of the newer types of French manufactures. After 1820 the rising tariff scale in France made French exporting in some cases even more difficult, owing to the reprisals made by other governments on French products. For example, the high tariff on iron reduced by over a half the exportation of wine from Bordeaux to Sweden and Russia. French external commerce grew, however, from 502 million francs' worth of goods exported in 1818 to 544 million in 1825. Imports consisted almost exclusively of raw materials.

Internal commerce in France was already highly developed before the Revolution. The gradual abolition of internal custom boundaries during the eighteenth century was a great aid in improving the conditions of local trade. In local districts the center of trade was the neighboring country town. Here there were usually no shops except, as in the days before 1789, the workshops and stores of the local craftsmen — the shoemakers, the tailors, the furniture makers, and the rest. Such a workshop was usually the enterprise of a single family. The wife did the bookkeeping, the children waited on customers or helped the head of the house with his craft, while the housekeeping was often done by the eldest daughter. In these small towns there was usually a weekly market where peasant and townsman met. The peasant sold his farm produce, made his purchases in the town shops directly from the handicraftsman, and returned home. Sometime during the year a large fair was held in the more important towns. Here there were puppet shows and street entertainments to attract visitors. In the streets shops were set up which carried a wider variety of goods than the local market usually offered — spices, fancy types of cloth, various sorts of tools, and small luxuries. There was at these fairs a great deal of trading in the specialty of the region — horses, cattle, sheep, or flax, or whatever it might be. These annual fairs, which go back to the twelfth century or even earlier, were on the decline before the Revolution, though even in the twentieth century they have not died out in France. Some towns had general stores which sold everything from sugar and coffee to calico and candles. Besides the general store, the town market, and the annual fair, the country districts also knew one of the most picturesque of types — the local peddler. Sometimes he specialized in one product, though he usually carried a variety of articles in his pack, such as belts, gloves, clocks, and caps. A higher class of peddlers went about with a wagon, or a pack horse or two, carrying a larger and more varied stock.

The larger towns showed much greater specialization in their shopkeeping. There were streets of specialized though quite small shops which sold clothing, shoes, and other articles at retail — articles which were not made in the shop. It became commoner now to adorn such shops with large glass windows in which goods were displayed to the passer-by. There were also numbers of the older type of store where the shopkeeper did not come between the craftsman and his customer. It was considered an innovation when, at the close of the Restoration, M. Thernaux employed tailors and seamstresses to work for him on dresses and suits to be sold ready-made in his shop at the sign of Bonhomme Richard, Place des Victoires, in Paris. The first large "magasin de nouveautés" dates from the end of the Restoration.[1] The larger towns had special markets or "halles" where trading in large commodities was done. In these towns

1 Advertising was more common than before 1789. An example of the new advertising reads as follows: "We make our own products, hence our manufacturing costs are small, and our retail prices, as you can see, are below those of other houses." Modern advertising had such modest beginnings. (L. Cahen in *Revue d'histoire moderne*, 1930)

a merchant class handled the food supply. Special trades like the cotton industry of Mulhouse, the silk trade of Lyons, and the wine trade of Bordeaux were, as we have seen, elaborately organized. The markets for these products were wide, sometimes extending to foreign countries, and a modern capitalistic organization had been developed to handle them before the Revolution. Thus French commerce in the period from 1815 to 1830 continued its steady expansion from local to national and international markets.

V. MEANS OF COMMUNICATION

The government played a large part in the improvement of the means of communication which marked everywhere the earlier part of the nineteenth century. France had been famous in the eighteenth century for her excellent roads. Arthur Young speaks of these highways as "truly magnificent," and adds that "we have not an idea of such a road in England." There had been created in the reign of Louis XV a Corps des Ponts et Chaussées, to give more attention to the highways of France. The Ecole Polytechnique, founded during the French Revolution, was a government school of engineering which furnished the government with a good corps of engineers, who were especially useful in bridge, road, and canal building. The roads were classified under Napoleon's rule as imperial and departmental highways, the care of the latter falling on the local authorities. Many of the French roads suffered from neglect during the later years of the Empire, and especially during the campaigns of 1814 and 1815. The chief road enterprises of the Restoration were extensive and thoroughgoing improvements rather than new constructions. Bridges were far less numerous than they are today, and packhorses and vehicles were used to splashing through a ford. The gradual increase in commerce through the early nineteenth century was marked by the appearance of greater numbers of heavy wagons and carts, and by more numerous diligences. The latter, with the passengers crowded inside and the luggage piled high on the top, gave a certain picturesqueness to the highways of France that was lost with the advent of the railroad. At certain seasons of the year the roads were crowded with droves of cattle, sheep, pigs, and waddling geese being driven to market. Transportation by pack horse or wagon was possible only for valuable articles. For many kinds of heavy materials the cost of transportation so increased their value that it was out of the question to transport them any distance.

A work of the Restoration more striking than its road construction was the building of canals. Again this represented the continuation of a program that went back into the days of the Ancien Régime. In the reign of Louis XIV the first great French canal had been built, connecting the Mediterranean with the Atlantic through the Garonne River — an achievement which had moved Arthur Young to say, "Here, Louis XIV, thou art truly great!" An important canal through Picardy was begun under Louis XVI and completed under Napoleon. In 1818 a regular program of canal building on a large

A DILIGENCE, 1828

SÉGUIN'S LOCOMOTIVE, 1827

scale was undertaken by the government. It was in this same period that much canal building was going on in England and in the United States. In 1821 and 1822 new laws were passed which encouraged the digging of canals. The expense was borne now partly by state loans and partly by private companies to which the concession of collecting tolls was sold. By 1830 over nine hundred kilometers of canals had been added to the twelve hundred kilometers already in existence. These canals formed a vast network, most of which had been built to connect the four great river basins of France — the Seine, the Loire, the Garonne, and the Rhone. In regions where the river navigation was poor, lateral canals were built. The greatest canal built during the Restoration was a canal connecting the Rhine and the Rhone. There was still insufficient communication between the North and the South. The Rhone was almost useless in its upper course, and many of the river-ways needed dredging, as well as adequate quays and wharves. The merchandise from Provence, to reach Paris by water, had to pass by Gibraltar — at least until 1829, when a canal was opened connecting the Saône and the Seine.

Boats were towed by horses or men. Successful steamboats were first used in 1822 on the Saône, following some experiments of the Marquis de Jouffroy in 1816. In 1829 the first successful steamboat of the Rhone took seven days to go up the river from Arles to Lyons, a difficult trip owing to the swift current of the Rhone. Steam mules were not used until after 1830. The first steamboats used on the open sea were small pack boats that plied between Corsica and Marseilles. Commerce on the high seas during the Restoration was still handled in wooden sailing ships.

The construction of railroads began under Napoleon, when cars were moved on rails — usually wooden — in and about mines. These cars were drawn by men or mules. The first horse cars on rails used for any distance were employed near Saint-Etienne after 1823, where they were used to haul coal to the Rhone and the Loire. It was in this year, 1823, that the government made the first important railroad concession. There was some prejudice against these concessions, and two new towns, Saint-Chamond and Rive-de-Gier, near Saint-Etienne, refused to allow a new line of horse cars to pass through their limits. In 1827 the first successful steam locomotive was used to haul coal cars near Saint-Etienne. The use of the locomotive did not affect commercial conditions until after 1830. No one, except the Saint-Simonians, had the least idea of the future importance of steam railways. As late as 1838 Thiers saw nothing in a railroad built near Paris but a "plaything for children and for Parisian pleasure seekers." The *Producteur*, the organ of the followers of the Socialist prophet, Saint-Simon, however, looked forward to a time when "railroads would work a vast revolution in society and make provincial towns mere suburbs of the capital." That time, though, was still well in the future. The telegraph, like the steam railway, belongs to the history of the July Monarchy. However, the government had, since the Revolution, used semaphore poles for signaling. There were nearly five thousand kilometers of this system by 1830. The operation of this system was expensive, as each pole required an operator, and signaling was only possible when the weather was clear. The service was used only by the government, and had no commercial significance.

The chief means of communication was the diligence. The diligences were run by the government, though in places they were supplemented by local omnibuses, some of which were owned by the municipalities and some by private companies. There was also one large and well-managed private company of diligences which sent out about three hundred coaches from Paris every day. From Paris, to go to Chartres (about 54 miles) took one day, to Metz or Tours two days, to Lyons or Nantes four days, and to Bordeaux eight days. The total number of passengers carried on both the public and private diligences doubled between 1816 and 1828. In the South and East of France much of the travel was done on horseback. Horses were changed along the way. The baggage was sent ahead, sometimes in a wagon, but usually on horseback. It was in charge of the "messager en chef," who also saw that meals and sleeping quarters were ready. In Paris the first city omnibuses with regular routes were inaugurated in January, 1828. They had places for fourteen persons, and charged a fare of twenty-five centimes for all rides. By October, 1828, there were forty omnibuses in use, and the service had become very popular.

The postal system attained the most rapid rate of

speed. The average rate of eight and a half minutes to a kilometer in 1816 was reduced to five and three fourths by 1830. In 1830, to send a letter from Paris to Bordeaux took forty-five hours, from Paris to Lyons forty-seven hours, and from Paris to Toulouse seventy-two hours. Postage stamps were not issued until 1847. Letters were taxed according to the distance sent, and the cost of sending was paid by the person who received the letter. After 1819 each postal diligence took a few passengers. Only four persons could travel in one mail carriage, and the price of a seat was much higher in these conveyances than in the regular diligences. The improvement in the postal system gives evidence of the great improvement in communication in this period just before the railroad. The number of letters distributed in Paris rose from 28,000 a day in 1816 to 43,000 a day in 1828. Compared, however, with contemporary conditions, the postal service was still very backward, especially in the provinces. Of 37,367 communes in France, 35,587 had no postoffice. In 1828 the price of postage was raised, and in the July Monarchy a new era in the French postal system was inaugurated.

The student of this period cannot but conclude that, with the credit facilities, with the kinds and amount of merchandise handled, and with the facilities of transportation, the economic life of the Restoration resembles that of the Ancien Régime far more closely than that of contemporary France. It was the building of railroads and the changes which they made that were, of all the phenomena of the Industrial Revolution, most fundamental in marking the transition from the old economic order to the new. The Restoration saw the interesting beginnings of this transformation. Wealth in mines and industries had not yet eclipsed wealth derived from agriculture, but the banker and the industrial capitalist played a greater rôle in French life than they ever had before.

CHAPTER IV

THE STATE OF SOCIETY

THE social life of the Restoration presents those interesting contrasts which always mark any society in a state of change. In such a transition some classes are little affected by new forces, while other groups owe their very existence to the new conditions.

After 1815 the life of the aristocracy and of the clergy retained much of the atmosphere and flavor of the Ancien Régime. Although they were forced to recognize parvenu groups which shouldered in beside them,— the nobility of the Empire and the newer industrial bourgeoisie of the cities,— they tried to hold themselves aloof, and would have maintained the older life had it been possible. During the period of the Restoration the life of the peasants was least affected; their daily round continued much as it had been before the Revolution. Their lot was perhaps somewhat easier, but not essentially changed.

The new economic forces were developing two new classes — the rising bourgeoisie of the towns, and, in sharp contrast, the working classes of the cities. Among the workers the abuses of the Industrial Revolution caused much misery and wretchedness. The new proletariat, however, was almost without class consciousness. Trade-unionism was just beginning to develop, in spite of laws against it, and isolated groups like the Saint-Simonians conceived the first programs of social action for the workers. As in England before the Reform Bill of 1832, the workers, so far as they envisaged reform, joined forces with the bourgeois Liberals in working for the extension of the franchise and for the freedom of the press. All over Western Europe the ballot box was at this time regarded as the new Ark of the Covenant. Mill owner and mill hand had hardly begun to realize their divergent economic and political interests.

In the large towns there was an inevitable fusion of the new and the old. The old nobility, the nobility of the Empire, and the new industrial plutocracy were more or less thrown together by common interests; in effect they were the ruling classes, though some of them looked to the future while others looked to the past. The industrial bourgeoisie were proud of their newly acquired wealth and social position as well as of the political power which they had gained through the Revolution. Moreover, they preserved from the Revolutionary period a marked distrust of hereditary kings, of nobles, and of priests. It is true that the women of the middle class still went to church and looked upon the priest as their truest guide, but the men leaned more and more to Liberalism in politics and to anti-clericalism and free-thought in all that pertained to religion. Much of this was in direct opposition to the traditional position of the old aristocracy, and to a lesser extent to the interests of the Napoleonic nobility, but as a whole the old nobility and the new plutocracy were opposed to the peasants and the working classes, and they had common interests in social life, in art and literature, and to some measure in politics.

This newer, composite society appeared in the larger towns and in the cities. The older social forms, and distinctions, and ways of thinking persisted in the country districts. As always in France, the cities, with the capital at their head, were the foci of reorganization.

I. PARIS AND THE PROVINCIAL CITIES

In the life and activity of the nation Paris dominated everything. This concentration of the forces of French society in the capital had become more marked with every stage of French history since the Middle Ages. The Revolution had accelerated this age-long process by destroying the old provinces, and the Napoleonic regime had completed this centralization with a thoroughness that could be equaled in no country of the Western World.

After 1815 the Court lived in Paris, not at Versailles. Economically Paris dominated France as never before, while the Chambers focused all political attention on the capital. Paris, moreover, drew to herself most of the talent of the country, and after 1815 was the artistic capital of the whole of Europe. The gaiety and charm of its society, its intense artistic and intellectual activity, its unrivaled theaters and cafés, made it the favorite resort of every people in Europe. Paris was especially popular, after 1815, with the English. There were so many English in the city that an English newspaper,

Galignani's *Messenger*, was established. After the reactionary settlement at Vienna in 1815, the city was also full of political refugees, and as Vienna was to all European Liberals the City of Darkness, Paris from 1815 to 1848 seemed the City of Light.

The Paris of the Restoration was still, by present standards, a small city. According to the census of 1817, the population was about 715,000. By 1830 it had increased to 800,000. The city remained in many ways quite mediæval in appearance, in spite of the improvements that had been made by Louis XIV, Louis XV, and Napoleon — modern Paris, in fact, is largely the work of Baron Haussmann, and dates only from the Second Empire. At this period most of the streets were narrow, ill paved, and dirty, and the houses were crowded together. The congestion was worst on the Ile de la Cité and in the central part of the old city on both the Right and Left Banks of the Seine. The occasional Gothic doorways, the many dark passages, and the jumbled masses of old buildings were greatly admired by the rising Romantic generation, but they were looked upon as a disgrace by the new industrialists.

In the period of the later Middle Ages the city had begun to spread rapidly on to the Right Bank. Here was the enormous pile of the Louvre and the Tuileries, the sixteenth-century Hôtel de Ville, the old noble Quartier du Marais, the wholesale and trading district of Saint-Antoine, and finally, bounding this solidly built mass, a ring of boulevards built under the last Bourbon kings before the Revolution. Beyond this half-circle to the west, along the Seine, lay the Champs Elysées and the Cours La Reine. These formed a sort of ill-kept and open forest through which were scattered a number of out-of-door summer restaurants. At the end of the Champs Elysées rose the half-finished Arc de Triomphe, which Charles X proposed to complete in honor of the Duc d'Angoulême and the Spanish Campaign of 1823. This absurd project was not carried out, and it rose above the trees a strange, unfinished mass of masonry until its completion during the July Monarchy. The present fashionable quarter about the Arc de Triomphe was at this time occupied by a few small houses and truck gardens.

The Place Louis XV (after 1815 the Place de la Concorde), between the Tuileries Gardens and the lower end of the Champs Elysées, was a huge ill-paved square, impressive for its size, but not much frequented except on Sundays and holidays. The Tuileries Gardens were then, as they are now, a favorite promenade. On the river side of the Place Louis XV a bridge led across to the Palais Bourbon. During the Restoration this belonged to the Condé family, who rented it to the government as a meeting place for the Chamber of Deputies. On the fourth side of the Place stood the two beautiful pavilions built by Gabriel during the reign of Louis XV. Between them ran a wide street which revealed the incomplete façade of the Madeleine. The obelisk, the fountains, and the statues of French cities which now decorate the square had not yet been set up.

From a corner of the Place Louis XV Napoleon had

constructed the rue de Rivoli, which led down the side of the Tuileries Gardens to the square in front of the Palais Royal. This fine street, with its arcaded walk, is one of the great building achievements of the Empire. It was a favorite promenade during the Restoration, but its shops were considered much inferior to those of the Palais Royal. Behind the Madeleine, and beyond it to the west in the direction of the Champs Elysées, there were a few scattered houses. The district was quite open, and most of the better houses had fine gardens. Here was the Faubourg Saint-Honoré, where lived many of the Napoleonic nobility and a group of wealthy bourgeois families. In the opposite direction, to the east of the Madeleine, the city was more closely built, especially in the old part between the circle of boulevards — built in the seventeenth century on the site of the old fortifications — and the Seine. Besides the Louvre, the Hôtel de Ville, and a number of large churches, this section included the Place Vendôme and the Palais Royal. Here were many of the most fashionable shops. In one part of the quarter, the Chaussée d'Antin, lived a group of very wealthy bourgeois families. Further to the east, following the river, was the Marais, once the home of the old nobility where the fine eighteenth-century houses of the Rohans and the Soubises are still to be found. After 1815 this quarter was largely occupied by the lesser bourgeoisie. Finally, at the extreme east of the city, near the site of the old Bastille, was the poorest quarter of Paris, the Quartier Saint-Antoine, famous for its rôle in the Revolution.

Crossing to the Left Bank, one found there was less differentiation of classes and districts. At the west end of this bank, across the river from the Place de la Concorde and the Tuileries Gardens, was the Faubourg Saint-Germain, where after 1815 the old aristocracy lived in indignant seclusion. The principal buildings on the Left Bank were the Luxembourg Palace, where the Chamber of Peers had its sessions, and the Panthéon, reconsecrated in 1815 as the Church of Sainte-Geneviève — an amusing anomaly when one remembers that Mirabeau, Voltaire, and Rousseau lie buried in the crypt. In the center of this part of the city on the Left Bank was the Latin Quarter, with its old traditions and its new Romantic Bohemia. Here, as elsewhere in Paris, were many old gardens belonging to private individuals and to religious houses, some of them quite extensive. There are remnants of these still in Paris. One knows of their existence only by the tall chestnut trees that hang over high forbidding walls, or by an occasional glimpse through an open doorway.

Paris was still very much as it was in the eighteenth century. The Restoration made fewer changes than had been made during the Empire. Some of the street names were changed after 1815. The rue d'Arcole, for example, became the rue de Beaujolais, while the rue Napoléon was renamed the rue de la Paix. Very little public building was done between 1815 and 1830. A bronze equestrian statue of Henry IV was set up on the Pont Neuf in 1818. It was cast by a Napoleonic sympathizer, who is said to have put a statuette of his hero into the arm of

leaving the Tuileries and five geese waddling in! The Duc d'Angoulême, the elder son of Charles X, was gruff, awkward in his movements, and hesitating in his speech. He had been pushed by his family into the Spanish war of 1823, where he had acquired a manufactured reputation as a soldier. He always seemed to be without either emotions or opinions. His education had been neglected, and added to his ridiculous ignorance of affairs was a certain conceit that made him indulge in facial tricks and peculiarities of gait. Even the Ultras thought him unfit to be king. His wife, whom he had married in exile, was his first cousin, the daughter of Louis XVI and Marie Antoinette. An unattractive woman, severe in manner, and very devout she was to the French the symbol of the hatreds and prejudices of the Ancien Régime. She had, however, proved herself a person of vigor and courage in 1815; Napoleon said she was "the only man in the royal family." She had no children. The younger brother of the Duc d'Angoulême, the Duc de Berri, was a vigorous but stupid man with a rough manner. His assassination in 1820 improved his reputation. His young wife, the Duchesse de Berri, a daughter of the King of Naples, was a small and vivacious woman, who in the reign of Charles X presided over the Tuileries.

The life of the Court, even under Charles X, was quiet. After the great entertainments and pomp of the old monarchy at Versailles, and even after the sort of parvenu display at the Tuileries under Napoleon, the Court life of the Restoration was insipid. In the evening at the Tuileries a dozen or fifteen dukes and their wives sat about the salon. Some played whist, the favorite game of Charles X; the Duc d'Angoulême preferred chess. The Duchesse d'Angoulême embroidered. Politics were forbidden in the conversation and as the guests were usually ignorant of science and literature, they were not discussed. Most of those who appeared at Court were very old, even decrepit — members of the old nobility who had suffered exile with the royal family. The nobility of the Empire, by choice rather than by decree, were rarely seen at Court. As one writer of the time remarked, "anyone might be called a patriot so long as he had nothing to do with the King. One had to be a Vendéen, a Chouan, a Cossack, or an Englishman to be presented at Court."[1] James Fenimore Cooper observed in 1828 that the public were indifferent to the royal family. He went to the races, where the Duchesse d'Angoulême held up her little nephew, the Comte de Chambord. An Englishman applauded, two Americans took off their hats; the French paid no attention whatever, and remained covered. The life of the royal family showed clearly that the great interests of the nation were no longer centered in the Court. The scientists, the statesmen, and the writers who were laying the foundations of nineteenth-century France were living and working quite outside the Court, which had now dwindled to scarcely more than a family circle.

Class lines had been broken down to some extent during the eighteenth century through the rapid growth of the bourgeoisie. The upheaval of the Revolution, how-

1 Charléty, p. 38.

ever, had done more than the whole previous century to obliterate old class lines. First the nobility were abolished; then Napoleon created a new nobility; then in 1815 the old nobility were reinstated. It would seem that under such circumstances most of the old social distinctions would have disappeared. Some of these nevertheless survived after 1815, though the progress of democracy was each year more marked. The words "aristocracy," "bourgeoisie," and "the people" still meant in the years 1815 to 1830 something much more definite than they do now. Each class had its own life, its own customs, and its own amusements. At the top of the social scale were the old aristocratic families; then between this class and the richest industrialists stood the Napoleonic nobility; next came the wealthier bourgeoisie, then the petite bourgeoisie, and finally the workers and the peasants. The first three classes were the only ones which counted greatly in politics or in the movement of ideas.

The old aristocracy in Paris lived mostly in the Faubourg Saint-Germain. Many of the families that stayed in the provinces lived on their ancestral estates. Especially was this true after the indemnification of the old nobility in 1826. The Faubourg Saint-Germain held as its highest distinction, next to an ancient title, a seat in the Chamber of Peers. According to the caricaturists of the time, this society was dominated by strange old dowagers returning from years of exile, and broken nobles with little left but their titles. Their piety was usually very marked, and an abbé was always a figure in the home life of this group. In upper-class families, both noble and bourgeois, the mother and her daughters were especially devout. The ladies embroidered altar cloths, patronized the priest, gave him money for his poor parishioners, and attended Mass regularly. Monsieur le curé was for such families a sort of earthly providence who baptized, helped to educate, and married the children, at the same time giving advice on everything. Piety was one of the surest marks of social respectability. This old aristocracy, both in the Faubourg Saint-Germain and in the provinces, disliked Louis XVIII because he seemed too lenient, and they looked upon Villèle as a dangerous radical. Charles X was their idol.

Life among the aristocracy in Paris went by routine, six months in the country and six in Paris, with balls during carnival time, and concerts and special sermons during Lent. This class went to the theater very little, and almost never traveled. They brought up their children very carefully. The first lessons in writing, reading, and arithmetic were usually given at home by the priest, who might also teach his pupils some Latin and a little sacred and profane history, the last often put into simple verses. The dancing master gave the young people lessons in deportment. This was all very much as in the days of the Ancien Régime. The girls might learn to play the harp or the piano, which was just coming into drawing-rooms. The convent of Sacré-Cœur was highly esteemed as a place for the education of girls. Boys must learn to hunt. They were ordinarily sent to

A READING OF THE *DRAPEAU-BLANC* IN THE FAUBOURG SAINT-GERMAIN

a Catholic collège, and went finally into the army, the diplomatic service, or, more rarely than in former years, into the church.

In the noble and in the wealthier bourgeois families the arrangements for marriage were of great concern to both the families involved. Marriages of inclination were looked upon as belonging only to the lower classes. There was, in these higher circles, little faith in love or in conjugal fidelity, and only mariages de convenance were considered. The marriage negotiations were usually opened by the mothers of the young people, and concluded, after many visits back and forth, by the fathers. Marriages were usually contracted when the betrothed were both young, and still unformed in character; hence they frequently proved more successful than might have been expected.

If a young woman felt that she did not love the man she was marrying, her mother assured her that she would learn to, and the priest told her that a well-bred young woman always loved her husband. Usually the bride-to-be was so showered with presents and so occupied with parties that she had little time to think or wonder. There were two weddings — a civil marriage at the mayor's office, and one at the church. For a year after marriage the young wife never went out into society without her husband, her mother, or her mother-in-law. After this first year, husband and wife often frequented different salons. It was supposed to ruin the gaiety of a salon if it was frequented by both husbands and wives. Little wonder that the young Romanticists and the Saint-Simonians were both in violent revolt against such a social regime.

The salon was still the center of fashionable social intercourse. Nearly every aristocratic and wealthy bourgeois family received guests on certain days in the week. Here one might meet interesting people, or encounter the most stupid ones, depending on where one went. Dinner was served at six, and the guests generally arrived about eight. The evening was spent in conversation, which was still cultivated in an eighteenth-century way. Sometimes there would be dancing, though cards and billiards were much more popular. The talk was often clever and witty enough, though, except in certain literary and political salons, usually of little consequence. A young Pole visiting Paris in 1829–30 found that in this society thinking was usually quite unnecessary. Writing of the aristocratic salons of the Quartier Saint-Germain, Stendhal says: "So long as you do not speak lightly of God, or of the clergy, or of the King, or of the men in power, or of the artists patronized by the Court, or of anything established; so long as you do not say anything good of Béranger, or of Rousseau, or of Voltaire, or of the opposition press, or of anything that allowed itself the liberty of a little freedom of speech; so long, above all, as you did not talk politics, you could discuss anything you pleased with freedom!"[1] The men still joined in this society. The retreat of the men to smoke cigars apart, or the fashion of spending the evening at the Jockey Club, did not come in until after 1830.

1 *Le rouge et le noir*, Chap. 34.

Intellectual and artistic interests brought together to some extent, the Faubourgs Saint-Germain and Saint-Honoré and the Chaussée d'Antin. In the salons where moved the intellectuals of the day there was still much of the wit and finesse of the eighteenth century, together with a certain seriousness that the Revolution had brought. It was more possible to maintain an intellectual salon now than it had been under the Empire, when snobs and adventurers flourished. Life was more settled, and society no longer had the air of being temporarily encamped between two campaigns. Money had not yet come to take the place it was to occupy in the society of the July Monarchy and of the Second Empire. Great expense and elaborate display counted for little. Cooper, who found this society charming, remarks that a person never hesitated to say that he was too poor to own a carriage.

In the early years of the Restoration Madame de Staël and Madame Récamier still received. In these years Madame de Staël spoke of her salon as a "hospital for the wounded of all parties." Later the best-known literary salon of the Faubourg Saint-Germain was that of the Duchesse de Duras, whose sentimental novel, *Ourika*, had a tremendous vogue and gave its name to fashionable hats and shawls. The salon par excellence of the political Ultras was that of the Duchesse de Trémoille. Madame d'Ancelot welcomed both Classicists and Romanticists in one of the most diverting salons of the period. Here Alfred de Vigny fell in love with the young poetess Delphine Gay, whom he would have married had his mother not interfered. Mademoiselle Gay was a very characteristic figure, and, as Madame de Girardin, was also a great personage in the July Monarchy. Born in Aix-la-Chapelle, she was said to have been baptized on the tomb of Charlemagne. She had the pale face and the air of mysterious beauty — "ce visage de keepsake"[1] — so admired by the Romantic School. Every important occasion, public or private, was celebrated with one of Mademoiselle Gay's poems. Her lyre, it was said, was "one of her household utensils." Her popularity in the salons of the Restoration amounted to a furor.

Fortune telling and spiritualism were much in fashion, and society was beset by a number of charlatans, most esteemed of whom was a German, Dr. Koreff, described as "the prophet of illuminism, vampirism, occultism, and the interpreter of dreams." In the salon of Madame d'Agoult the songs of Schubert and the "Symphonie fantastique" of Berlioz were heard in France for the first time. Music played a larger place in the salons than earlier, though Heine thought that the craze for virtuoso piano playing was ruining conversation and "turning people into sentimental idiots." Rossini was most sought after to direct these private musicales. Malibran, Sontag, and Rubini were the favorites in the salons, as at the Opéra. It was in this period that the young virtuoso Liszt was introduced by Rossini as a

1 A "keepsake" was an album inscribed with sentimental verses, sketches, and autographs, and decorated with pressed flowers. It was the immediate ancestor of the family photograph album.

prodigy. His playing of Beethoven introduced this composer's works into France. Politics was a subject of salon conversation in many circles, though it was the custom for the host or hostess to call a halt if the discussion became too acrimonious. In literary salons, Chateaubriand, and later Hugo and Lamartine, were much lionized.

The most cosmopolitan group, gathered from all corners of Europe, was to be found at the home of Baron Gérard, the portrait painter. Besides a miscellany of duchesses and bohemians, it included young Thiers, a little man wearing great spectacles and talking wittily on all subjects, Cuvier the scientist, Balzac, a great blustering hulk of a man, Bertin, the brilliant and fearless publisher of the *Journal des Débats*, whose features still live in Ingres' magnificent portrait, the wily old Talleyrand, who said little but whom all feared and most respected, the Russian Ambassador, Pozzo di Borgo, and Delacroix, the young Romantic painter. At the home of Laffitte, the banker, generals and army officers and the more prominent Liberal deputies foregathered—Général Foy, Benjamin Constant, Paul-Louis Courier, Manuel, Béranger, and Casimir Delavigne. At the Palais Royal the Duc d'Orléans was a lavish entertainer. The refreshments were considered the finest in Paris, but the Duchesse was regarded as a stupid hostess. Ternaux, one of the richest manufacturers in France, had a salon in the Place des Victoires. It was frequented by the Doctrinaire group, Guizot, Royer-Collard, and Camille Jordan, who also met in the drawing-rooms of the Duc and the Duchesse de Broglie. At the salon of Madame Davillier, the daughter of a great Alsatian industrialist, were to be found the more radical deputies — Lafayette, Manuel, Dupont de l'Eure, Général Foy, Casimir-Périer, and Voyer d'Argenson.

The Faubourg Saint-Honoré and the Chaussée d'Antin became more friendly during the Restoration. The marriage of Mademoiselle Laffitte with the Prince de la Moskowa was much commented upon as symbolizing the alliance of the Napoleonic nobility with the industrial bourgeoisie. The Faubourg Saint-Germain remained the most aloof. Both Louis XVIII and Charles X tried to break down some of this aloofness by inviting both Napoleonic nobility and certain great capitalists to the Tuileries. A number of wealthy foreigners — especially Russians, Poles, Italians, and English — came to live in Paris and opened salons. The rise in society of Baron James de Rothschild, who was on the best terms with Villèle, marks the entrance of the rich Jewish banking group into the highest French society. In this society of the Restoration there was still much of the charm which characterized the society of the Ancien Régime.

III. THE BOURGEOISIE

The bourgeoisie formed, next to the peasants, the largest group in French society. The very rapid growth of this class, whose origins went back into the Middle Ages, dated really from the eighteenth century. Commerce and manufacture had improved the standards of living for the mass of the bourgeoisie and had at the same time raised a small capitalist group to the top. The social life of this upper group was, even before the Revolution, very much like that of the nobility. The mad scramble for money, and the vulgar nouveaux-riches, hardly appeared before the July Monarchy.

The great mass of shopkeepers, clerks, government officials, and professional men formed a larger group. Their virtues one may see fairly set forth in the comedies of Scribe. Their vices are furiously pilloried in the diatribes of the Romantics, and later in the novels of the realists, Stendhal, Balzac, and Flaubert. The desire for security in their social and economic position characterized this great mass of the French bourgeoisie. Their "stratégie des intérêts" is marvelously set forth in Balzac's *Comédie humaine*. These French bourgeois, as he portrays them, were matter-of-fact to the last degree, regarding the successful marriage of their children as their greatest social obligation. Balzac expresses their ideal in his *La Grande Betèche*, quoting an epitaph in Père Lachaise Cemetery, "Good husband and good father." Scribe's *Avant, pendant et après* of 1828 is their most complete apology. Here the hero is a manufacturer, and the play a panegyric of industry and of the bourgeoisie. It so angered the Duchesse de Berri that it was withdrawn from the repertory of the Théâtre de Madame.

In general, the middle class was Liberal, though not yet Republican, in politics, industrious and cautious, and very fearful of both atheism and clericalism. I loved order, security, and authority, provided this authority were not so oppressive as to throw the country into revolution. It was inclined to philanthropy towards the inferior classes so long as they were inclined to remain inferior. The bourgeoisie, both high and low, lacked democratic idealism, and a taste for art, literature, or philosophy. Their favorite organization was the National Guard, called by radicals "l'épicier janissaire," in which the bourgeoisie saw themselves as defenders of the state and the home. Their hope was in the ballot box, and their highest social ambition was to be decorated with the Legion of Honor.

French fashions and manners changed slowly during the periods. In 1814 and 1815 some individuals in each class showed their political sentiments in their dress, ignoring the current fashions of the day. The Ultras wore clothes reminiscent of the Ancien Régime. Short trousers and large shoe buckles for men were de rigueur at Court until after 1830. The women wore hats à la Sévigné or Henri Quatre. Republicans and Bonapartists, in some cases, affected various styles of the period 1789 to 1815. The steady evolution of styles was, however, very little modified by these eccentrics, who chose to carry their political opinions on their backs. In general, the styles for women of the Restoration are ugly and without the grace and elegance of the styles of the eighteenth century. They stand midway between the "Athenian" styles of 1793 and the "Cæsarian" modes of the Empire on the one hand and the simple and graceful styles of the July Monarchy on the other. By 1815 the Classic styles of the Empire had been modified, so that there is no abrupt change at the beginning of the Restoration. The ideal after 1815 came to be, according to Leroy, the greatest costume designer of the period, "skirt a bell, of the body a bobbin, and of the head and hair a monument."[1] The result, if one may judge from the pictures of the period, was fearful.

Plays, novels, and public events gave their names to womens' costumes. There were Atala collars, Mary Stuart coats, Ourika articles de luxe, and in 1823 Trocadéro ribbons in honor of the capture of the Spanish fort by the Duc d'Angoulême. The dress of the men varied slightly as the wearer was an Anglophile, an Ultra, a Democrat, a Bonapartist, or a Romantic. These variations appeared chiefly in the style of the cravat and the height of the hat and collar, both of which were usually very high. Except for a few Court functions, powdered hair and knee breeches, even for aristocrats, slowly went out of style after 1815, as did also the long, ugly Napoleonic moustaches.

The most amusing forms of dress and manners were developed by the young Romanticists, who, though they were in the beginning a very small group, came to have an influence, especially during the reign of Charles X. Historic plays in the theaters and at the opera and the great vogue of costume balls helped to spread the Romanticists' taste for the mediæval and the exotic. The "style moyen âge" included the fourteenth, fifteenth, and sixteenth centuries, and was usually most

1 Ch. Simond, I, 656.

unhistorically conceived. At the same time all sorts of mannerisms were affected. Women tried to look seraphic. At no time in French history were women so frequently spoken of as "angels." After 1830 they became more frequently "vampires" and "devils." In the early poems of Lamartine and Hugo women are represented as daintily dressed in soft stuffs, and consumed with "virginal yearnings for an ideal poet-lover." The statuesque and decisive woman of the Empire was succeeded by the frail type who sometimes drank vinegar to look pale and Byronic, as if she were devoured with passion and disappointment. "She bowed," as one of the Romantic poets writes, "in exquisite languor, like a frail reed before the breath of love."[1]

The Romantic young man affected English dandyism, always combined with a certain Byronic cynicism. He smoked many cigarettes, and enjoyed "l'orgie echevelée," which usually amounted to little more than an evening of drinking. Long hair in the "style Mérovingien" was affected. The pale face and sighing were much in vogue. The mal du siècle of Chateaubriand's René was imitated, and these young men, says Gautier, loved to "talk sadly and fantastically about death."

These young Romanticists were really a mutual-admiration society encouraging each other's eccentricities. They felt the need of standing together to assert themselves against the dead weight of tradition, and many of their most extreme affectations were due to the

1 C. H. Wright, *The Background of Modern French Literature* (Boston, 1926), p. 102.

AN HOUR BEFORE THE CONCERT

ROMANTIC HOUSEKEEPING IN THE EIGHTEEN-TWENTIES

power and stupidity of the older generation. Those who were most affected were usually not men like Hugo, Lamartine, or Nodier, who maintained a certain dignity, but young students, especially art students, who claimed, as Ingres said of Delacroix, the right to paint with a drunken broom. They liked to turn up their collars when passing a Classical painting, lest they catch a cold. Many of these members of Jeune-France were mere révoltés and poseurs. Some, says Gautier, "were Byronic, some passionate, some mediæval." They almost all, at times, affected beards and a disheveled appearance, so that no one might confuse them with neatly dressed and smooth-shaven bourgeois. Gautier describes one young man who, converted to Jeune-France, rushed home, smashed in his tall hat, cut the collars from his shirts, burned the works of Boileau, Racine, and Voltaire, and called his father "garde nationale."

Alfred de Musset, with a mixture of insight and rhetoric, describes this Romantic generation in his *Confessions d'un enfant du siècle.* "During the wars of the Empire, when their husbands and brothers were in Germany, the distracted mothers gave birth to an ardent, pale, and nervous generation. Conceived between two battles, raised in schools to the roll of drums, thousands of children looked about them with a somber eye. From time to time their fathers, stained with blood, appeared, raised their children to their bespangled breasts, then put them down to ride off again."[1]

1 De Musset, Ch. I.

IV. THE WORKING CLASS

At the bottom of the social scale in the towns were the skilled and unskilled workers. Their condition in the larger cities had by 1830 become thoroughly distressful. The old economic order before the Revolution gave the workers some of the benefits of association; the new regime of universal suffrage in the later nineteenth century was to make it possible for them to improve their condition through the ballot box. Between the great Revolution of 1789 and the Revolution of 1848, however, their conditions of living and working were usually very wretched. Both the employing classes and the government were largely indifferent to their distress, and the doctrine of laissez-faire held by those in power was against all attempts on the part of the state to modify "economic laws."

The worst conditions prevailed in the cotton industry, particularly in Lille and in Mulhouse. According to Villermé, our best source on all these matters, the silk workers were less miserable, though certain parts of the silk industry were ruinous to the worker's health. The conditions in the woolen industry were better, but the industry was so subject to periods of unemployment that the workers at times suffered terrible privations. Villermé found that most of these unhappy industrial workers had come to the city from the surrounding country districts. They had been attracted by the larger wages in money and had failed to estimate the fall in their net income. They were likewise unaware of the bad housing and working conditions and of the grave dangers of unemployment.

There were many indications of this wretchedness. The infant mortality was very high. There was at the same time a steady rise in the number of illegitimate children, from 62 per 1000 births in the period 1814 to 1818 to 72 per 1000 in the period 1826 to 1830. At Lyons the number of abandoned children doubled between 1814 and 1828. The living conditions of the workers were frightful. Large families were crowded into damp and ill-ventilated rooms. Unspeakable filth, undernourishment, and sickness prevailed in the quarters where the workers lived. The cities of France were unprepared to take care of the great numbers of factory hands who crowded into them. Besides inadequate housing conditions, no proper provisions existed for supplying the population with water, and for sewage disposal. Moreover, the food of the workers was inadequate, consisting chiefly of soup, bread, potatoes, and milk, a diet deficient in meat and vegetables, and in bare quantity often wholly insufficient. The working day was usually thirteen and a half hours, in some cases even rising to as high as seventeen hours. Work usually began at five o'clock in the morning and lasted until eight or nine o'clock in the evening, with a half-hour for lunch and an hour for dinner. The worst conditions prevailed amongst the ill-paid and overworked women and children in the textile industries. They were usually paid a half or a third the wages of a man. The children were no longer apprentices, as they had been before the Revolution; they had become mere factory hands. Children were particularly useful in the textile industries, not only because they were cheap, but also because their supple fingers were excellent for mending threads, and they could easily crawl under the looms. These factory children were frequently degenerate and sickly. In some factories the children were regularly beaten. Villermé found children as young as four years old working long hours. Under the circumstances, sickness, alcoholism, and prostitution increased rapidly and aggravated other conditions.

To make the life of the workers still more unbearable, there were, during the period 1815 to 1830, both a gradual rise in the price of foodstuffs and a decline in wages. The cost of living for a Parisian worker, including living quarters, food, heat, and light, but not clothing or other expenses, rose from 890 francs in 1810 to 950 francs in 1820 and 985 francs in 1830. Duchâtellier in 1830 estimated that at the same time the worker's income had decreased 22 per cent since 1800. Wages decreased in almost all trades, and in some of the textile industries the worker's income was reduced two-thirds between 1815 and 1830. A period of unemployment or sickness, or an accident, plunged the worker's family almost at once into destitution. Their misery is indicated by the fact that, in 1828, out of 224,300 workers in the Department of the Nord about Lille, 163,000 were registered with the various charitable agencies. At Paris the charitable agencies helped in their homes 86,415 in 1815, 200,000 in 1821, and nearly 300,000 in 1829.

In some industries, particularly in the building trades and in industries that had not been transformed by mechanization, conditions were much better; the number of workers was usually smaller, and their living and working conditions less crowded. Villermé estimates that in 1840 the average daily wage for a man in the textile industry was two francs, but that in mining, in glass factories, and in forges the average rose to three francs, while in the building trade, the largest group of all, the average stood as high as four francs. Wages were even higher in printing and in ship construction. It was in these trades, as we shall see presently, that compagnonnage existed, and that eighteenth-century conditions of apprenticeship and working still prevailed. In the smaller towns the workers usually had gardens and detached houses, and conditions prevailed that were in every way more sanitary and attractive than those of the slums of Lille, Paris, Lyons, or Mulhouse. In 1847, the first year for which we have reliable statistics, there were — out of a population of thirty-two millions — in 63 departments only 254,000 women, 131,000 children, and 672,000 men in factories employing more than ten persons. So while the condition of many of the workers was frightful, they formed a very much smaller proportion of the population than they do in any industrialized state today, or than they did in contemporary England, where misery was far more widespread.

In the face of such conditions, labor had not yet come to a consciousness of its own solidarity or power. Even if it had, the laws prevented any very effective sort of labor organization. The economic legislation of the French Revolution had been guided by very individualistic views. In this, the Revolutionary legislators expressed the interests of the rising bourgeoisie, which demanded the removal of all obstacles to individual initiative. In March, 1791, the old guilds were abolished and an era of free competition established. In spite of this, some trade-unions were organized, but in June, 1791, the Le Chapelier law was passed. This stated that "citizens of certain trades must not be permitted to assemble for their pretended common interests. There is no longer any competition in the state; there is but the particular interest of each individual and the general interest. It is necessary to abide by the principle that only by free contracts between individual and individual may the working day for each workingman be fixed." Other terms of the same law were even more detailed in their prohibition of workingmen's combinations. In the same law, the chambers of commerce, organizations of employers, were specifically sanctioned. The only protection for the workers was the vague statement that employers must not lower wages "unjustly." In 1803, and again in 1810, further severe laws were passed against strikes and against any sort of collective action on the part of the workers. Other Napoleonic laws prohibited associations of any sort of more than twenty persons. One article of the Civil Code provided also that in all circumstances "the master's word is taken both for the rate of wages and for the payment of salary." Each worker had to carry a "livret," a small book, in which was set down the time and places of his employment, the amount of his wages, and the conditions of his change from one employer to another. The livret had to be signed by the mayor or the police. It was, in practice, a real instrument of servitude, for if the employer or the civil authorities refused to sign it the worker could find no employment. Thus the law was used by the bourgeoisie to keep the worker down.

At the same time, the Napoleonic government, while pretending to stand for a complete laissez-faire policy in regard to industry, had passed a number of laws directly in contradiction of such a policy. A law of 1803 prohibited work in manufacturing establishments before 3 A.M. A police ordinance of 1806 prescribed the hours of work for certain workers in the building trades. In 1813 and in 1814 a comprehensive set of laws regulating work in mines was passed. Hence it is clear that had the government cared to act after 1815 to protect the workers, there was, in spite of any Revolutionary legislation in the matter, good precedent for government interference. The only law added by the Restoration to the labor code was one of 1814 which forbade all except necessary labor on Sunday and ecclesiastical holidays. At every point the laws favored the employer. The government during the Restoration was still living in the past, and was too concerned with old political and religious questions to pay much attention to new social and economic problems. It did something, as we have seen, to aid agriculture. That was due to the agitation of the landed aristocracy. It passed high tariff laws because they were desired by the rich manufacturers and the great agricultural landowners in the Chamber of

Deputies. It did nothing for the worker except to give him a certain amount of poor relief.

Acute suffering brought, as it was bound to, widespread discontent among the workers. The government reports give a table of strikes and the penalties imposed during the last five years of the Restoration. The number of illegal strikes — all strikes were of course illegal — was highest in 1825 with ninety, and lowest in 1829 with thirteen. There were some attempts on the part of the workers to break up the new machines, though in comparison with England "Ludditism" was practically unknown in France. In most cases these strikes seem to have been spontaneous outbursts of discontent among unorganized workingmen, though they were sometimes directed by organizations of workers which existed in spite of the law. These labor organizations were of three sorts — compagnonnage, the mutual-aid society, and societies of resistance.

The "compagnonnages," the most important working-class organizations of the Restoration, go back to the fifteenth century, though their rapid growth belongs to the eighteenth century, when the tendency toward aristocracy in the regular guilds had increased the membership of the compagnonnages. The members of a compagnonnage organization consisted of bachelor journeymen; if a member married or became a master, he left the organization. Admission depended on technical skill and the ability to pay the dues. It included only the élite of those who earned their living by such old trades as had not been greatly affected by the new machine process. Miners, bakers, shoemakers, and textile workers were not admitted. Compagnonnage was commoner in the South of France, and was best organized in the building trades. Their organization was simple. All the members of a single trade lived together in an inn kept by the "mère." Here they held their meetings, kept their records, and admitted new members. To this inn came "compagnons" arriving from other towns in search of work; for a tour about France to learn the trade in divers places formed part of a compagnon's training. A member found wherever he went comrades ready to help him on the way, to find work for him, to sing and carouse with him, and to tend him in sickness. All the compagnons of France were divided into three orders called "devoirs": The Enfants de Solomon, the Enfants du Maître Jacques, and the Enfants du Maître Soubise. Each of these devoirs had strange legends of its origins, and each traced its history to the time of King Solomon.

"There was," says Clapham, "an old-world flavor about these compagnons, with their legends and their rites of admission, their passwords and elaborate greetings when they met on the highway, their canes and ribbons full of symbolism, and the speed with which they fell to brawling for the honor of Solomon or Master James, or for the right to wear ribbons and to wear them in a particular way."[1] They had lived on in secrecy under the Ancien Régime, and they continued to flourish until after the railroad destroyed the condi-

1 Clapham, p. 80.

tions under which they had prospered. Their organizations had a value in keeping up a professional and moral standard, and by boycotting certain employers they were frequently able to improve their wages. They were one of the ancestors of the modern French trade-unions.

Next to compagnonnage, the mutual-aid societies were the most common form of labor organization. These were friendly or benevolent societies, usually called "bureaux de bienfaisance" or "caisses de secours mutuels," for aid in cases of sickness, accident, retirement or death. None seems to have offered insurance against unemployment. In 1823 there were 160 such organizations in Paris, of which it is known 132 had a membership of 11,143. The average membership seems to have been under eighty, though 33 had more than a hundred members, while five had more than two hundred. They were very common in the provinces. In 1828 there were 113 in the Department of the Nord alone. La société philanthropique de Paris, founded in Paris under Louis XIV, had undertaken, as a work of charity, the organization of these societies. The Société weathered the Revolution and remained during the Restoration the central agency of all these mutual-aid societies. Like compagnonnage, these societies excluded many workers who were unable to pay its small fees. The central society in Paris guaranteed the docility of its daughter societies, encouraging them and acting as their intermediary with the government. They were technically illegal, but so long as there were no strikes the government ignored the laws and allowed them to exist. Employers often looked favorably on these societies as a means of keeping the workers quiet.

The newest form of workingmen's organization, called into being by the new economic conditions, was the Société de résistance, a type of organization designed primarily to exercise control over the conditions of employment. Their existence had to be secret, and they assumed various names, one of the most famous being the Devoir Mutuel of Lyons, founded in 1828. These societies usually had no benefit features, and their secret statutes emphasized their purpose of obtaining better wages and improved conditions of employment. Much of the early history of these societies is unknown as most of their records have been lost or destroyed. Such societies are indicative of the rise of a new class spirit which was to be a great force in the mechanism of modern society. At this time all that was necessary to suppress sporadic uprisings due to such organizations was simple action on the part of the police. The Liberal newspapers and the Liberal deputies during the Restoration never concerned themselves with labor problems. Even the proposals to establish the old guilds seem never to have been considered seriously. It seemed that the only legitimate public interests were those represented in the Chambers; all others were merely private affairs to be regulated by "economic laws."

Charity was thus the only method of ameliorating the lot of the working classes. An exception to official indifference was a workshop and home for beggars created by the city of Bordeaux in 1827. The first workingmen's savings bank was established in Paris in 1818 by Benjamin Delessert and the Duc de la Rochefoucauld-Liancourt, the famous philanthropist. It accepted deposits as low as one franc. Its funds were invested in government bonds. This bank had remarkable success, for in the year 1829 it received 6,278,134 francs from 138,722 depositors. From 1819 to 1830 thirteen more such banks were founded in other cities of France. Two other large philanthropic societies were founded—one in 1821, the Société pour le placement des jeunes apprentis, another in 1828, the Société des amis de l'enfance. Both maintained employment offices in some of the French cities.

The Church distributed alms in a somewhat random fashion, while the Société de Saint Joseph, founded by the Jesuits, acted specifically as a means of helping workingmen either with money or by finding them employment. There were houses for convalescent working women, societies that visited the prisons, orphanages where poor children were taught various trades—all of them maintained by the Church. Scattered over France were a number of "salles d'asile," where the small children of workers were looked after during working hours. The first ones were established near Strasbourg by the Alsatian pastor Oberlin. They represented the beginning of a type of charitable work that was to be greatly extended during the century.

The government provided one official agency for bringing justice to the worker. These were the Conseils des prud'hommes, where individual workers might present their grievances. These councils, however, were made up entirely of employers and foremen, and no real representative of the wage-earning masses ever sat on them. The government also, as before the Revolution, supported many charity hospitals, and maintained an elaborate system of poor relief. This last had frequently to be distributed on a large scale. Villeneuve-Bargemont estimates that in 1834, out of a population of 163,000 in the city of Lille, one sixth received poor relief. No wonder that later in the century the workers demanded justice in place of charity.

V. THE PEASANTS

The great majority of the French population lived, as in the days of the Ancien Régime, in the country districts. A statistical report of 1826 divides the population of 31,851,545 into three groups — 22,251,545 agriculturalists, 4,300,000 workers, and 5,300,000 merchants, clerks, government officials, and professional men. Intellectual inertia, incessant manual labor, and an almost unbroken routine marked the life of the peasant. Usually he was poor and dirty. His food had little variety, vegetables, bread, and various milk products forming the basis of his diet. If the peasant had money, his tendency was to hoard it rather than to spend anything on improving his home or his way of living.

From a distance, the peasant village stood out a simple gray mass of buildings clustering around the high nave and tower of a church. Within the village there was usually one long street of cottages. Scattered farms were rare. The poorer peasant cottages often had but one large room which served as a kitchen and general living-room. A table with benches, a great chest, a heavy cupboard, a bread trough, and a bed or two constituted the furnishings. On one side, opposite the low door, was a huge fireplace. Glass was not common, and when the weather was bad and the heavy wooden shutters had to be closed the only daylight that crept in came from above the door and windows and through the low, wide chimney. The walls were ordinarily unplastered and blackened from the fire. Above was a loft reached by a ladder and used for storage, or sometimes as sleeping quarters. The floor was of beaten earth. As a peasant became more prosperous, he might pave the floor with flat stones, replace his clothing chest with a larger cupboard on whose shelves he loved to see the family linen piled high, — a sign of affluence, — and substitute mattresses for straw on his beds. Connected with the house were a number of buildings to house the animals. These were usually built around a large open space into which the manure from the stables was thrown and where his chickens and children were allowed to run. The food and the living conditions of the peasants, however, showed improvement since the eighteenth century. They were, for example, eating more meat, more pure wheat bread, more butter and eggs. The annual consumption of meat, which rose slowly from 39 pounds per person in 1789 to 61 pounds in 1848, is an index of the improvement. The prefectoral reports show that leather shoes were replacing wooden sabots. They show also a steady decrease in begging.

The peasant was usually contented, kind to strangers, and jovial. He accepted his lot in life, whether easy or hard, as a part of the order of things, and it did not occur to him to question the organization of society. The peasant was not possessed with the modern notion that everything must show progress, evolution, and change. His ideal was contentment, and his aim was to preserve the world as he found it. Book learning hardly existed for him. Rarely could he read or write. Anyone who could easily read a document at the notary's office was considered a learned man. Books on agriculture were very little read. Why should a man cultivate his acres differently from his father and grandfather? "The sun rises equally on the ignorant and the learned," the peasants were wont to say. "See so-and-so, who knows how to read: he is not as rich as I am." It is estimated that in 1819, out of about twenty-five million adults, fifteen million could neither read nor write.

The most popular book among those peasants who could read was *L'Albert*, a curious compend, known to the eighteenth century and often reprinted. It contained remedies for sickness, prescriptions to maintain beauty, recipes for preparing food, and methods of preserving butter and fighting insects. There were also annual almanacs. During the ministry of Decazes, who realized their influence, Royalist almanacs were sold. Anti-clerical propaganda took the form of pamphlets containing *Le testament du curé Meslier*, the *Ruines* of Volney, Dupuis' *Origines des cultes*, and the various writings of Voltaire and Diderot. On the other hand, the Rousseauistic type of primitivism had no appeal for the peasant. The young men who could read bought from the itinerant book peddlers the works of Piron and of Grécourt, and the *Ass* of Lucian translated by Paul-Louis Courier. Such works as the *Livre d'amour* and the *Tableau de l'amour conjugal* had a large circulation. On the walls of his cottage a peasant sometimes hung cheap lithographs. On the mantelpiece one usually found in the South an image of the Virgin, in the North a bust of Napoleon.

Many peasants believed in sorcerers and goblins and haunted places. Nothing was done without taking account of occult influence and of certain prescriptions. Before sowing the peasant must make sure that the moon was in the right phase and that the day and the hour were also propitious. To make the grain grow well, he took care to carry it into the field in the tablecloth used at the Christmas dinner. On the first of April salt was placed at the four corners of the pasture to preserve the animals from all ill. Sheep sheared during the week of Corpus Christi would die during the year. The peasants had hundreds of notions of this sort, many of them centuries old. These beliefs and customs varied greatly from district to district.

The long days in the country were spent in the routine of work, each peasant working most of the time in his own field, though many also worked out part of the year at sawmills, charcoal works, or potteries in the neighborhood. Many often found extra things to do at home, especially during the long winter months, such as making barrels, baskets, and wooden shoes. As the peasants lived in villages, it was natural that they should to some extent work for each other. One might make shoes on the side; another might be a tailor. The women did weaving of one sort or another, and exchanged their own cloth for the kind made by their neighbor, or sold it to a traveling dealer. A peasant who made farming his only occupation was rare.

The peasants' lives were passed close to the soil. They very rarely traveled. Only in the case of military service was a peasant ever taken from his home, and as it was not very costly to send a substitute, only the poorer peasant boys had this advantage forced upon them. Many of these boys soon found the food and life in the army better than at home, and they frequently reënlisted. Ignorance and the monotony of life killed all curiosity. Fenimore Cooper found that the peasants usually knew nothing about the country even a few miles from home. They took little interest in politics. According to one story, the mayor of a village, on receiving Napoleon's "Acte Additionnel" in 1815, wrote to the prefect that he had received this "constitution respectfully, as he had received all others." Another story has it that in 1830 a peasant thought the Charter, "La Charte," was the wife of Louis Philippe. Only in the reign of Charles X, when it seemed that the old feudal rights might be restored, were the peasants aroused to any interest in politics. Of course, in all these matters conditions varied greatly from one part of France to another, but in general the South of France was more backward than the North.

Each peasant village had its local characters. City civilization, with its inspected schools, its newspapers, and its standardized products, has not yet come in to bring uniformity. Among these local characters there was usually an old Napoleonic veteran who retold for the thousandth time some vivid bit of a campaign. The principal authorities were the mayor, the priest, and sometimes a nobleman who lived near by on his ancestral estates. The last was often a very picturesque figure, a great drinker and a hearty eater, conservative to a degree, whom the name of Napoleon or the sight of a tricolor drove into a rage. The priest was most influential in the West of France and in a part of the South, though, as we have seen, his influence had waned since the day of the Ancien Régime. The peasant, as he is shown in the novels of Balzac, liked to make fun of and to tell bad stories about the priests — which did not, however, prevent his confessing in case of a grave illness. The mayor was usually one of the most well-to-do men in the village, and one who felt his importance to the very limit. Sometimes the local innkeeper combined his functions with that of being mayor and head of the local unit of the National Guard. The school-teacher, if the village had a school, was often an old soldier who had learned something in traveling about the world but who was in most ways almost as ignorant as his pupils. The town furnished him lodgings and between one and two hundred francs a year. The rest of the meager income was made up by the small contributions of his pupils, and by various minor jobs he might find in the village. Doctors were not numerous. Where there was a doctor in the village, he found it difficult to collect money for his services. The stingy peasant often refused to consult a physician until his malady was so far advanced that medical attention was of no use. The peasant in sickness preferred to consult a quack who employed old tried remedies, and who could, if the situation demanded it, use magic formulæ.

The chief occasions in the village were still the Church festival days, especially the local saint's day, when the peasants dressed in their best, and after the ceremonies enjoyed a banquet. In a peasant's family the chief days were those when the children of the household received their first Communion and when they were married. On the day he married his child even the most stingy peasant took his money from his woolen stocking — the peasant's bank — and spent it on the food and drink he offered to all comers. Many local costumes, which did not disappear until after 1840, gave variety and picturesqueness to these peasant fêtes. It was commonly said that the peasants in the East of France were more revolutionary and more democratic in spirit, in the West more religious, in the North more ambitious, and in the South more gay and easy-going. Certain regions, such as Auvergne, Limousin, Poitou, and Provence, had an aversion to military service, though the belligerent departments in the East, especially in Alsace, always furnished enough extra soldiers to fill all vacancies in the regiments.

All in all, no social type in France has changed so little as the peasant. A few verses of Thomas Hardy tell his story:

> Only a man harrowing clods,
> In a slow silent walk,
> With an old horse that stumbles and nods,
> Half asleep as they stalk.
>
> Only thin smoke without flame
> From the heaps of couch grass:
> Yet this will go onward the same
> Though dynasties pass.

VI. SOCIAL AND ECONOMIC THOUGHT

The currents of social and economic thought present an interesting commentary on the actual conditions of life, and help to explain them. The Restoration, next to the later eighteenth century, is the most fecund period in the history of modern French economic and social thought. The schools of the eighteenth century, with their gospel of Liberty, Equality, and Fraternity, and their faith in progress, were after 1800 merged into new schools of thought, some scientific and some radical, but all faced with the new problems of modern industrialism. The majority of Liberal thinkers considered the doctrines of Voltaire and Rousseau as sufficient, and set up an ill-defined liberty as their social panacea. Others, while admiring the destructive side of the eighteenth century, felt the need of a new and more positive faith. The work of destruction accomplished by the Revolution was, they believed, an important one, but it had left a spiritual vacuum; and there still remained the work of constructing a new society on the ruins of the Ancien Régime. Moreover, many new problems had arisen in the meantime, and were crying for settlement. It is from this second, much smaller, more radical, and more original group — and especially from the work of Saint-Simon — that the course of social doctrine and social reform for the whole nineteenth century proceeded. The period began with the economic doctrines of laissez-faire in full command of the field. Slowly there develops, in the work of Sismondi, and then in the writings of Saint-Simon and Fourier, an attack on the evils and abuses of private property and the whole laissez-faire regime established by the French Revolution. This attack commences as an attack on idleness and waste and develops into Socialism, and even into modern Anarchism.

In the economic field, the Revolution, as we have seen, had abolished the old guilds and most of the old trade regulations, and had established a laissez-faire regime founded on the "liberty to work." The Bible of these theories was Adam Smith's *Wealth of Nations*, well known in France before the Revolution, when similar doctrines had been spread there by Quesnay, Turgot, and the Physiocrats. The greatest representative of these laissez-faire ideas during the Empire and the Restoration was the economist J.-B. Say. Say popularized

Smith's ideas on the continent by arranging and classifying them, though it is not correct to regard him as merely an imitator of Adam Smith. Say began his career as a business man, and his work shows a thorough and first-hand knowledge of business conditions. From 1803, when he published his *Traité d'économie politique*, he devoted his attention primarily to economic theories. In 1816 at the Athénée he delivered a course of lectures on political economy which were among the first lectures on this subject delivered anywhere in Europe. These were published in 1817 as the *Catéchisme d'économie politique*. In 1819 he was called to the newly founded Conservatoire des Arts et Métiers, where he continued his teaching and writing until his death in 1832.

According to Say, political economy is a science of observation. The rôle of the economist is not to give advice, but to study and analyze economic activities and describe their working. In 1820 he wrote to Malthus that "the economist must be content to remain an impartial spectator. What we owe to the public is to tell them how and why such and such a fact is the consequence of another. Whether the conclusion is welcomed or rejected, it is enough that the economist should have demonstrated its cause, but he must give no advice." Say found, through his study of economic facts, that individual interest left to itself was the chief basis of all economic progress. The "laws of supply and demand" fix the value of commodities, and any attempt to interfere with the working of these "laws" is folly. Free competition increases production by stimulating and sharpening the inventive faculties. It works justice, moreover, by giving the greatest riches to the most active and the strongest. Increased and more efficient production — and it is always production rather than distribution that interests Say — favors the consumer by lowering prices. He developed the usual argument for free trade, showing that true competition among the nations has the same beneficial effect as free competition in any given national society. A people engaged in active production has need of wide markets, and should devote itself to producing those commodities for which it is peculiarly fitted by soil, climate, and general situation. The world must become a single coöperative union of producers. His ideal was a busy, productive world-society without customs duties and without war. Government would be reduced to a minimum, and should then be maintained only for public safety. Above all, government must not interfere in the relations of capital and labor. Wages must not rise above the subsistence level; otherwise production would be slowed up. If social ills exist, private charity can look after them.

Such was Say's credo. Its ultimate aim, which ran through every argument, was the increase of production to the very limit. His praise of liberty, his love of peace and of coöperation among the nations, particularly after the Napoleonic Wars, give Say an important place in the economic thought of the century. The radicals hated him, and later did their best to make a caricature of his theories. In reality Say's weaknesses did not lie in his positive doctrine so much as in what he omitted and ignored, and in his confusion of the mere mass of national wealth with the well-being of the rank and file of men. His doctrines naturally pleased the growing class of industrial entrepreneurs, whose credo was well expressed after 1830 in Guizot's famous admonition, "Enrichissez-vous."

In contrast with Malthus and Ricardo, the pessimistic followers of Adam Smith, the disciples of Say were optimistic and saw in increased production a bright economic future. Say's two most devoted followers were his son-in-law, Charles Comte, and Dunoyer. In 1817 they began to publish a journal, *Le Censeur*, which preached Say's doctrines. The brilliant engineer and statistician Charles Dupin shared much the same enthusiasm for Say, and in 1829 published an able two-volume study of French industry and commerce. Unfortunately none of these men saw the necessity of completing Say's theories, but devoted their efforts to defending them — at best a poor sort of discipleship.

A more interesting group who followed the growth of Say's doctrines, but whose real connections were with the eighteenth-century Physiocrats, were a number of philanthropists. Chief of these was the Duc de la Rochefoucauld-Liancourt, whose interest in improving agriculture and in the Société philanthropique has already been mentioned. Others were Lasteyrie, Alexandre de Laborde, Benjamin Delessert, and Gérando. They encouraged vaccination and sanitation among the poor. They were behind the movement for "l'enseignement mutuel" to extend primary education — a movement which, as we have seen, the Church blocked at every turn. They started savings banks and mutual-aid societies for workers. Laborde's *De l'esprit d'association* and Gérando's *Traité de la bienfaisance publique* are among the earlier works on the type of charities demanded by a modern industrialized society.

The school of J.-B. Say met its first sharp opposition from Sismondi. Sismondi, born in Geneva, and a close friend of Madame de Staël, had already made a reputation as a literary historian when he turned to take up the cause of the workingman. He is the first of a line of economic thinkers whose attitude, without being what was later to be called Socialist, was severely critical of the abuses of a laissez-faire regime. In 1803 he published his first economic work, which, like J.-B. Say's first book, was based largely on Adam Smith. Not until sixteen years later, in 1819, did he publish a second work, *Principes d'économie politique*. In this long interval he had seen industrial conditions in England and France at first hand, and his second work shows him clearly at odds with both Adam Smith and Say. Sismondi objects that both these economists made of political economy only a science of wealth, whereas he conceived its true object to be the study of the well-being of all. Wealth only deserves the name in a society where it is proportionately distributed. Machine methods increase the total national wealth, — he was too intelligent not to see the benefits of the new industrial regime, — but machine methods also pauperize the workers, who deserve to enjoy better wages and shorter hours. "The earnings of an entrepreneur," he writes, "sometimes represent nothing but the spoliation of the workingmen. A profit is made, not because the industry produces more than it costs, but because it fails to give the worker sufficient compensation for his toil."[1] This was a new note in modern French economic thought.

Sismondi is most effective in attacking Say's identification of the interests of the individual with "the general interest" and the total sum of national wealth. These, he insists, are in no wise identical. He is too conservative, however, to hope for a general overthrow of capitalistic society, and is content to remain a grieved spectator of the helplessness of mankind in the face of the evils of an industrialized society. Sismondi is nevertheless the first important modern thinker to express the belief that the Industrial Revolution separates society into two distinct classes, those who work and those who possess. This was, in fact, a much more thoroughgoing division than that of Saint-Simon, who separated society into "the busy and the lazy." Free competition, Sismondi believed, hastened this fatal separation of capital and labor, causing the gradual disappearance of the intermediary ranks and leaving only the capitalist and proletarian classes. He stopped short of Socialism, and criticized the impracticability of the program of Robert Owen. His only remedy was government regulation. Society must somehow intervene in industry to set a limit to individual action. He held that the belief

1 Sismondi, *Principes d'économie politique* (1819), I, 92.

of the laissez-faire school that all government control was bad had gone too far. Property was not sacred; it must be used for the good of society, and the state must regulate its use. Sismondi is thus the first important French advocate of state intervention for the amelioration of the lot of the working classes, and though his immediate influence was small, he is a precursor of great importance. After Sismondi, it was no longer possible to forget the awful misery and suffering which lay beneath an appearance of economic progress.

Sismondi's chief followers were Fodéré, the mayor of Strasbourg, who in 1825 published an *Essai historique et moral sur la pauvreté des nations*, Villeneuve-Bargemont, a prefect during the Restoration, whose three-volume work, *Economie politique chrétienne*, the result of years of investigation, did not appear until 1834, and Buret, who in 1842 published his *De la misère des classes laborieuses en Angleterre et en France*. These men shared Sismondi's ideas, backing up his theories with great masses of statistics and with more detailed accounts of the whole industrial situation. If they added any new idea, it was a demand for a better-organized system of state charity. Fodéré proposed the creation in each department of a Council of Commerce and Industry to determine economic policy, to fix salaries, and to improve working conditions. Villeneuve-Bargemont is often considered the father of Christian Socialism. Buret's work was used by the Socialists of the July Monarchy, especially by Louis Blanc and Pierre Leroux, as an arsenal of facts for condemning the whole capitalistic regime. Before 1830 the proposals of the followers of Sismondi never came to any practical results, though there were occasional echoes of their ideas in the Chamber of Deputies, as when in 1822 one deputy, Beauséjour, spoke of "the vices of present social organization," and referred to "those who eat and those who are eaten," and again in 1828 when Voyer d'Argenson, the redoubtable old revolutionary, called the attention of the deputies to an "economic order that condemned an immense number of human creatures to forced labor." Even the radical Général Foy, however, considered such ideas as vain and silly wanderings, and a tiresome interruption of the real business of the Chamber of Deputies. As we have seen, the vast majority of the members of the Chambers simply had no conception of the existence of these great social problems — another proof that the politics of the Restoration were in many ways a mere continuation of the old animosities of the Revolution.

In the meantime, several solitary thinkers were laying the foundations of modern Socialism and Anarchism. While Sismondi had raised many new questions, it never seems to have occurred to him to attack private property. Every English and French economist of the eighteenth and early nineteenth centuries, with the possible exception of Babeuf, had treated it as a thing apart, a fact, indisputable and inevitable. Suddenly a number of thinkers laid their hands on the sacred ark and attacked the institution of private property with wholehearted vigor, though neither Saint-Simon nor Fourier were true communists in the modern sense of the word

Nevertheless, by 1830 nearly every idea which was to become a commonplace of later nineteenth-century Socialism had found a place somewhere in one of their systems.

The earlier of these was Saint-Simon, a nobleman, whose unhappy life was a thing of shreds and patches. At sixteen he had served in the American Revolution During the French Revolution he had renounced his titles, but had made a fortune in land speculation. After a short period of imprisonment, he began to proclaim himself a Messiah. In 1803 he published his first work on social reform, a pamphlet entitled *Lettre d'un habitant de Genève*. As the result of an unhappy marriage and the loss of his fortune, he was by 1808 living on the charity of an old servant. After her death he was so poor that in 1823 he attempted suicide. With aid from his relatives and from a few of his disciples he spent the last few years of his life in comparative comfort. It was in the period after 1820 that, first the young Augustin Thierry, who later became one of the greatest of modern French historians, and then Auguste Comte, the philosopher, served him as private secretary. During his last years — he died in 1825 — he published a series of pamphlets, which, though extremely unsystematic in their form, furnished to his followers the basis of his doctrine. This powerful mind which conceived both Socialism and Positivism was never able to compose a consistent treatise.

Saint-Simon's doctrine was an outgrowth of the economic thought of Adam Smith and Say, for whose work on the negative side he had great respect, but which he found wholly insufficient on the positive side. As a young man, Saint-Simon had inherited the unbounded optimism and the belief in human perfectibility of the early years of the French Revolution. He inherited too, from the political and social experimenting of the Revolution, the belief that society might be entirely reconstructed along lines set down in some paper scheme. The great upheaval from 1789 to 1815 had profoundly impressed him as being the birth of a new society, but he had not found that after the Revolution this new society had been achieved. Indeed, men did not seem even to have conceived the terms of its achievement. Hence Saint-Simon looked on the political struggles of Ultras and Liberals during the Restoration with the same contempt with which Voltaire had regarded the controversies of the Jansenists and the Jesuits of the eighteenth century. Nothing, from his point of view, was to be gained from threshing old straw. Only he himself, and a few of his followers, really comprehended the problems of this new society — a surprisingly conceited attitude, but one not far from right.

Saint-Simon envisaged a new industrial society divided into three orders, never too clearly defined — namely, the entrepreneurs, the workers, and the scholars and artists. All distinctions not based on labor and ability must disappear. He did not, it is interesting to note, believe either in uniformity or in complete equalization, though he hated "idlers" and had a profound sympathy for the suffering of the working classes. Saint-

Simon did not have in mind the conflict of capital and labor so much as a more general conflict between the "workers" and the "idlers." Society should be organized in such a way that all must work. Men should cease exploiting one another, and should turn to exploiting the earth. This last emphasis on the great value of all effort turned toward production shows clearly the influence of Adam Smith and J.-B. Say. The state must provide work for the unemployed in draining marshes, in building roads, bridges, and canals, and in other public works.

He illustrates some of these ideas with his famous parable published in 1819. "Let us suppose," he writes, "that France suddenly loses fifty of her first-class doctors, fifty first-class chemists, fifty first-class physiologists, fifty first-class bankers, two hundred of her best merchants, six hundred of her foremost agriculturalists, five hundred of her capable iron masters"— and so on, enumerating the principal industries. "Since these men are its most indispensable producers, the minute it loses these the nation will degenerate into a mere lifeless body. . . . Let us take another supposition. Imagine that France retains her men of genius, whether in the arts and sciences or in the crafts and industries, but has the misfortune to lose on the same day the King, the King's brother, the Duc d'Angoulême, and all the other members of the royal family, all the great officers of the Crown, all ministers of state . . . all the marshals, cardinals, archbishops, bishops, grand vicars, and canons, all prefects and sub-prefects, all government employees, all the judges, and, in addition to all these men, a hundred thousand landed proprietors — the cream of her nobility. Such an overwhelming catastrophe would certainly aggrieve the French, for they are a kindly-disposed nation. But the loss of a hundred and thirty thousand of the best-reputed individuals in the state would give rise to sorrow of a purely sentimental kind; it would not cause the community the least inconvenience."[1]

The nation should be organized as one vast workshop —a single coöperative community so adjusted as to procure the greatest advantage to the greatest number. "Society," he says, "should be the union of men devoted to useful tasks." Government then will be largely unnecessary, and will be confined to seeing that each is rewarded according to his capacity and use. Capital as well as labor will then receive its remuneration in a proportion more just than in the society he sees about him. Saint-Simon was not definitely opposed to private property, and he allows a reward to capital when it is in the form of what he calls "an investment worthy of compensation." None of these matters is, however, made very clear.

A high place in this new society would be given to the banker, to the entrepreneur, and to the scholar. In 1803 he wanted the control in the hands of scholars; by 1819 he had come to believe that it must be jointly in the hands of scholars and industrialists. He comments on this in various ways from 1819 to 1825, but this remained his final view. Government is for the people,

1 *L'organisateur* (1819), Part I, pp. 10–20.

but by a body of scholars, artists, and industrialists. Saint-Simon's devotion to science is twofold: he believed in it, in the first place, because it would furnish practical knowledge that would be of value in improving production, and, in the second place, because it would furnish a positive religion and a new code of ethics — a "Scientific Breviary," as he first called it, and a "New Christianity," as he finally named it. This side of Saint-Simon's doctrine was developed by Auguste Comte into Positivism and the Religion of Humanity, while from his economic theories came most of the doctrines of Socialism, from Marx and Engels to Lasalle and Jaurès. There is much, too, of the contemporary Romantic Movement in Saint-Simon. His dogmatism, his pose of being a prophet, and his idealization of genius show clearly this relation to the thought of the new Romantic School.

Weill, one of Saint-Simon's biographers, calls him a "precursor of Socialism" rather than a Socialist, and from the point of view of the economic thought of the later nineteenth century Saint-Simon's doctrine is very hard to classify. His proposals for public ownership of utilities, and his belief in reward according to social worth, clearly anticipate modern Socialism. On the other hand, his dependence on the classes rather than the masses to bring about a better society, and his plans for the bureaucratic administration of industry, without proper democratic safeguards, are greatly at variance with the ideals of later Socialistic schools. In any case, he was the first important thinker to see clearly that in modern society the scientist would replace the priest and that the new industrial capitalist was replacing the old feudal lord.

Saint-Simon's doctrine was taken up by an interesting group of engineers, artists, and professional men, who formed themselves, after Saint-Simon's death, into what is generally known as the Saint-Simonian School. These disciples proved to be much more radical than their master and they soon developed his doctrine into a system of communism. During one year, 1826, this group — chief of whom were Bazard, a former leader of the Carbonari, and Enfantin, an engineer — published an interesting little paper, *Le Producteur*. Auguste Comte occasionally wrote for it. It preached the necessity of invention and the improvement of machinery, along with the need of a better distribution of wealth. In 1828 the school was more elaborately organized under the rulership of a number of "fathers," and it took on the forms of a new religion which was to supplant decadent Catholicism and outworn Liberalism. During the years 1829 and 1830 Bazard gave a series of public lectures, in the preparation of which he was aided by Enfantin. They were published in the *Exposition de la doctrine de Saint-Simon*. Among the young men who attended these lectures were Carrel, who with Thiers founded the *National* in 1830, Ferdinand de Lesseps, who was later to build the Suez Canal, Pierre Leroux, one of the founders of the *Globe*, Franz Liszt and Félicien David, the composers, and Michel Chevalier, who negotiated the reciprocity treaty with England in

1860. From 1829 to 1831 Enfantin and the mystical group had the upper hand; Enfantin took a group to Egypt on an absurd and pathetic search for the "Mother Messiah," and the school as an organized group rapidly fell to pieces.

The doctrine of Bazard and Enfantin's *Exposition* of 1829 demands that everyone occupy a position becoming his capacity and receive a wage according to his labor. This was, of course, directly derived from Saint-Simon. They go further, however, in holding that all privileges of birth and all rights of inheritance must be abolished. "All instruments of production, all lands and capital, the funds now divided among individual proprietors, should be pooled so as to form one central social fund, which shall be employed by associations of persons hierarchically arranged, so that each one's task shall be an expression of his capacity, and his wealth a measure of his labor."[1]

Part of their doctrine was based on an elaborate interpretation of history. Saint-Simon had suggested this historical interpretation, Comte, as we have seen, made it the basis of his system of Positivism, while the Saint-Simonian School elaborated it in a different form and passed it on to later schools of Socialism. Society, they held, had moved through three stages: a Theological one down to the sixteenth century; a Metaphysical stage in the seventeenth and eighteenth centuries; and now finally a Positive and Scientific stage had dawned. Society moved through these stages by a law of progress,

1 *Doctrine de Saint-Simon, Exposition, Première Année* (1829), Appendix.

passing at the same time from isolation to unity, from war to peace, from antagonism and exploitation to association. Association and coöperation always were on a larger and larger scale, starting in early civilization with the family, and rising through city, nation, Christendom, to humanity. This ascent was made possible by three great creations of human activity, art, literature, and science. These early Socialists had the same faith in historical laws — most of which they themselves made up — that the early Christians had in Providence. Their doctrine was a strange mixture of realism and utopianism, patched together from Vico, and from Kant, Herder, and Hegel, — known chiefly through the description of their ideas in Madame de Staël's *Sur l'Allemagne*, — from Saint-Simon, and from Joseph de Maistre, whose praise of mediæval unity and whose insistence on the dangers of individualism and the benefits of solidarity these Saint-Simonians shared enthusiastically. The leaders of the school seem to have known nothing of Robert Owen or of Fourier until 1829. Mixed with the rest of their notions were extraordinarily forward-looking ideas about the future use of railroads, about intellectual interchange and coöperation in scientific work, about the need of better credit facilities, about methods of improving housing conditions among the workers, and even about the necessity of relating the fine arts more closely to contemporary life — an idea derived, as we shall see, from the contemporary theorists of Romanticism. The Saint-Simonians never had many followers, and their practical influence until after

1840 was very slight. The attitude of the average middle-class Liberal toward all this was well expressed by Laffitte's remark to Enfantin, "You place your mottoes so high, no one can read them."

The most isolated economic and social theorist of the Restoration was Charles Fourier. When a boy of five in his father's clothing shop, he was severely punished for telling a customer the truth about a piece of goods. At nineteen, while working for a business house at Marseilles, he was ordered to throw overboard a quantity of rice which had been held to raise the price during a famine. These two instances of dishonesty and waste, he tells us, made an indelible impression on him and started him on the development of his doctrines. The outward circumstances of his later life were uneventful. His maturer years were spent as a bookkeeper at Lyons, then at Paris. He was a very shy man and refused to speak in public, preferring to state all his ideas in writing. He always hoped to find a philanthropist who would help him to start one of his co-partnership communities, and for many years he stayed in his room for a certain time each noon expecting, though always in vain, that such a philanthropist would appear.

Fourier's doctrine is set forth in a great number of writings, the most important of which are the *Théorie des quatre mouvements* of 1808 and his *Nouveau monde industriel* of 1829.[1] Fourier's doctrine, like that of Saint-Simon, is a strange mixture of insight and fancy.

1 One of the best statements of Fourier's ideas is to be found in the work of one of his followers, Victor Considérant's *Doctrine Sociale*.

His own personal eccentricities color and often disfigure his work. His conceit was enormous, and he had a great contempt for the doctrines of other reformers. He regarded the work of Robert Owen, his Scotch contemporary, as "too pitiable to be worth refuting," and he "shuddered to think of the Saint-Simonians and all their monstrosities," especially their declaration against property and hereditary rights. Fourier went so far in his angry refutation as to say that inequality of wealth, and even poverty, are of divine origin. He worked alone, and such influence as he had came indirectly and long after his death.

The basis of his scheme for regenerating society was the "phalange," which he describes in the most clear-cut and minute detail in his *Nouveau monde industriel.* A "phalange" was a great co-partnership community composed of from four hundred to eighteen hundred individuals living together in one great building. This building, which had the characteristics of a vast summer hotel, was to contain all sorts of rooms — concert halls, lecture halls, and working rooms to suit all tastes. Fourier's insistence on this form of life, the only really communistic element in his doctrine, lies in his profound belief that no solution of social evils is possible until a new environment is produced that will create a new type of man.

The "phalange" must be located in a healthy and attractive spot, near a stream. Here we are reminded of the garden cities of modern England and Germany. Around the huge central building was to be an area of four hundred acres, the whole set down in the midst of a capitalistic society. The four hundred acres were to include scattered farm buildings and industrial establishments, and were to constitute a little self-sufficing world producing everything, or nearly everything, it consumed. There was to be nothing compulsory in the scheme, the joining of such a community being purely voluntary. Fourier feared the growing concentration of the population in large cities, and he wished also to avoid the high rental of urban land for his communities. This back-to-the-land side of his doctrine likewise emphasized his belief in the value of manual labor, though it must be a manual labor that was in itself varied and interesting. Too much effort, he maintains, had always been put into the raising of cereals, which is much harder and much less interesting work than fruit culture and vegetable gardening. Diet would have to be modified to allow a greater place for fruits and vegetables. Hence in his scheme horticulture would largely replace agriculture. Thus Fourier's fundamental panacea was a return to a coöperative regime, largely agricultural and based on hand labor. Here he differs from both Owen and Saint-Simon, who accepted an industrialized society, which they wished to improve.

The "phalange" would be more economical and more efficient because of its coöperative character. It would also — and this was of prime importance — create sympathy among men, gradually replacing the present regime, "with its ascending scale of hatred and its descending scale of contempt." He was especially impressed with the bitter struggle for profit among producers and the keen competition for wages among workingmen. Such a combination could result only in the degradation of the workers. As for the wage-earners, Fourier believed that they must be transformed into coöperative owners. As we shall see, he was not aiming at the abolition of property, but at a more reasonable coöperation of labor and capital. Each "phalange" was to be established as a joint-stock company. The ownership of private property was to be transferred into the holding of stock. Capital was to receive a third of the profits, labor five twelfths, and "ability" (management) three twelfths.

Fourier insists, not only that competition must be curbed, and misery abolished, but that labor must be made more attractive. Whereas work is now regarded as a curse, he longs to see men work for the love of it. This would be possible, he believes, if every man were assured of enough to live on. Each one in the "phalange" would choose his own employment. Labor would be assured for everyone, and the worker would be spared monotony by being allowed to move from one task to another every few hours. In a properly regulated society a man should be able to produce enough between the ages of eighteen and twenty-eight to live, if he cared to, in comparative leisure the rest of his life. Work was to take, for anyone who joined the "phalange," only about a quarter of his time. Labor would be divided into three classes — necessary labor, useful labor, and agreeable labor. The first received the highest award, the last the smallest, as it implied the least sacrifice. A minimum income was fixed for all members.

The most exaggerated side of Fourier is represented by his elaborate psychological formulæ, with his scheme of a dozen passions; his "Law of Attraction," an ever-present power in the world drawing men together in united action; his ideas of a new science that would harness lions to draw carriages from one end of France to another in a day, make whales pull vessels across the sea, and turn the ocean into a kind of lemonade; and finally his "Theory of Universal Unity," which held that the world was just passing out of its infancy, and that on adopting Fourier's plans it would enter on a millennium of seventy thousand glorious years. Caricaturists twisted some of his suggestions that human beings might develop new organs and keener senses through the improvement of physical and moral conditions, and they made pictures of Socialists with long tails for ornaments and as defensive weapons, each tail terminating in an enormous eye.

Fourier exaggerated nearly every aspect of the thought of Rousseau, from whom he derived much. He believed naïvely in the noble savage, and in unlimited possibilities of human perfectibility. He hated restraints of all sorts, and joined with the Romanticists in insisting that reason must abdicate in favor of the passions, which are the great drawing forces in men. Obstacles had hitherto been placed in the way of passions and the "Law of Attraction," and as a result men were led into anti-social paths. When these obstacles were removed universal harmony would prevail. Here we are reminded of Godwin and the argument of Shelley's *Prometheus Unbound.* He assumed that everyone is enlightened and wants to work. If anyone is lazy or criminal, Fourier says, he is to be punished by not being allowed to work. Fourier's craze for self-expression in education, in work, and in love have led recent critics to class him as an Anarchist rather than as a Socialist.

Yet out of some of Fourier's exaggerated ideas on education Froebel developed the kindergarten, and it is well to remember that Fourier saw clearly the necessity for the emancipation of woman, in which, however, he was not unique, as the Saint-Simonians had also envisaged this ideal. He understood the future of large-scale production, and was one of the earliest ardent anti-militarists. He played a large part, too, in the development of modern factory legislation, as well as in the growth of modern Socialism and Anarchism. He is one of the fathers of the Coöperative Movement and of what we now call Industrial Democracy.

These Utopias of Fourier and Saint-Simon were strange combinations of penetrating criticism of the present, of profound insight into the course of economic evolution, and of gross historical and economic fallacies and sophistries. Their gospel of economic justice and of the suppression of misery was taken up by later men and was also spread among the masses, who found in such schemes a new religion. The happiness of which both Saint-Simon and Fourier dreamed was to come, in some degree at least, through increased production combined with a more equal distribution. The Saint-Simonians and Fourier, however, differed greatly in their methods of social reorganization. The Saint-Simonian reform, in placing authority in the hands of scholars and industrials, was bureaucratic. In accepting the new machine process, it anticipated modern industrialism. The reform of Fourier, on the contrary, was individualistic, even anarchistic, and was based on hand labor and agriculture. The real influence of these ideas comes after 1830, but it is to the honor of these rejected and neglected prophets of the Restoration that they furnished some of the great seed ideas of the nineteenth century.

CHAPTER V

THE ROMANTIC REVOLT

THE generation of the eighteen-twenties showed — so far as the intellectual classes were concerned — much interest in the rise of a new school of literature, music, and art, and groups that discussed the franchise, the press, and clericalism began also to discuss the merits of Classicism and Romanticism.

As is usually the case in France, men saw political and social implications in literary doctrines. The *Globe*, for example, was Liberal and anti-clerical in politics, while Hugo, the recognized leader of the Romantic group, was in the beginning a Catholic and an Ultra-Royalist. He scored his first success by reading an ode on "Quiberon" at a meeting of the Société des Bonnes Etudes, a branch of the Congrégation. In spite of this, the *Globe* insisted that Hugo's literary doctrines be given a hearing — for the period a surprisingly generous attitude. The *Constitutionnel*, the chief organ of political and religious Liberalism, was, on the other hand, violently anti-Romantic in all its literary reviews. The editors believed that it was a betrayal of the cause of liberty to attack the literary style of Voltaire, or the models of Greek and Latin literature wherein the republican virtues of antiquity were set forth. They were angry, too, at the Romanticists' admiration for the literature of England and of

ROMANTIC DRAWING

VICTOR HUGO

Germany, the victors of Waterloo, and irritated with the Catholic mediævalism of Chateaubriand, Lamennais, and Hugo. The sympathy of some of the Romanticists for Victor Cousin indicates the same confusion. Cousin was in his æsthetic theories a Neoclassicist, though he was a political Liberal, which made him acceptable to such Romanticists as happened to be political radicals.

The Ultramontanes, Bonald and Lamennais, on the contrary, were sympathetic toward Romantic doctrines, because they believed that Romantic mediævalism, and the Romantic sentiment of the unattainable and the divine, would help to recover the spiritual devotion lost in the eighteenth century. Gallican churchmen, like Frayssinous, with much better insight into the drift of Romanticism, condemned the movement, holding that its assertion of freedom in the selection of subject-matter and style made it akin to political and intellectual Liberalism. The Saint-Simonians, finally, disapproved of Romanticism, because of its overemphasis on individualism and its indifference to producing a great art for the masses.

Little wonder that it was hard for contemporaries to understand the movement. The more recent attempts to relate Romanticism to contemporary social and political conditions, except in a general way, usually seem rather fantastic. There is much in French Romanticism that is in no wise a mirror of the period. Literature, music, and the fine arts have their own life and laws, which may or may not bear much relation to the political and economic life of the times.

I. ORIGINS OF THE ROMANTIC REVOLT

The French Romantic School of 1830 was not so original as it liked to imagine itself. Indeed, the development of Romanticism from 1815 to 1830 marks but the continuation of changes which began near the opening of the eighteenth century and which would have come to a fuller development decades earlier had not the French Revolution intervened. Long before 1789, in the midst of a society usually characterized by its faith in reason and by its literary and artistic Classicism, a great intellectual and artistic revolt had slowly gathered force. The first stirrings of this movement seem to have come from England early in the eighteenth century, though these English influences would have had little effect had the French themselves not begun to move away from the Classicism of the Age of Louis XIV. Before the middle of the century expressions like "the sweep of the imagination" and "the delicious agonies of the heart" begin to appear in French literature. Ennui, melancholy, and vague desires, the unlimited, the infinite, and the fantastic, — indeed, anything that ran counter to the reason, measure, and clarity of French Classicism,— are to be found pushing their way into poetry, fiction, art, and manners. Poems, novels, and engravings are set in strange backgrounds of moonlight, cascades, wild, rocky scenery, ruined castles, tombs, and Gothic churches. A revolution in taste was clearly in progress even before 1750.

It was in Jean-Jacques Rousseau (d. 1778) that the

movement found its greatest expression before the nineteenth century. The magic of this disordered genius, of whom Madame de Staël justly remarked that "he invented nothing, but set everything on fire," was felt everywhere. In France, no works of the century approached the popularity and influence of Rousseau's *Nouvelle Héloïse* (1761), his *Emile* (1762), and his *Confessions*. Here, more than in the work of Diderot or any other of Rousseau's contemporaries, the individualism of the whole Romantic Movement, its emotionalism, and its lyric subjectivity find their first glowing expression. It is from Rousseau, more than from any other man, that the Romanticism of the nineteenth century proceeds.

The bridge between the Romanticism of Rousseau and his generation and the School of 1830 is to be found chiefly in the work of Madame de Staël and of Chateaubriand. Madame de Staël furnished the Romanticists with many of their theories. Chateaubriand furnished an ideal and an example. Madame de Staël's great contributions to French literary doctrine were in her insistence that modern literature must be national and Christian, — that is, that it must seek beneath a crust of seventeenth- and eighteenth-century Classicism the indigenous culture of the Middle Ages, — and that neither rules nor models, especially classical ones, should cramp spontaneity and individuality. She believed, too, that the mediæval literature of Northern Europe, with its vague melancholy, its reverie, and its mystic exaltation, offered a mine of rich literary material for a generation in France that had exhausted the old Neoclassical tradition. Madame de Staël was not a great creative thinker, and she gathered together ideas held by a number of her contemporaries, some of whom were more original than herself, but she had an extraordinary ability to popularize and spread these new ideas.

The reputation and influence of Chateaubriand were exerted on the side of a new literature. A poet — though he wrote in prose — rather than a thinker, his melancholy, his eloquence, and his richly picturesque prose style mark him as the great successor of Rousseau. He presented to his generation the perfect Romantic type. Incapable of any sustained action, yet dreaming of every sort of heroic deed for the sensation it would bring, he fled from the real into a dream world. Like Byron and the young Goethe, he represented to his age a kind of dilettante of revolt. Chateaubriand's literary style was in itself a revelation, for he handled words not as symbols of thought, as had the writers of the Classical French tradition, but as the means of evoking reveries or sensations. His importance lies in the fact that after the empty formality of much eighteenth-century Neoclassical literature he restored to French letters a deeply emotional style, and showed the generation that followed him the possibilities of a subjective and emotional literature which drew its inspiration from nature, — though often from the exotic nature of distant lands and climes, — from the art and poetry of the Christian Middle Ages, and from the sensibility of the heart. Romanticism in France had many precursors, but none more important than Chateaubriand.

The period from 1780 to 1830 was marked, too, by a great influx of foreign influences into French literature. "Modern poetry," wrote Lecomte de Lisle in 1852, "is the blurred image of the fiery personality of Byron, the sensual religionism of Chateaubriand, the mystic reveries of German thought, and the realism of the Lake poets."[1] The Emigration had brought hundreds of Frenchmen into first-hand contact with foreign intellectual and artistic movements, and was a very important element in the introduction of foreign ideas into French literature. Among the English writers who were most influential in the French Romantic Movement after 1800, Shakespeare must be placed first, though Scott, Byron, and Ossian were nearly as important. Shakespeare's ignorance of the rules of classical drama, his use of history as dramatic material, and, above all, his poetic fire, made his name the rallying cry of the Romanticists. In the eighteen-twenties Villemain and Guizot were both preaching the glories of Shakespeare at the Sorbonne, and in 1822 Stendhal used Shakespeare as the Romantic counterblast to Racine. In 1827 an English company played Shakespeare with great success in Paris. Delacroix, Hugo, Gérard de Nerval, Alfred de Vigny, Dumas, and Berlioz followed these performances with worshipful enthusiasm. Scott's novels were translated as they appeared, and by 1820 several had been dramatized and put on the stage. Scott's commonsense view of life and his sober Protestant morality did not interest the young Romanticists. What they ad-

1 J. G. Palache, *Gautier and the Romantics* (London, 1927), pp. 27–28.

mired were his display of crossbows, his mediæval adventures, and his romantic old castles. It was the wild passion, the melancholy, of Byron, "the Bonaparte of poetry," and his glorious death in Greece, that made his reputation in France. Byron's paradoxes fascinated the young Romanticists. He asserts that love is all, and then again that it is the curse of man; he adores nature, and again despises it. He calls philosophy the vanity of vanities, and at the same time urges men to think that they may defy God. He affected a disdain for society, and yet was himself a perfect dandy. None of the French Romantic writers and artists entirely escaped Byron's influence.

The chief German literary influences in the first years of the nineteenth century were Goethe, the Schlegels, Hoffmann, Herder, Schiller, and the nature poets, Haller and Gessner, though the work of none of these men had the influence in France exercised by Shakespeare, Scott, and Byron. The German fountains and rivers, where dwelt elves and fairies, and the haunted mountains with their witches and gnomes, made Germany seem like a Walpurgis-Nacht dreamland. The most popular German work in France was Goethe's *Sorrows of Werther*. *Faust*, his masterpiece, was less influential, though it inspired Delacroix to make a great series of lithographs for its illustration. E. T. A. Hoffmann had some vogue in France. The French Romanticists admired his combination of wild fantasticality and sharply defined pictures. It was Schiller's plays, translated into French by Barante, that made his French reputation. Their freedom from the classical unities, their mediæval subjects, and their fervent poetic style made Schiller seem to the generation of 1820 to 1830 almost the equal of Shakespeare.

Many of the æsthetic theories of the German Romanticists reached France through Madame de Staël's *De l'Allemagne*, a work suppressed by Napoleon but widely circulated after 1815. Most influential of these theorists whom Madame de Staël made known in France were Herder, the Schlegel brothers, and Schiller. Herder had discovered the glamour of the Middle Ages. He also preached the value in art of intuition and feeling, both of which he placed above observation and reason. The Schlegels denounced the unities, the sterile harmony, and the abstraction of the French classical drama, and at the same time, like Herder, praised the folk poetry of the Germanic barbarians and the Gothic art of the Middle Ages. Schiller made a famous distinction between naïve and sentimental poetry, bringing into literary doctrine much of the Rousseauistic praise of everything that was primitive and spontaneous. The great foreign influences on French Romanticism were from the North of Europe, though among the Italians Dante and Manzoni were greatly admired, and the mediæval Spanish stories of the romancero and the drama of the Spanish Renaissance were much studied after 1800. On the whole, the French Romanticists seem to have admired these foreign literary men rather than to have imitated them. They invoked the name and fame of a Shakespeare or a Dante to justify their own work in the face of hostile criticism.

No great figure appears in French letters between 1810 and 1820, though the Romantic traditions of Chateaubriand were continued in such minor works as Sénancour's *Obermann* and Constant's *Adolphe*. The later years of the Empire, with their lack of freedom of expression and with their great opportunities for a life of action, were unfavorable to literary development. The best energies of the nation were diverted into channels of politics, military enterprise, and civil administration. The fall of the Empire changed all this. The spirit of adventure could no longer carry a young man to Moscow or Madrid. There was left only the road to Xanadu. There was also much genuine disillusionment after the failure of the Revolution to realize the optimistic promises of the Philosophers. After 1815, the present seemed to many quite intolerable, and the Romantic answer was to carry oneself away in imagination to an East impossibly oriental, to forests impossibly primeval, and to periods impossibly mediæval. The Romanticist was straining to escape into a dream world to muffle the ache of the actual.

The closing of the salons, the arbiters of taste, at the time of the Revolution had also given literature a greater freedom. No longer did all ideas have to be reduced to the level of good conversation and witty repartee. Moreover, it must be remembered that the young men who had grown up during the Revolution and the Empire had received their education in a very irregular fashion and that the dead hand of Greece and Rome had not been so heavy on this rising generation. It was easier for the poet to see the world through his own eyes when he was ignorant of Theocritus, of Horace, and of Boileau. It is in the years after 1820, from among the same generation that developed Eclecticism, Positivism, and Socialism, that the young Romanticists gathered their forces. In 1820 the *Méditations* of Lamartine appeared, in 1822 Hugo's *Odes* and the *Poems* of Alfred de Vigny. It was evident that a new literature was coming into being, though there was still no school, or even — what one would expect in France — a manifesto. For some years, however, a controversy over Classic and Romantic values had been going on. After 1815 there was less stirring news to fill the newspapers, and more space was given to literary discussion. The first important manifesto, though by no means the first statement of the claims of Romanticism, was Stendhal's *Racine et Shakespeare* of 1822. There is little that is either new or very clear in Stendhal's statement, but it is interesting because it was the first manifesto of Romanticism that was much read. Stendhal makes ennui and servile imitation the notes of Classicism, and his plea is for more liberty of expression for the artist and for a literature more closely related to life. "Classical literature," he says, "is that which pleased our great-grandfathers; Romantic literature is that which pleases us."

The first Romantic school or cénacle was in the meanwhile forming about Charles Nodier, the author of many fantastic and exotic tales, who was also the librarian of the famous Arsenal Library. At his house in 1823 there began to meet a group which included Emile and Antoine Deschamps, Alfred de Vigny, and occasionally Victor Hugo. In 1819 Hugo and his brother had founded *Le Conservateur littéraire*, which lasted less than two years. This was the first periodical which championed Romanticism, though, at this time, Hugo was still rather conservative and uncertain in his views. In 1824 the *Globe* began to appear, and while it can hardly be said to have championed Romanticism whole-heartedly, it demanded at least that the new school be given a hearing. The *Globe*, as we have seen, is the most interesting of a number of literary journals of the Restoration, and for the next six years it printed the best reviews and criticism of the books of the Romanticists as they appeared. Romanticism was slowly gathering its forces, and the reading public was beginning to take notice of the new school.

Gradually the points at issue between Classicism and Romanticism became clearer. It is interesting to follow the growing boldness of Hugo from the introduction of the *Odes* of 1822, through the preface to the *Ballades* of 1826, to the *Préface de Cromwell* of 1827. In 1822, and even in 1826, he maintains that there are only two sorts of poetry, good and bad, and that the discussions about Classic and Romantic values are rather futile, though in 1826 he insists on the necessity of liberty for the artist and on the evils of limiting the literary genres in choice of subject-matter and in style. The *Préface de Cromwell* was, however, a veritable trumpet-blast. Full as it is of gross historical inaccuracies and of bombast, it seemed at the time a successful attack on the rules of Classical taste. It was in any case clever propaganda, with its appeals to the examples of Ariosto, Cervantes, Rabelais, and Shakespeare. Like his contemporaries Saint-Simon, Fourier, and Comte, Hugo had an interpretation of history. There was no manifesto in the first half of the nineteenth century — political, literary, or philosophical — that did not begin with some sort of elaborate historical justification. Hugo distinguishes three literary periods — a primitive period, whose poetry is lyric; then the period of ancient civilization, when it is epic; and finally the modern period, the age of Christianity, which is the period of the drama. The only thing very original about this famous preface, except the noise made over it, was its assertions that art must contain a contrast between the ugly and the beautiful, that art must be free, and that things must be called by their right names. The whole breathes fire and brimstone on the formal pomposity of the whole Neoclassical school of rules.

A third manifesto, which stands alongside Stendhal's *Racine et Shakespeare* and Hugo's *Préface de Cromwell*, is Sainte-Beuve's *Tableau de la poésie du XVIe siècle* of 1828. Here Sainte-Beuve tries to link up the new Romantic poets with the poetry of the sixteenth century and so to give the new movement a glorious ancestry in the work of Ronsard and his school. The literature of the eighteenth century in France had taken as its models the ancient classics and the French classics of the seventeenth century. Now, quite rightly, the Romanticists were turning for inspiration to the Middle Ages and the Renaissance, and also to the literatures of other countries — England, Germany, Italy, and Spain. According to Sainte-Beuve, the whole history of French literature justified the new movement.

In these years a series of original Romantic works were appearing in rapid succession. Besides the first volumes of Lamartine, Hugo, and Alfred de Vigny, there appeared between 1825 and 1829 Mérimée's *Charles IX* and his *Théâtre de Clara Gazul*, Alfred de Vigny's *Cinq-Mars*, Dumas' *Henri III et sa cour*, Sainte-Beuve's *Pensées de Joseph Delorme*, and Balzac's first novel, *Les Chouans*. The year 1830 was marked by a remarkable series of Romantic works: Lamartine's *Harmonies poétiques*, Nodier's *L'histoire du roi de Bohême*, Stendhal's *Le rouge et le noir*, Alfred de Musset's *Contes d'Espagne et d'Italie*, his first work, Sainte-Beuve's *Consolations*, Gautier's first volume of poems, and Hugo's *Hernani*. A new cénacle, which met at Hugo's house, had been formed in 1827. This included Sainte-Beuve, Hugo, Dumas, David d'Angers, Delacroix, Alfred de Vigny, and Alfred de Musset. Between the *Préface de Cromwell* of 1827 and the fight over *Hernani* in 1830 the quarrel of Classicists and Romanticists waxed into a veritable fray. To the younger men it seemed a literary war of liberation. Artists, poets, and musicians joined the movement. Poems were read in painters' studios. Delacroix and his friends sang Hugo's ballads. Berlioz admired Shakespeare more extravagantly than did Hugo. The whole group were closely allied to rout the enemy. They gave each other inspiration, courage, and criticism.

By the end of 1830 the battle was practically won, partly through the success of *Hernani*, and partly through the bold and clever manœuvres of this group of young poets, artists, and musicians. Hugo's play *Hernani* had been well advertised by its enemies of the old school, who had listened at the door during the rehearsals, and, having picked up single lines, parodied the play in the newspapers. When the play opened Hugo gave away three hundred tickets for each of the first three nights. Madame Hugo later described the spectators who came to fill these seats as "a troop of wild, extravagant creatures, with beards and long hair, dressed in every fashion except that of the day, in woolen jerseys and Spanish cloaks, and Henry III caps." The leaders were all young men; Hugo was twenty-seven, Dumas twenty-six, Musset nineteen, and Alfred de Vigny thirty-two. The moment the curtain rose the storm broke, and it continued for many nights in succession. The enemy took boxes and left them unoccupied in order that the newspapers might report a poor house. At other times they ostentatiously read newspapers and banged the doors. An appeal to stop the play was made to Charles X by six members of the French Academy. His characteristic answer was, "My place is in the parterre with the audience." The play itself is one in which every emotion is strained to the highest pitch, and what the younger generation saw in it was the expression of their own defiance and thirst for independence.

The success of *Hernani* marks the decisive turn of the Romantic battle, and after 1830 Romanticism held the field. If one turns from the story of this long literary war and tries to understand the real nature of Romanticism, he is at once faced with both vagueness and contradiction. The definitions of Romanticism made by the Romanticists themselves between 1820 and 1830 differ greatly. These definitions can best be followed in the *Globe*. To Thiers, the movement stood for "nature and truth," to J. J. Ampère it was "originality opposed to imitation," for Sismondi it was the "faithful image of modern civilization," — a view shared by Stendhal, — and for Hugo it was "liberalism and freedom in literature."

The more recent attempts to define the movement show likewise an immense divergence. They range all the way from Beer's restatement of Heine's assertion that Romanticism was a return to the Middle Ages[1] to the contemporary studies of Lasserre, Paul Elmer More, and Professor Babbitt, who find in Romanticism a whole revolution — and that a bad one — in ethics and politics.[2] Whatever the definition used, it is now generally recognized that Romanticism, even on its purely literary and artistic side, was a great international movement which gathered its forces in the eighteenth century and in one form or another dominated European art

1 H. A. Beers, *English Romanticism in the Eighteenth Century* (New York, 1899), Chap. I.

2 P. Lasserre, *Le romantisme français* (1907); P. E. More, *The Drift of Românticism* (1913); I. Babbitt, *Rousseau and Romanticism* (Boston, 1919).

and literature until past the middle of the nineteenth century.

As this great movement affected the generation of 1830 in France, it manifested itself in an attempt to renew poetry, the drama, the novel, the fine arts and music, after all of these had seemingly exhausted themselves in the sterilities of Neoclassical formalism. Whatever the classical tradition may have meant to earlier generations, it had, in the France of the eighteenth century, come to be little more than a set of rules and formulæ. The formal garden with its clipped hedges, the witty and artificial conversation of the salons, and a poetic style slavishly imitated from models were indication enough that the arts and letters lacked individuality and spontaneity. Classic form had degenerated into a dead formalism. The upshot of this, as we have seen, was a turning of men's attention to wild nature, to solitude, to the Middle Ages, and to the art and poetry of Northern peoples whose artistic traditions were less affected by the canons of an enfeebled Classicism, and, finally, from reason to an expansive emotionalism. The result was, for good or for ill, a fiery and glowing art and literature, fully developing every caprice of thought. An artistic movement was launched which resembled the Renaissance.

II. THE ADVENT OF A NEW LYRIC POETRY

The Romantic Movement was everywhere a great period in the history of lyric poetry. Schiller and Heine, Wordsworth and Byron, Lamartine and Hugo, their work stretching across a hundred years, are but representatives of a golden age of lyricism. In France, Neoclassicism, against which Rousseau and Chateaubriand had led the revolt in prose, was in 1815 still supreme in poetry. Nothing could be drier and more sterile than the verse of the Empire, the last stand of decadent Classicism. "The Empire," says Lamartine, "was the incarnation of the materialistic philosophy of the eighteenth century." He speaks of its literary dictators as the "geometric men" who seemed to say to the young men of the time, "Love, philosophy, religion, enthusiasm, liberty, poetry, are nothing. Calculation and force, figures and swords, rule." [1] The sudden overthrow of Napoleon and his Cæsarian regime in 1815 seemed a great release. Lyric poetry might at last develop.

The enthusiasm with which the poems of André Chénier were received in 1819 indicates the eagerness of the time for lyric poetry. Chénier's poems, though the greatest literary work of the period of the Revolution, were not known before 1819. They are refined in sentiment, and as finely chiseled in style as the verse of Keats. Their popularity was very great, and for the next few years overshadowed the success of some of the early Romantic poets. The new age of poetry really begins with the publication in 1820 of the *Méditations poétiques* of Alphonse de Lamartine.

This young man, who at the time was still wholly unheard of, had spent a happy childhood on his father's

1 *Premières méditations poétiques*, Introduction.

estate near Mâcon. A trip to Italy in 1811 and a somewhat irregular schooling had given him a taste for literature and a love of nature. In these formative years he read and absorbed Rousseau, Bernadin de Saint-Pierre, and Chateaubriand. In 1816 he went to Aix-les-Bains for his health, and while there he fell deeply in love with a Madame Charles. Her death in 1818 inspired his first volume of verses, the *Méditations* of 1820. The success of the volume was immediate. Even a man of the Ancien Régime like Talleyrand tells us that he was so stirred by these verses that he was unable to sleep the night he read them. It was the intense sincerity and the simple flowing style of these poems that made them seem so novel and so beautiful. Lamartine's poetry and himself seemed one — as Gautier remarked, "Lamartine, c'est la poésie même."

When he speaks of nature, of love, and of regret, he seems penetrated with these sentiments. At his best, Lamartine is one of the most natural and exquisite of all French poets. His style seems completely without effort, so close to pure inspiration is it, though the form is in many ways still Classical. One of his few remarks on technique — and he seems to have been particularly indifferent to questions of poetic technique — was that "One must be Classical in expression, and Romantic in thought." [1] Lamartine never wanted to appear as a man of letters, and it is only the part of his work which represents a pure and spontaneous inspiration that reveals him at his best. He had almost no capacity

1 J. Giraud, *L'école romantique française* (1927), p. 19.

to rework his poems, and his later work shows this deficiency. Fifty years later, writing of the extraordinary impression made by this work of 1820, Sainte-Beuve says, "One passed suddenly from a poetry that was dry, thin, and poor to a poetry from the heart, overflowing and divine."[1] In 1822 appeared a second volume, *Nouvelles méditations*, and in 1830 his *Harmonies poétiques et religieuses*, perhaps his greatest work. After the July Revolution he turned his attention to social and political questions. Lamartine never actually joined the Romantic School, though his work represents one of the finest achievements of that movement.

Two years after the appearance of Lamartine's *Méditations*, Alfred de Vigny published a slender volume of poems. They differed greatly from Lamartine's verses in being much less personal, though in their style they showed clearly a relationship to the new artistic ideals. The Comte de Vigny spent his formative years (1815–28) in the Royal Guard, and this military experience, in the midst of which he published his first volume of poems, forms the only active part of his career. In this period of his youth he met Victor Hugo, and he was a member of the two Cénacles of 1823 and 1829.

During a long life de Vigny wrote only about thirty poems, a few dramas, and several prose works. His poetry, which explains his inner life, is always written in the same mood. Forty years lie between *Moïse* of 1822 and the *Mont des Oliviers;* yet one perceives no change in his pessimism. Throughout his work his one

1 Giraud, *p. 21.*

theme is the distress of the soul which accompanies the sense of isolation and solitude. De Vigny is the most sincere and the most bitterly logical of all the descendants of Chateaubriand's René, of Byron's Manfred, and Goethe's Werther. There is no suggestion of pose about the "mal du siècle" of this man, who adored the ideal at the same time that he had lost the capacity to believe in it. Men are hostile or indifferent; nature is cold and impassive; God, if he exists, is silent. It is the melancholy of Chateaubriand without the consolation which Chateaubriand found in a beautiful dream world, and the deep disillusionment of Pascal without the power of a saving Christian grace. Man is utterly alone, as his *Moïse* of 1822 says:

> O Seigneur, j'ai vécu puissant et solitaire
> Laissez-moi m'endormir du sommeil de la terre.

De Vigny's only admonition is "Souffre, et meure sans parler." His stoicism, so far as it is relieved at all, is tempered only by a certain tenderness and by his belief in the duty of pity. What a contrast to Lamartine's view of man and nature:

> Tout est bien, tout est bon, tout est grand à sa place!

Both Lamartine and de Vigny represent an attitude that is profoundly personal, and both write from a deep experience. The eighteenth century had seen in nature fauns and dryads; the Romanticists saw only themselves, and hence each one saw something different. Romantic isolation and melancholy proved to be one of the spiritual maladies of the nineteenth century, and nowhere does this melancholy strike so sublime a note as in some of de Vigny's poems.

These poems usually represent some single idea over which he had long reflected, and finally developed in a severe and highly polished manner — a style, as George Brandes remarks, "that has the sheen of ivory." His conciseness and his studied power were derived partly from the study of André Chénier, whom de Vigny greatly admired. "The final impression of Alfred de Vigny," says Faguet, "is of a solitary force working apart, in the midst of a great sadness and under a dreary sky, without haste and without attracting attention, producing now and then a beautiful and precious work."[1] Though, as Sainte-Beuve said, "de Vigny dwelt in an ivory tower," he took a more active part in the work of the Romantic School from 1820 to 1830 than did Lamartine.

The natural leader of the school was Victor Hugo. He, above all the other poets, painters, and musicians of the group, possessed the energy, the courage, and the ability to lead the movement, and these qualities early brought him into prominence. The son of a Napoleonic general, Hugo had as a child traveled about Europe with the army. His earliest memories were not of France, but of Spain and Italy. Left much to himself during his youth, he naturally acquired a very indifferent education, though he was early possessed with the idea that he "would be Chateaubriand or nothing." When he was only fifteen years old, he received a literary prize, and at twenty he was granted a pension by Louis XVIII.

1 Faguet, *Etudes littéraires du XIXe siècle* (1887), p. 152.

From this time (1822) until his death in 1885 his life was to be one long series of literary triumphs.

Before 1850 Hugo's best-known work was in the drama and the novel, though his early poetry is more representative of the central movement of Romanticism than that of either Lamartine or de Vigny. Hugo wrote with a fire and energy that marked the advent of the full tide of Romanticism. In each new volume — 1822, 1826, and 1829 — the verses were orchestrated with a more magnificent sweep and amplitude, in which all the resources of the language seemed to be exhausted. He painted with a brush as mighty as the pine which Heine would fain have torn from the Norwegian cliffs and dipped in the fire of Etna to write the name of his beloved across the heavens.

Hugo was in these years an omnivorous reader of all sorts of works — technical books, old romances, sixteenth-century poets, memoirs, and histories. From all these he, like a number of his fellow Romanticists, drew words and expressions which he used in his verse, often with brilliant effectiveness. The French language was being enriched by Hugo and his contemporaries as in the days of Ronsard and the Pléiade. Hugo proclaimed that he had, in his wide choice of words, "mis le bonnet rouge au vieux dictionnaire." Hugo boasted, too, that he always "called a pig a pig." In verse forms he was also a bold innovator, especially in his use of enjambement — that is, the carrying of a thought without a break through more than one line of poetry. Romanticism brought back into use a great mass of Mediæval and

Renaissance words and expressions that the Neoclassical grammarians had weeded out of the language. The movement meant thus a great enrichment of the French language, and in this process Hugo holds first place.

Hugo drew freely upon all his contemporaries, Byron, Chateaubriand, Delacroix, Walter Scott, and Sainte-Beuve, reflecting in some way the special interests of each. The physical world about him, too, left its vivid impressions. The color, the outline, the movement, of everything he had seen are caught in his verses. Sensitive in the extreme, he wrote poems which, like the *Ballades* and the *Orientales*, are frequently just a series of sensations devoid of ideas, but glowing with all the colors of the rainbow. It was hardly evident in these years before 1830 that Hugo was later to be given to empty rhetoric, and that he was also in many ways a petty and humorless man. He was still, in 1830, the White Knight of the Romantic forces, their most vivid and fearless figure, and their natural leader. Little wonder that the young Romanticists followed him with an ardor that knew no bounds.[1]

III. THE WAR OF LIBERATION IN THE THEATER

The rise of the Romantic drama during the Restoration attracted much more attention than did the first volumes of the new Romantic verse. Indeed, the popular interest in the whole Romantic Movement dates

1 I have omitted any discussion of the work of a number of other Romantic poets — Sainte-Beuve and Madame Desbordes-Valmore because their work is less interesting, and Gautier and Alfred de Musset because they belong rather to the later history of Romanticism.

really from the performance of three plays, Dumas' *Henri III et sa cour* (1829), de Vigny's *More de Venise* (1830), and Hugo's *Hernani* (1830).

The origins of the Romantic drama go back to the tearful comedies of La Chaussée and of some of his contemporaries in the eighteenth century. The handling of the humble as well as of the extravagant and the pathetic was a first step away from the artificialities of the Neoclassic drama. The hard-and-fast separation of comedy and tragedy, and the rigid adherence to the three unities of time, place, and action, had also received a severe blow just before the Revolution, through the tremendous success of the plays of Beaumarchais. The greatest contributing force in emancipating the drama came, however, from the popular melodrama given in the boulevard theaters. By its brutal and pathetic effects which mixed tragedy and comedy, by its choice of subjects from exotic, from mediæval, and from foreign sources, by its indifference to the three unities, and by its composition in prose, it accustomed the public to a type of play far removed from the sort of stilted dramas given at the Comédie-Française. These melodramas gave the public a taste for mediæval settings, fierce tyrants, persecuted souls, honest and kind-hearted outlaws, and the persons stricken by an evil destiny. The great master of this style was Guilbert de Pixérécourt, who wrote over a hundred melodramas between 1789 and 1834. In his boyhood Hugo loved these plays, but when he began to write for the stage himself he was so afraid that the public might think his plays melodramas that he wrote them in verse and was careful to confine the time of action to two days.

Romantic poetry had developed spontaneously, but the new Romantic drama of the Restoration represented rather the application of theories that were thoroughly discussed beforehand. The newspapers and certain of the literary salons took a great interest in these discussions of the nature of the drama. It formed the chief topic of conversation of a cénacle which met usually at the home of Viollet-le-Duc, the architect. This literary group included Stapfer, who made a translation of Goethe's *Faust*, Prosper Mérimée, and Charles de Rémusat. The dictator of the salon was Stendhal. The discussions turned on Shakespeare, the French translation of whose plays had just been revised by Guizot, on Barante's translation of certain of the plays of Schiller, on a new translation of Schlegel's *Dramatic Literature*, and on an eloquent plea by Manzoni for more liberty in the drama. This group criticized the contemporary examples of Neoclassical drama — plays like Raynouard's *Templiers*, where, to preserve the unity of time, the Templars are arrested, tried, condemned, and executed in a single day, and Brifaud's *Ninus II*, originally laid in Renaissance Spain, but, to please the censor, transferred without any changes to ancient Assyria! Out of these soirées Stendhal drew most of the theories of his *Racine and Shakespeare* (1822) and by them Mérimée was inspired to write his *Théâtre de Clara Gazul* (1825).

According to Stendhal, as we have seen, "Romanticism is the art of presenting to the public literary works which in the present condition of their habits and beliefs will give them the greatest pleasure possible." Following this doctrine, Sophocles, Euripides, and Racine were Romantic in their time. Although he praised Shakespeare, Stendhal wanted a new school of drama written in prose and closely related to the ways and interests of contemporary life. His manifesto, though an able attack on the limitations of the Neo-classic drama, was a plea rather for Realism than for Romanticism. It was in advance of its time and was the work of a man who said a few years later that he would "begin to be understood about 1880." Mérimée's *Théâtre de Clara Gazul, comédienne espagnole* is a pastiche of Shakespeare and Calderon written with a strange mixture of fantasy and irony. In 1828 he published an historical play, *La Jacquerie*. Laid in the fourteenth century, it presented a collection of historical pictures of monks, bourgeois, and nobles, but it can hardly be called a play. These plays of Mérimée were not performed, though they influenced Dumas and Hugo. They were the first literary successes of the Romantic drama, and they prepared the way for later successes on the stage.

Of all the theoretical discussions of the period before *Hernani*, none was of more interest than Hugo's *Préface de Cromwell* of 1827. We have already noticed his fantastic division of the literary ages into the lyric, the epic, and the dramatic. Behind much that was absurd in this manifesto there lay Hugo's sincere desire to put all life, its comedy and its tragedy, into the drama, giving to each situation and character its exact "local color." He would achieve this by abolishing the unities and by wiping out the old distinctions between comedy and tragedy. Hugo was here merely repeating the phrases of his Romantic contemporaries. His insistence on the use of contrast was, however, novel. To achieve the effect of life, the sublime and the ridiculous, the beautiful and the ugly, must be set in sharp contrast. He justified this by the contrasts in Gothic art and in the plays of Shakespeare. Except for some of the writings of Wagner, the whole Romantic Movement shows no more sublime egotism than this *Préface de Cromwell.* Hugo would prove that *Cromwell* was the kind of work for which mankind had been waiting through the centuries — indeed, that it was the culmination of a progress that began with Genesis and the Book of Job.

Part of Hugo's argument for a poetic drama is an answer to Stendhal, who argued for a drama in prose. In 1829 de Vigny, in his preface to the *More de Venise*, stated much more simply all that Hugo had tried to say. The drama, he says, "should present a large picture of all of life, instead of a picture narrowed to show the catastrophe of an intrigue." The brilliant performances of Shakespeare in Paris in 1827 by an English company made Shakespeare seem like a contemporary advocate of the new Romantic theories of the drama. Curiously enough, this new Romantic drama, which found Shakespeare both useful and inspiring, was to imitate much that is weak in him, at the same time that it failed utterly to achieve Shakespeare's marvelous analysis of character.

In the midst of all this theorizing, Alexandre Dumas in 1829 presented the first Romantic play that was a success on the stage, *Henri III et sa cour.* The author, who was the grandson of a Creole and a negress and the son of a Revolutionary general, had received practically no regular education, and he was only twenty-four years old at the time this play was produced. *Henri III* throws the unities to the winds and its story is drawn not from the ancient classics but from a chapter of the history of France. The critics greeted it with tirades, but the public liked it and applauded it to the echo. It seems, if read today, hardly a play at all, but only a series of gorgeous tableaux of the days of Catherine de' Medici and the Guises. A large number of other pieces of the same sort were being put on at the time by several minor dramatists, though none had the success of Dumas' play. Much of Dumas' somber coloring, — and this is also true of other Romantic plays and novels, — in his massacres, imprisonments, escapes, and murders, was inspired by the scenes of the French Revolution, which were still fresh in men's minds. Whatever were its excesses and weaknesses, *Henri III et sa cour* was popularly acclaimed because of its striking contrast to the insipid and inane Neoclassical plays that were produced in the better theaters of the Restoration.

In the same year Alfred de Vigny's *More de Venise*, a translation of Shakespeare's *Othello*, was given its first performance in Paris. The play is a magnificent handling of the original, and its presentation gave those who could not understand Shakespeare's plays in English their first opportunity to see him in his full power. Shakespeare had been played in France before the Revolution in the translation of Ducis, and one of Voltaire's best plays, *Zaïre*, is a rehandling of *Othello*. Ducis' translation of *Othello* is an interesting gauge of the limitations of Neoclassical taste. Ducis changed the names of most of the characters to make them sound more like the names in the plays of Racine. He did not dare to place the second act in Cyprus, but kept the whole play in Venice so as to preserve the unity of place. Desdemona's handkerchief, which was too inelegant for eighteenth-century taste, was replaced by a diamond tiara; the pillow which smothered her became a sword; Othello had a very fair complexion, lest in looking like a Moor he should be mistaken for a negro! De Vigny's version put the true *Othello* on the French stage, and the play was enthusiastically received in Paris in 1829.

Also in 1829 Hugo tried to present a new play, *Marion Delorme*, but, on the petition of seven members of the French Academy, Martignac refused to allow the play to appear, giving as an excuse that its treatment of Louis XIII was too unfavorable to royalty. The play, which was performed in 1831, is picturesque and full of splendid verse. Like Dumas, Hugo draws from Shakespeare, Scott, and Schiller, though the handling of the material is his own. *Hernani*, written after *Marion Delorme* had been refused production, was Hugo's first play to be performed. This play, over which the Romantic battle was finally fought in 1830, is laid in the Spanish Low Countries in the sixteenth century. Like

Marion Delorme, it is an extravagant mixture of history and melodrama, weak from the dramatic point of view, but full of superb poetry. The play seemed a veritable Bible to the young Romanticists, who fought for its acceptance, and its success marks the turning point in the history of Romanticism.

The Romantic drama held the field during most of the July Monarchy, though it represents the weakest aspect of French Romanticism. The whole movement was primarily a renaissance of lyricism, and the drama, with its demand for action and for a variety of characterizations, was not suited to the literary capacities of a group of lyric poets. Though their artistic value is not great, the comedies of Scribe are much better adapted to the stage than any of the plays of Hugo.

The Neoclassical drama presented characters that were abstractions of jealousy, ambition, or avarice. The Romantic dramatists always claimed that they were putting individuals, not types, on the stage, but with the exception of some of the comedies of Alfred de Musset, written between 1833 and 1836, the Romantic drama was a failure, and a failure largely because of the same lack of real characterization that had marked the Neoclassical drama. These Romantic dramas are overemphatic, often puerile in their motivation, and monotonous in their characterization. Much of the success of *Henri III et sa cour* and of *Hernani* was due to successful propaganda and to the great ability of the actress Mademoiselle Mars, who played a leading rôle in each. Balzac's contemporary judgment of *Hernani* is a just estimate of at least the dramatic quality of the whole Romantic drama. "All its tricks are old," he says, "its story is impossible, its characters false, and their action contrary to good sense."[1]

IV. ROMANTICISM IN THE NOVEL AND IN THE WRITING OF HISTORY

Among the literary genres the novel was the earliest to be freed from classical canons. The school of Louis XIV had neglected the novel as an inferior literary form. Profiting by this neglect, the novels of the eighteenth century presented many direct portrayals of contemporary life. The novel in France thus reflects the changing life of this interesting century, its manners, its aspirations, and its weaknesses, much better than does lyric poetry or the drama. All sorts of novels appeared — romances of adventure, novels of character analysis, exotic and historical romances, and novels with a thesis.

The greatest novels of the latter part of the century — of the period from 1760 to 1815 — were studies of sentiment rather than of manners. From the *Nouvelle Héloïse* of Rousseau (1761), Bernadin de Saint-Pierre's *Paul et Virginie*, and Chateaubriand's *Atala* (1801) and *René* (1804), to the *Delphine* (1802) of Madame de Staël, Sénancour's *Obermann* (1804), and the *Adolphe* (1816) of Constant, there is an unbroken tradition of lyric confession in the novel, combined usually with some philosophic thesis and a series of picturesque impressions of nature. There is almost no description of manners. Only

1 Le Breton, *Le théâtre romantique* (1922), p. 61.

one or two of the characters have any reality, and these are usually the hero and his beloved. What is not autobiographical is unreal. Most of these novels follow the epistolary form, wherein the French novel from Rousseau to Constant owed a great debt to Richardson and some of the great English novelists of the eighteenth century.

At the beginning of the Restoration two of these confessional novels, the *Obermann* of Sénancour and Constant's *Adolphe*, played an important rôle in the formation of the French Romantic School, though their immediate influence was greater on lyric poetry than on the novel. The style of *Obermann* is rather dry, and its best passages are descriptions of landscapes set down as states of the soul. The book, however, is rich in ideas. The central theme is the spiritual agony of the hero, the story of a religious nature left without a religion. Like many of his generation, Sénancour was a man saddened by the loss of friends and relatives in the Revolution and in the bloody wars that followed it. His "mal du siècle," however, was not a mere literary affectation. For him, the religious faith of the seventeenth century was gone, as was also the humanitarian faith of the eighteenth. Voltaire and the Philosophers had discredited religion; then the Terror and Napoleon had discredited the Philosophers, who had promised the return of the golden age and the discovery of happiness in freedom. An old society was dissolving and a new society was slowly taking shape. Sunset and sunrise were simultaneous, and many thinking men were perplexed and consumed with vain regrets. To Obermann, as to many of his generation, life lacked a purpose. In Chateaubriand it is the heart that is tormented, in Sénancour it is the intellect. The book was later much admired by Matthew Arnold, and was widely read after 1815 by the young Romanticists in France.

The *Adolphe* of Benjamin Constant presents all the phases of his unhappy love for Madame de Staël. In his cold analysis of himself, Constant is one of the precursors of later nineteenth-century Realism. The confessional form of the book, and its appearance just a few years before the *Méditations* of Lamartine, show its relationship also to the lyricism of the new Romantic Movement. The tradition of *Obermann* and *Adolphe* was carried through the Restoration by such novels as the *Ourika* (1824) and the *Edouard* (1825) of the Duchesse de Duras, in the many novels of Pigault-Lebrun, and in the sentimental tales of the Vicomte d'Arlincourt.

The type of novel most cultivated by the Romanticists after 1820 was the historical romance. Instead of choosing its subjects from the life of the time, the characteristic novel of the Romantic School, like the typical Romantic drama, preferred subjects from the history and legendry of times past. This is all part of the Romantic desire to escape into a dream world where the author can invoke, down the long vista of the past, sublime dreams of a world completely in contrast with the drabness and dullness of the life about him. The historical novel was not new in France, but after 1820 its popularity grew very rapidly. In seventeen months in the years 1824 and 1825 over a hundred and thirty historical novels appeared. Most of them are now, of course, utterly unknown and unread. Ironically enough, though all of them are based on history, they have all of them long since been condemned in the name of history.

Hugo's first book was an historical novel, *Bug-Jargal.* Written in 1818, it was first published in 1820. He rewrote part of it and brought out an improved edition in 1826. *Han d'Islande*, his second historical novel, was published in 1823. Both works are full of the youthful impressions of Hugo, especially of his reading of Chateaubriand's *Génie du christianisme*, *Les Martyrs*, and *Atala*, and of a work by Mallet on Scandinavian lore. In 1821, the year after the first publication of *Bug-Jargal*, Hugo met Chateaubriand, who was so impressed with the young man that he offered him a position — which Hugo refused — in the French Embassy in London. These first novels of Hugo also show the influence of Shakespeare's historical plays, Byron's narrative poems, and the novels of Scott, from whom the French historical novel really derives.

Bug-Jargal is a story of the insurrection in Santo Domingo in 1791, told by an army captain. The hero is a humble negro who loves a white girl, and in the insurrection, of which he becomes the leader, he carries her off, and then generously saves her white lover who is his enemy. Its hair-raising adventures and its exotic descriptions of the tropics, make it a highly picturesque book, and in Hugo's insistence on the essential nobility of the negro slave it is in harmony with the Romantic beliefs of the period. The book is, however, without any real character analysis or depth. *Han d'Islande* is a story of Norway in 1699, a tale of murder, insurrection, and intrigue. Some of the local color — always the chief interest in the Romantic historical novel — is drawn from *Hamlet*, though in its plot and its handling Hugo is much nearer to the melodramas of Pixérécourt than to Shakespeare's play. The hero, Han d'Islande, is a monster of the type often set forth by Byron. These first historical novels of Hugo are mediocre works, though they contain some splendid passages worthy of the genius that was later to write *Notre-Dame de Paris* and *Les Misérables*.

The first historical novel of distinction was Alfred de Vigny's *Cinq-Mars*, which appeared in 1826, when de Vigny was only twenty-nine years old. It is a romance based on the famous rivalry of Richelieu and the Marquis de Cinq-Mars in the reign of Louis XIII. The interest is centered in a striking contrast between an ambitious young nobleman who owed all his force to the depth and sincerity of his love, and a cold old prelate who knew everything, was suspicious of everyone, and pardoned nothing. The novel is laid in the spacious days of the Renaissance, when never a day passed at Court without its intrigue or its duel. The work is full of gross historical anachronisms, like the meeting in 1642 of Milton, Descartes, Molière, and Corneille, as well as of inaccuracies in characterization, such as when the author makes a selfish climber like Cinq-Mars appear a true friend, and when he vents his rage on

Richelieu because de Vigny disliked Richelieu's treatment of the nobility. De Vigny tries to excuse these inaccuracies in his introduction, where he maintains that art must deal with ideal truth, and that in handling historical subjects the novelist should follow popularly accepted legends rather than fact. *Cinq-Mars* is best in its descriptions of settings, costumes, architecture, ceremonials, and mass movements. The finished style in which the novel is written has kept it alive.

In 1829 Balzac published his *Chouans, ou la Bretagne en 1799*. The son of a notary's clerk of Tours, Balzac had by 1829 established himself in Paris and had published several works anonymously. *Les Chouans* was his first success. The novel, which follows Scott's *Ivanhoe* in its method of construction, is a thrilling picture of the rising of Brittany against the Revolution. The book resembles Scott more than any other romance of the period in the way in which individual interests and passions are identified with the interests and passions of a whole people. The true subject of the book is Brittany during the Revolution, its profound hatred of the new regime, and its fanatical spirit that would fight everything for which the Revolution stood. Balzac shows everywhere a wonderful knowledge of the Breton country and the Breton people. Both the individuals and the masses live as in no other historical novel of the Romantic School. De Vigny had tried in *Cinq-Mars* to describe mass movements, but he was too much the aristocrat to succeed as did Balzac. Balzac's greater power of imagination and his knowledge of the common people give his scenes the rough vitality of a Jan Steen painting. Balzac resembles Scott, too, in his excellent handling of dialogue. Men and women talk as in ordinary life. If the novel shows Balzac's clumsy style and his lack of taste, it shows also his extraordinary power. After 1830 he turned to contemporary life for his subjects, and *Les Chouans* remains his only important historical novel.

Les Chouans was not, however, quite to the Romantic taste. It was not laid in a time remote enough to seem really picturesque, and this novel proved to be less popular than de Vigny's *Cinq-Mars* and Mérimée's *Chronique du temps de Charles IX*. Mérimée, though still a young man when he published his *Chronique* in 1829, was already known as a writer of plays. The *Chronique* was his first novel. It is evident in reading the book that Mérimée had read more history than either de Vigny or Balzac or Hugo, and that from this reading of old chronicles and memoirs he had gleaned a great deal of local color and a great variety of anecdotes. He was especially fond of characteristic anecdotes, saying that he would gladly give up Thucydides if he could have the memoirs of Aspasia! In spite of all his historical learning, the novel is both historically and artistically a rather indifferent success, and is quite inferior to Mérimée's later novels, *Carmen* and *Colomba*. The story lacks unity and reality. Like Dumas' play *Henri III et sa cour* and de Vigny's *Cinq-Mars*, it is really nothing but a series of pictures which he attempts to hold together by carrying a love intrigue through the events of the Massacre of Saint Bartholomew. On finishing the novel one finds it hard to decide just what is the subject of the book. Mérimée is chiefly occupied with the life of the Court, where the gentlemen are concerned with their love affairs and their honor. If the book has a leading idea, it is that, beneath the superficial differences of Catholic and Protestant, love and ambition are the real motives of men. The chief quality of the novel lies in its condensed and vivid style, and in its excellent handling of situations in which the action and conversation of his characters, rather than mere descriptions, give the setting and the mood. Mérimée was always a scrupulous artist, and this, like the rest of his work, is brilliantly finished.

All in all, the Romantic historical novel in France is in its achievement — and one must include in this Hugo's *Notre-Dame de Paris* of 1831 — inferior to the best of Scott. It did, however, mark a step beyond the confessional type of novel. In that sense, the historical novel and the historical drama of the Romantic School form an important transition between the lyricism of the followers of Rousseau and Chateaubriand and the rise after 1830 of Realism, with its greater objectivity and its more faithful representation of life. After 1830, in the work of Stendhal, of George Sand in her later years, and of Balzac, we pass from the historical romance to the novel of contemporary manners.

Closely connected with the rise of the historical novel and drama, the Romantic Movement was also marked by a great revival of historical writing, a renaissance that in its achievement outdistanced any other literary aspect of Romanticism except perhaps that of lyric poetry. There had been almost no great historical writing in France since the close of the Middle Ages. Bossuet's *Discours sur l'histoire universelle* in the seventeenth century was really a theological discussion, while Montesquieu's *Grandeur et décadence des romains* in the eighteenth was primarily a work of political theory. Among all the great literary figures of two centuries of French Classicism, Voltaire was the only one to concern himself with history. His *Siècle de Louis XIV* is one of the first successful attempts to write a history of a whole civilization, and the "New History" of our time counts Voltaire as one of its founders. He left no immediate followers, and to know the sort of history that was read in France during the eighteenth century one has to turn to the work of utterly second-rate men. Their work is wooden, and everything is sacrificed to elegance and to large generalities. The people are all alike, a Merovingian king and a general of the time of Louis XIV being described in the same terms. These eighteenth-century historians had no interest in the origins of institutions and usages, and hence no historical perspective. Even Voltaire said of the centuries between the fall of Rome and the time of Louis XIV that "they no more merited a place in history than the story of bears and wolves." [1]

While a new interest in history begins to appear about 1800, neither the Revolutionary government nor

1 G. Pelissier, *Le mouvement littéraire au XIXe siècle* (11th ed., 1928), pp. 199–200.

Napoleon was favorable to historical studies. The Jacobins looked on the past as a prison from which a human spirit had at last escaped, and the National Assembly ordered a burning of records of noble families in the Place Vendôme. Under the Empire, history was a state monopoly, and, like literature, received recognition in so far as it glorified the Emperor. In this stifling atmosphere historical research was impossible. There were, however, many signs that a renaissance of historical studies was beginning. During the Revolution Lenoir opened a remarkable museum of mediæval monuments in the cloister of the Petits Augustins in Paris. These he had gathered together after the fury of the Terror had left many Romanesque and Gothic buildings in partial ruin. The collection was assembled and exhibited at a time when no French works of art of any period were admitted to the Louvre. This superb collection was dispersed in 1816, when most of the monuments were returned to their original sites, though another collection of the same sort made at Lyons was bought by the government and installed in the Louvre in a gallery of mediæval sculpture opened in 1824. These collections were a great inspiration to the young men of the Romantic generation. Michelet says that he discovered his profession in Lenoir's museum.

In 1804 Napoleon had appointed Daunou director of the National Archives, and an extensive work of reorganization and of collecting new manuscript materials was begun. The opening of a part of these archives to students in 1815 was a great aid to historians. In 1805 the Académie Celtique, later the Société des Antiquaires, was founded to stimulate the study of mediæval history. In the meantime, the Institut de France had taken over the work of the Benedictines of Saint-Maur on their great *Histoire littéraire de la France.* Several historical works were also indicative of the beginning of a new era in historical studies. Michaud in 1808 began to publish a history of the Crusades, which was the first attempt to understand and interpret sympathetically this great chapter of mediæval civilization. In 1817 Sismondi undertook the publication of an extensive work on the mediæval Italian city states. The next year Lemontey brought out his *Essai sur les établissements monarchiques de Louis XIV*, one of the first works of the nineteenth century to be based on a careful study of manuscript sources. Another great stimulus to historical studies in the period before 1820 was the work of Fauriel. Thoroughly acquainted with the revival of historical studies in Germany, and a master of Greek, Arabic, and Sanskrit, he spent his best years studying the civilization of the south of France. He published little, but all of the younger historians, especially Thierry, Guizot, Thiers, and Mignet, owed much to his teaching and example. In 1821 the Ecole des Chartes was opened to train librarians and archivists, especially in the study of mediæval documents. After 1815 there was also a great deal of publishing and republishing of old memoirs. Between 1819 and 1829 Petitot and Monmerqué published a hundred and one volumes in their *Collection des mémoires relatifs à l'histoire de*

France depuis le règne de Philippe-Auguste, and Guizot edited thirty-one volumes of a *Collection des mémoires relatifs à l'histoire de France depuis la fondation de la monarchie française jusqu'au XIIIe siècle* and twenty-six volumes of *Mémoirs relatifs à la Révolution d'Angleterre.* In 1823 Michaud published eight volumes of memoirs and documents of the Crusades. Between 1820 and 1828 Berville and Barrière edited sixty volumes of memoirs of the French Revolution, and Buchon forty-seven volumes of a *Collection des chroniques nationales françaises écrites en langue vulgaire.* The craze for memoirs seemed to know no bounds, and to supply the market a number of forged memoirs, mostly of the period of the Revolution, were published.

The literary movement of the period is likewise indicative of a new interest in history. Between 1800 and 1820 there appeared a long series of epic poems and plays written on historical subjects. Hugo's *Odes* are almost entirely historical in their subjects. The speeches in the Chamber of Deputies from 1815 on abound in historical allusions. The greater interest in history, moreover, owed much to the rapid and dramatic changes of the immediate past. The years 1789 to 1815 had seen more changes than the preceding five or six centuries. Under the rather monotonous reigns of Louis XIV, Louis XV, and Louis XVI the common man had had no sense of the movement of history. Suddenly after 1789 one new regime had succeeded another; Robespierre had been followed by Napoleon, and Napoleon by the returning Bourbons. Men had now a sense of history as never before, and they began to question the meaning of the past.

Thus by 1820 a new movement in historical studies was clearly under way, though no really first-rate new work had yet appeared. Soon a whole group of younger men — Thierry, Barante, Guizot, Michelet, Thiers, and Mignet — were publishing. Different as they were in temperament, this new generation of historians had many things in common. All, except Barante, were from the substantial middle class, of whose history they were proud and whose opportunities they wished to see extended. All admired England as the home of modern liberty, and all wished to stimulate and justify the Liberal cause in France.[1] They had in common also a great admiration for Chateaubriand and Walter Scott. The *Génie du christianisme* and the *Martyrs* were not historical works at all, but they were full of glowing pictures of the past, and all the historians of the Restoration were stimulated by these works. Guizot addressed a poem to Chateaubriand, and Thierry declared that his reading of the *Martyrs*, as a schoolboy in Blois, had revealed to him his vocation. Scott was nearly as influential. The new school of historians learned from Chateaubriand and from Scott — "that great master of historical divination," as Thierry calls him — that

1 Ruggiero remarks (p. 171): "Continental thought was following the opposite path to that pursued by contemporary England: the former felt the need of tempering its abstract revolutionary attitude by the introduction of an historical point of view; the latter the need of infusing new life into its traditionalism by contact with a rationalistic point of view. Each bestowed upon the other the element most peculiar to its own historical and national genius."

the past could be brought to life by the power of the imagination.

The first of these younger historians to publish was Augustin Thierry. In 1817 there appeared his *Sur les révolutions d'Angleterre*, a work marked by a mastery of the sources combined with vivid historical coloring. Thierry interpreted the English Revolution as a great popular reaction against the old Norman domination. The work has a strong Liberal bias, and he wrote with one eye on the French situation in which he was living. He began the fashion in France of trying to find parallels between English history in the seventeenth century and French history since the Revolution. In 1820 a second work, *Histoire de Jacques Bonhomme*, showed Thierry as an apologist for the common man, who through twenty centuries of French history had been ground down by Roman landlord, Frankish chieftain, feudal baron, and Revolutionary and Napoleonic tyranny. The work shows clearly the influence of Saint-Simon, for whom Thierry served as secretary for several years, and whose ideas left a deep impress on the younger man.

It is only with his *Lettres sur l'histoire de France*, which began to appear in 1820, that Thierry came into his full powers. Here he is less a propagandist and more of an historian. In these *Lettres* Thierry studied the Celtic, Roman, and Frankish institutions of old France as they varied from province to province, in order to explain the process by which the French monarchy had been built up. He shows a remarkable ability to construct a vivid and unified picture of the past. Writing years later of Thierry as a blind old man, Renan, who helped him, says: "I never witnessed without astonishment the promptness with which he seized a document and adapted it for his narrative. The least fragment revealed to him an organic whole."[1] In 1825 Thierry published his *Conquête d'Angleterre*. His thesis here is the long continuation of the conflict in England between two races, the Anglo-Saxon and the Norman. He exaggerates this conflict, though the work is still interesting for its striking descriptions. One has only to compare Thierry's work with anything that preceded it in France to realize that, whatever might be his errors, he was a great innovator in historical studies. Like the work of his contemporaries in the fields of the novel, the drama, and painting, Thierry evoked the past and tried to make it live again, and it must be acknowledged that in this no one approached his powers except some of his own fellow historians.

A writer whose style was much like that of Thierry, but who had far less interest in interpretation, was Barante, the first volume of whose *Histoire des Ducs de Bourgogne* appeared in 1824. The work shows throughout the influence of Scott's *Ivanhoe* and *Quentin Durward*. It is a series of picturesque scenes put together with little organization. He places before us a long succession of tournaments, marriages, and intrigues, based almost entirely on chronicles of the time. Like many of the historical writers of the first half of the nine-

1 E. Renan, *Essais de morale et de critique* (1857).

teenth century, Barante ignored a great mass of documentary evidence, which is harder to study and much slower in yielding results. He says, in speaking of his method, that he "wanted people to see the fifteenth century instead of hearing it described." The work charmed his own Romantic generation by the color and sweep of its narrative.

A far greater artist than Barante was Jules Michelet, who was just beginning his remarkable career. He came from a poor family, and his early life was a hard struggle with poverty. As a young man he owed much to the teaching of Cousin, who urged him to study German and turned his attention to the writings of Vico and Herder. Michelet in these formative years was much impressed with Cousin's notion that the events of the external world are ruled by an internal world of Ideas, which Cousin had probably learned from Hegel. This Idea became later the point of departure for Michelet's symbolism in the treatment of history. From Cousin he derived the notion that a nation is an Idea and the conflict of nations a conflict of Ideas. For example, Asia represents the infinite, Greece the finite, the combination of the two, Christianity. Progress is continuous, and the Idea that is victorious is the best. These Ideas are realized historically through three manifestations: the natural setting of climate and soil, which demands a study of geography — a new element in historical studies; the heroes who set forth the great Ideas; and the people.

In 1828, at the instance of Cousin and Quinet,

Michelet went to Germany, where he extended his knowledge of the philosophies of history of Herder and Hegel, and was introduced to the new study of folklore, whose leader in Germany was Jacob Grimm. During these formative years Michelet was gradually coming to conceive of history as the story of the life of a whole people. Like his fellow Romanticists, he wanted to mix the old literary genres and to create a new history which was to be "a combination of epic, drama, lyric, metaphysics, and painting." In 1827, the year in which appeared Quinet's translation of Herder's *Philosophy of History*, Michelet published his first two books, a translation of Vico's *Scienza Nuova* and a little textbook on modern history. In Vico, Michelet found some of the same ideas that Cousin and his young friend Quinet had shown him in Herder. Especially was Michelet impressed with the emphasis of both Vico and Herder on the contribution of the masses to civilization, and on the importance of understanding the laws and literature of any people as a reflection of its life. His second book, a school text, caused a revolution in the teaching of history in French secondary schools. At a time when history was just coming into the curriculum, Michelet provided a brief sketch of modern history with a verve and clarity that made the book a classic. In this work he rejects Thierry's theory of races and shows that all races are mixed, and that in the formation of any national culture many things count besides race. The subject-matter of this textbook likewise represented a great innovation. Religion, social and political institutions, the economic movements, and the development of art and literature, have a large place, while the annals of wars and politics are reduced to a minimum.

Michelet's best work was done after 1830. His great history of France, on which he spent his life, began to appear in 1833. Here he was to see France as a living person and to paint the epic of her soul. In this he became one of the greatest expounders of that emotionalism of the earlier nineteenth century which merged humanity with the divine and evolved a mystical pantheistic myth of the goodness of democracy and of the perfection immanent in the people. Both Michelet's power and his weaknesses lay in his imagination and his passion. "If I am superior to other historians, it is because I have loved more." Taine compared him to Delacroix, and Monod speaks of him as "a great musician." His judgments are often false, his erudition inadequate, and his hatreds unreasoning, but this young historian of 1827 was to become the greatest literary artist that ever devoted himself to historical studies in France.

Besides the school of Thierry, Barante, and the young Michelet, whose chief interest was in painting a picture of the past, there appeared in the eighteen-twenties a second group of historians whose object was rather to explain than to narrate. Chief of this group was Guizot. Before 1822 Guizot had become well known, first as a professor of history at the Sorbonne, and then as a member of the Conseil d'Etat and as one of the leading followers of Royer-Collard among the Doctrinaires. In

1822 his forced retirement from teaching gave him more time for writing. In 1823 he published his *Essais sur l'histoire de France*. It was based on a more careful study of documents than any other work of the period, and is the first study of the mediæval institutions of France to have permanent value. Guizot drew something from a detailed history of France which Sismondi had begun to publish in 1821, and something, too, from the ideas of Thierry and Cousin. The basis of his interpretation of the Middle Ages is an analysis of four great institutions — the Church, the feudal nobility, the monarchy, and the towns. In 1826 appeared his *Histoire de la Révolution en Angleterre*, a subject which interested the French very much during the Restoration. The events of the English Revolution are related to show the growth of political and religious liberty in England, and to prove the superiority of the English Revolution of the seventeenth century to the more violent French Revolution. He follows Thierry in his theory of races, finding in French history a long conflict between the Gallo-Romans and the Franks, and in the English tradition a similar conflict between the Anglo-Saxons and the Normans. He is, however, less insistent on these matters than Thierry.

In 1828 Guizot returned to the Sorbonne, where he gave the lectures that appeared later as his *Histoire de la civilization de l'Europe*. These are his best work. He dwells on the fundamental elements in civilization since the fall of Rome, with a special emphasis on the growth of the middle class. This little book is still one of the most suggestive surveys of the growth of Western civilization. Guizot followed this by another course of lectures on the history of French civilization, applying in greater detail some of the principles set forth in his earlier work. From these various series of lectures by Guizot, and from Carrel's *Histoire de la Contre-Révolution en Angleterre* (1827), the Liberals developed the famous parallel of French and English history which, as we have seen, was so effectively used against the government in the last years of the reign of Charles X. No one has ever equaled Guizot in the power of arranging and comparing great masses of facts. His work, however, suffers somewhat from over-simplification. Sainte-Beuve wrote that when he had finished reading one of Guizot's lofty discourses he took down a volume of the *Mémoires* of de Retz to remind himself of the actual material of history.

In 1823 and 1824 there appeared two important studies of the French Revolution by Mignet and by Thiers. Each was the work of a young man from Provence who had come to Paris in 1821 and had made himself known to Talleyrand, Laffitte, and Manuel. Mignet soon made a reputation for himself by a series of historical lectures at the Athénée. In 1824 he published his *Précis de la Révolution française*. Though this work is based on little research, Mignet had gathered material in talks with Talleyrand and others who had lived through the Revolution, and thanks to his remarkable gift for organization he became the first historian to present the Revolution as an organic whole. Madame de Staël's *Considérations sur la Révolution française*, published in 1818, had marked the beginning of an interpretation of the Revolution that was at once better poised and in clearer perspective than anything that had appeared earlier. Mignet's work, however, is better rounded out than that of Madame de Staël. He shows that the Revolution was not an accidental convulsion, but the logical result of the past. His tendency was, like that of Thiers, to make everything seem inevitable, and to excuse anything and everything because it was inevitable. This is why contemporaries spoke of Mignet and Thiers as belonging to the "Pessimistic School of History," as Guizot belonged to the "Philosophic," and Thierry, Barante, and Michelet to the "Descriptive" school.

Thiers, who had been writing brilliant articles in the Liberal *Constitutionnel* since 1821, published his first two volumes in 1824, and so began the first presentation of the French Revolution on a large scale. Eight other volumes appeared between 1823 and 1827, each volume showing a greater power of handling facts. His account is a steady setting forth in great detail, with almost no comment, of the movement of the Revolution. Thiers consulted a great many soldiers, statesmen, and financiers who had lived through the period, and his work thus abounds in interesting first-hand views of the Revolution. Sainte-Beuve said of Thiers' history that it had the effect of the "Marseillaise" and made one love the Revolution. In 1830 Thiers, Mignet, and Carrel joined in the editing of the *National*, a brilliant anti-dynastic journal which did much to hasten the overthrow of Charles X.[1]

V. THE FIRST TRIUMPHS OF ROMANTICISM IN THE FINE ARTS AND MUSIC

The decade from 1820 to 1830, as we have traced it in its various aspects, is surely one of the richest in the whole history of the French tradition. The same generation that created Positivism, Socialism, Eclecticism, Liberal Catholicism, and Romanticism in literature produced also a group of important painters and a new movement in music. All these currents of thought, as we have seen, crossed and recrossed, enriching and influencing one another. Delacroix, the painter, was a close friend of Hugo. Cousin influenced both the Romantic historians and the young Romantic novelists. Auguste Comte and Thierry began their careers as followers of Saint-Simon. Liberal Catholicism, the outgrowth of Lamennais' Ultramontanism, derived much from Chateaubriand and Scott and the new interest in the art and life of the Middle Ages, from which sources came also the first plays of Dumas, Hugo, and Alfred de Vigny. Positivism and Socialism, while less closely related to the movements in literature and art, represent

1 The Restoration was also a great period in the development of oriental studies, in which France took the lead. In 1822 Champollion, with the aid of the Rosetta Stone, worked out a key to Egyptian hieroglyphics which he described in his famous *Lettre à M. Dacier*. In 1827 he opened the first gallery of Egyptian art in the Louvre. In 1821 Abel Rémusat and Silvestre de Sacy founded the Société Asiatique, and in 1822 the first number of the *Journal Asiatique* appeared. During the Restoration the young Burnouf did his first publishing on ancient India and Persia.

the same ardent desire to turn from old controversies and dead issues to new ideas and new causes. It was indeed an age of great beginnings.

In the development of the whole of modern art, this Romantic generation holds a very important place. In fact, all great movements in nineteenth-century painting came from France. Whistler, Sargent, and Zorn, to mention only three painters of the later nineteenth century, used French methods of painting, though they worked in England, in the United States, and in Sweden. The history of the style and technique of modern painting is in the work of Frenchmen — David, Ingres, Delacroix, Corot, Millet, Daumier, Courbet, Manet, Degas, Monet, and Cézanne. The starting point in this great international movement, in which French painting came to hold a position comparable only to that of Italy in the Renaissance, lies in the work of David.

Louis David (1748–1825) received his first training in the studio of Boucher, one of the best known of the boudoir masters of the eighteenth century, whose art was gay, charming in color, and trifling in content, the very quintessence of an elegant and cynical society. After his first study with Boucher, the young David went to Italy. Here his style was completely transformed through a study of ancient monuments, and through the influence of a contemporary Neoclassical movement in Italy. The discoveries in Pompeii and Herculaneum, and the writings of the German archæologist Winckelmann, who was living in Rome, had aroused among the Italian and foreign artists in Italy a new conception of the meaning of their classical heritage. The purpose of art, as set forth by Winckelmann, the great theorist of the movement, was not to imitate nature, but to realize a generalized and abstract ideal of beauty. This ideal was best represented in classical sculpture, and the modern artist had only to imitate this sculpture. A number of other Frenchmen beside David helped to introduce Winckelmann's Neoclassicism into French art, among them Quatremère de Quincy, the Comte de Caylas, and Vien, but it was the genius and the energy of David that fixed these ideas on the art of his generation.

This Classical Revival at the end of the eighteenth century and the opening of the nineteenth, a movement that affected not only painting among the arts, but also sculpture, architecture, and interior decoration, — "le style Empire," — marks a kind of interruption in the slowly developing Romantic Movement. There were minor currents of sentimentalism, and of a taste for Orientalism, for Gothic art, and for mediæval legendry, in the art of the eighteenth century — currents which again came into prominence after 1820. This slowly rising tide of Romanticism, which extends roughly from about 1750 to 1840, was checked by the Classical Revival of David. Perhaps it would be nearer the truth to regard both Romanticism and the Classical Revival as movements of protest and discovery, as reactions against the growing sterility of the artistic canons of the Age of Louis XIV. Romanticism became the stronger, and though the Classical Revival in France counted such men as David and André Chénier among its chief figures, it showed as a movement less vitality than Romanticism. The Classical Revival held its own in architecture and in interior decoration long after Romanticism had captured literature, painting, and music.

In studying the work of David, it is evident that the classical art that was known to the later eighteenth century was the sculpture of the Hellenistic and Roman periods. David saw some casts of the Parthenon marbles toward the end of his life, and he realized that had he known and studied Greek art at an earlier period his own work would have had more value. According to the canon of David and his school, painting must become a sort of colored bas-relief. All emphasis was placed on drawing and form. The figures must be nude or only scantily draped. Composition was simplified, and color, atmosphere, and movement were relegated to a secondary place. Landscape painting practically ceased to exist, even for backgrounds. There were no models for it in the sculpture galleries of Rome and Paris!

Some of this emphasis on the classical was due to the contemporary admiration of Plutarch and of the forms of ancient government. The leaders of the Revolution dramatized themselves as followers of republican Rome; after the advent of Napoleon, everything that was reminiscent of imperial Rome was à la mode. David himself took an active part in public affairs. As a member of the Convention, he succeeded in getting this Assembly to abolish the old Académie Royale de Peinture

— a great help in making David secure in his position as artistic dictator. Later, when Napoleon established a new Académie des Beaux Arts as a part of the Institut, David was able to dominate it. It was this Napoleonic creation that caused so many artistic quarrels during the nineteenth century. The dead hand of David's Classicism lived on in this Académie after his death, and it was this same foundation that refused admission to Delacroix, Barye, Rude, Corot, Carpeaux, Millet, Manet, Degas, and Rodin. David and the official style of Napoleon's Academy pleased the Emperor. Never in its history did France have an art so completely official as during the Empire.

Fortunately David did not maintain his standards too strictly, and he deigned to paint some scenes from contemporary life. His "Tennis Court Oath," "The Distribution of the Eagles," "The Coronation of Napoleon," and a group of brilliantly executed contemporary portraits, represent about all of his work that is still interesting. At its worst David's painting is more demoded today than the work of any man of first-rate capacity in the history of French art. It must, however, be said of him that he brought back into French painting a dignity and a largeness of style which the Nattiers and Bouchers of the eighteenth century had lost. It was, though, a strange art, in which the strong passions of a tumultuous period were made to speak a language of pure abstraction. David had voted for the death of Louis XVI, and in 1815 he had to quit Paris for Brussels, where he worked until his death in 1825.

Some of David's followers brought greater freedom into their method of painting. Among these lesser men were: Guérin, nearest to David in his style; Girodet, best known for his "Burial of Atala," the subject of which is taken from the novel of Chateaubriand, and is handled with a romantic sentimentality unknown to David; Gros, whose masterpiece, "The Pest-House of Jaffa" (1804), painted to commemorate Napoleon's expedition into Palestine, is a work of originality and force, its subject not taken from the classics, but from a most disagreeable aspect of contemporary life; and Baron Gérard, who became the favorite portrait painter of the Restoration. In their handling of movement and of color, and in their selection of subjects from contemporary life and literature, the work of these followers of David shows clearly the breakdown of his artistic canon.[1]

One charming painter of the Empire and the earlier years of the Restoration who seems to have escaped the influence of David was Prud'hon. His paintings have an exquisite grace that is reminiscent of Praxiteles, while his vaporous color reminds one of Correggio. Prud'hon had a voluptuous eye, and he knew also how to handle light and shade. His beautiful use of color and of shadows at a time when David was doing tinted

1 A group of genre painters of this period did a number of little pictures of daily life somewhat in the style of the Dutch genre painters of the seventeenth century. Their work plays almost no rôle in the larger artistic movements of the time, but for the social historian these little scenes of contemporary life by men like Boilly and Granet are of the greatest interest.

bas-reliefs gives Prud'hon an important place as a precursor of the Romantic School.

After 1815, the removal of David to Brussels weakened his influence on French painting, though even before the downfall of Napoleon new forces were already at work breaking down the sterile tyranny of classicism. The opening of Lenoir's Musée des Monuments Français in Paris in 1792 proved to be a revelation of the beauty of mediæval art and an overwhelming contradiction to the rules of the school of David. We have already seen the recovery of the romantic Middle Ages in the work of Chateaubriand. In 1810 the restoration of mediæval monuments had its beginnings in an order to the prefects from the Ministry of the Interior calling for a statement of the condition of every château and abbey injured by the Revolution. Out of this was to come the work of Viollet-le-Duc and the Service des Monuments Historiques. In 1814 the Académie Celtique, founded in 1804, became the Société Nationale des Antiquaires de France, the first of a large number of French archæological societies devoted to a study of mediæval monuments. The first great publications on the French mediæval monuments appeared from 1807 to 1811, the work of Millin. Another series by Alexandre de Laborde were published from 1816 to 1836. In 1820 appeared the first part of Baron Taylor's *Voyages pittoresques et romantiques dans l'ancienne France*, with magnificent illustrations, many of them by Isabey and Bonnington. In 1821 the Ecole des Chartes was founded. Thierry was publishing his *Lettres sur l'histoire de France*. In

1814 the first of a veritable flood of reprints of memoirs of mediæval France appeared. By 1820 almost nothing seemed to be in vogue that was not mediæval.

An even greater contradiction than the art and romance of the Middle Ages to the official style of David were the great galleries of the Louvre, with their newly assembled masterpieces of Titian, Tintoretto, Veronese, Rubens, and Rembrandt. Passing from a dismal studio where a nude model was posed sitting on a plank to the color and gusto of the great painting of the Renaissance was in itself a revelation of the possibilities of art. All the younger men after 1815 seem to have been influenced more by these great masters, now first put on public view, than by their older living contemporaries in whose studios they were supposed to have learned the craft of painting.

The first fruits of a new movement in painting appeared in the work of Géricault, whose "Raft of the Medusa" created a sensation in the Salon of 1819. Géricault had grown up under the influence of David, but he had later traveled in Italy. Here he was greatly impressed with the work of Michelangelo in the Sistine Chapel. He had also made a sojourn in England, where he had turned to painting animals and landscape. Unlike the work of the School of David, whose chief inspiration is the antique, and that of Delacroix, whose subjects are often mediæval, the work of Géricault depicts the life which the painter saw about him. Géricault's handling of scenes taken directly from contemporary life make him in some ways even more the precursor of the

RAFT OF THE MEDUSA

GÉRICAULT

Realism of Courbet than of the Romanticism of Delacroix. His "Raft of the Medusa," however, was hailed as a manifesto against the Davidian School. It is a huge canvas representing a group of struggling figures on a raft in the midst of a storm-tossed sea. Its violent movement, its irregular and unsymmetrical composition, and its strong contrasts of light and shade, although prefigured by Gros' "Pest-House of Jaffa," were so at variance with the artistic traditions of the time that this painting was everywhere recognized as marking a revolution. Part of the furor it created was due to political reasons. The blame for the wreck of the ship *Medusa* in 1816 off the coast of Senegal was laid on the government, and the Liberals made great capital out of the incident. Hence many who knew little about art helped to make Géricault's work known. He died in 1824 at the age of thirty-three, perhaps the greatest loss that modern French art has known. The same year Gros and Gérard are said to have asked each other at Girodet's funeral, "What mighty hand will be able to defend the School of David?" Neither had authority enough to impose David's austere idea upon rebellious youth. Gérard was a mere Court painter, and Gros, a premature wreck, was bewailing the sins of his youth. By 1824 the old artistic order seemed dead.

The Salon of 1824 brought together Ingres' "Vow of Louis XIII" and Delacroix's "Massacre of Scio," which the Classical critics dubbed the "Massacre of Painting." This Salon of 1824 created a veritable war between Classicists and Romanticists, which resembles the war over *Hernani* that was to break out six years later. Ingres, who at the time was forty-four years old, had lived for years in Italy. He was a follower of David, though his enthusiasm for the drawing of some of the Pre-Raphaelite Italian painters made the Davidians look on him as a kind of heretic. He returned to France in 1824, and circumstances rather than choice made him the champion of the Classicists. Ingres' "Vow of Louis XIII" and his "Apotheosis of Homer," a declaration of artistic faith painted in 1826, show him as a follower of Raphael. Indeed, much of his work is hardly more than a pastiche of Raphael. His composition is often mechanical, and his color usually insipid and without depth, but his drawing is superb. The subtle line drawing of his portraits is unrivaled in the work of anyone since Holbein in the sixteenth century.

The immediate future, however, belonged to his young rival, Delacroix, who at the time was only twenty-five years old. Already in 1822 he had aroused interest by his "Dante and Virgil in Hell." The "Massacre of Scio" of 1824, a more original work, represented an incident in the Greek War of Independence, which in these years was arousing the sympathies of Liberals all over Western Europe. The painting was full of violent action, and it showed the influence of Géricault's "Raft of the Medusa" as well as of Rubens and Rembrandt, whom Delacroix ranked above Raphael. A group of writhing figures stand on a dismal plain against a gray, smoke-laden sky suggestive of pillage and ruin. Delacroix's color shows the influence of a group of English painters, especially Constable, Lawrence, and Bonnington, who were just beginning to be known in France and whose work in the Salon of 1824 was a revelation to the artistic public. This English work played something of the same rôle in the development of French Romantic painting later taken by the Japanese block print in the development of Impressionism. Commenting on the "Massacre of Scio," the *Globe* issued a manifesto of the new art. "It is now a question in art of making drawing truer to life and less academic, and creating compositions richer, and less sterile and systematic. Finally art must turn from the mythology of Greece and Rome to choose its subjects from all times, to conserve the picturesque and the ideal in all costumes, manners, and subjects."[1] Here we see Romantic literature and painting sharing a common ideal. Both waged war on Classical standards in the name of an art that was freer in its choice of subject-matter and in its definition of beauty.

In 1825 Delacroix went to England, where he had greater opportunity to study the painting of his English contemporaries. A prodigious worker, he was soon turning out a large number of paintings, all of them striking in color and in their contrasts of light and shade. There was nothing of the tinted drawing of David and Ingres about this work, nor was it the realization of some abstract ideal. It was all the expression of an individual soul in passionate protest against all legislation which fetters genius. His critics accused him of "painting with a drunken broom," and Delacroix himself once re-

1 Charléty, p. 221.

marked: "My picture is writhing. That blessed coarseness! I hate systematic painting." The great number of his sketches deposited in the Louvre after his death, however, are proof that his art was anything but "slipshod inspiration," as his critics claimed. He wanted freedom from the academic. As Hugo was trying to free the drama from classical restraints, so Delacroix was to free painting from antique modes and pyramidal compositions. For thirty years he continued to paint as if he were fighting.

As in the case of other Romanticists, disorder in execution apparently was sometimes to Delacroix an indication of genius and sincerity. He admired his own dreams so thoroughly that, like the Romantic dramatists and novelists, he refused to paint reality. The Romanticists always attacked Classicism in the name of Truth, and yet these same Romanticists had a great contempt for accuracy or for any reality except that of a dream world. Nothing could better describe the essence of Romanticism than Delacroix's remark, "The most real things I paint are the illusions I create." Like Hugo, he was furiously attacked as a painter of the ugly. The public never understood Delacroix, and he seems to have had more enemies at the end of his career than at the beginning.

The subjects of Delacroix's paintings, like those of the contemporary Romantic drama and novel, were taken mostly from the Middle Ages, and they show the influence of Dante, Shakespeare, Byron, Scott, and Chateaubriand. His mind teemed with conceptions. No wonder his painting sometimes gives the impression of an uneasy and feverish Rubens or Veronese. Matthew Arnold found the poetry of Shelley "not quite sane," and the same phrase might be applied to Delacroix's painting. He was forever experimenting with pigments and varnishes, and many of his best paintings have as a result gone to pieces. His exasperated sensibility led him to ignore simple colors and harmonies, and he often uses strange combinations. His paint is slashed on in staccato strokes, and though the result is usually excellent, there is often, as in Hugo's *Hernani*, something uncertain and rhetorical about his paintings. Some of Delacroix's best work, like that of his contemporaries, was in the newly discovered medium of lithograph. The books of the period were illustrated with lithographs even more romantic than the engravings in certain works of the eighteenth century: solitary poets, lyre in hand, dreaming upon tombs; delicate lovers embracing, spied upon by jealous eyes; women dragged by the hair; black dungeon cells, Gothic roofs with gargoyles and flights of bats, and witches on broomsticks. In this romantic world of the illustrator, devils were as numerous as Cupids had been in the art of the eighteenth century. The best-known illustrator of this school was Célestin Nanteuil. Delacroix did a magnificent series of lithographs for a French translation of Goethe's *Faust*. Goethe was delighted with them, and found in Delacroix's art the perfect illustrations for his great drama. After 1830 Delacroix turned more and more to mural painting, and in his great ceiling of the Gallery of Apollo in the Louvre and in his work in the Luxembourg Palace he established himself as one of the great decorative painters of the century. All in all, by opening wide the field of painting to experiment, Delacroix did more to create modern drawing and design than did any of his contemporaries. Here his position is similar to that of Berlioz in the development of nineteenth-century music. Delacroix, unlike Ingres, did not open his studio to students, and thus, in some ways, the immediate influence of Ingres was greater.

Delacroix's chief follower was Delaroche, a man of much less capacity than either Delacroix or Ingres, from both of whom he derived his art. He acquired some vogue just before and after 1830, through his painting of English historical subjects just at the time when the public was reading Thierry and Guizot on English history. A man of somewhat similar style was Devéria, who in 1827 exhibited his "Birth of Henry IV," and Ary Scheffer, a very uninteresting painter, but one who was very popular with the generation of 1830.

The greatest influence of Romanticism on painting, though it was not clearly manifested until after 1830, was in the renaissance of landscape painting. This genre had been completely neglected by the School of David, and even the first Romantic painters, Géricault and Delacroix, had shown only a slight interest in landscape. Romanticism, which in poetry had turned to nature to see therein, not the gay sylvan creatures of a golden classical age, but a reflection of the poet's mood, was almost certain to do likewise in painting. This attitude was characterized by Amiel when he said that "landscape is a state of the soul." There had been some landscape painting in the time of David, but it was the work of obscure men. Chief of these early nineteenth-century landscape painters was Michel. He has left a number of interesting landscapes, which show a turning away from the imitations of Italian landscapes that Poussin and Claude Lorrain had brought into French art in the seventeenth century, and an adaptation of the art of Hobbema, Ruysdael, and Paul Potter, the vigorous Dutch contemporaries of Claude Lorrain. The new note, however, in the work of Michel and a number of minor men working at the same time was their first-hand and sympathetic observation of familiar things — a band of road between a row of trees, an old mill, a barn-yard, or an open field. As Michel remarked, "a land-scape painter who cannot find all he needs within four square leagues does not know his craft."

Among the painters of this new school of landscape, Corot was the earliest to achieve fame. His genius first flowered as the result of a sojourn in Italy, where he painted the Italian landscape as he saw it, not as Salvatore Rosa, or Poussin, or someone else had seen it. On his return to Paris he revealed to the French the beauty of their own landscape. His first French pieces, exhibited in the Salon of 1827 alongside the work of Constable, showed that his originality lay in his wonderful handling of values of light and shade. His earliest paintings still rank among his best work. His trees, figures, and buildings stand in an atmosphere of their own which permeates and envelops everything. They are rich, too, with the poetry of his own perception and feeling. Much that is finest in Corot's early work reminds one of passages in Sénancour's *Obermann* and in the first poems of Lamartine.

A more vigorous painter of landscape was Corot's younger contemporary, Théodore Rousseau, who in 1830 had just begun to be noticed. He was a man who loved solitude and a life close to nature. Much of his early work is in water color, a medium much used at this time in England. Rousseau's work shows the influence of Hobbema and Ruysdael, as well as of the English landscape painters Gainsborough, Constable, and Crome. Not until years later was his painting really appreciated in France. After 1830 he became the leader of the Barbizon school of animal and landscape painters, a group which included Daubigny, Diaz, Troyon, Dupré, Rosa Bonheur, Millet, and Barye the sculptor.

The Romantic Movement did not affect sculpture as early as it did painting. Gautier, writing long after 1830, still finds it hard to conceive of any sculpture except classical. "Sculpture received from antiquity its definite form," he says. "Never was the hymn of the human body sung in more beautiful strophes. All sculpture is perforce classical."[1] The sculpture of the Restoration had the cold and pompous manner that had prevailed under the Empire. The charm of Clodion, of Houdon, and of the sculpture of the last days of the

1 Gautier, *Histoire du romantisme* (1874), p. 29.

Ancien Régime had by 1800 given way to a frigid Classicism of which the Italian sculptor Canova was the dictator as David was of painting. Canova had taught many French students in Italy, and after 1802 he made repeated visits to Paris to execute commissions. His enormous nudes with their smooth surfaces and flat muscles seem to have been modeled from cadavers. In sculpture the tyranny of Classicism was even more complete than in painting. David painted some scenes from contemporary life, while the followers of Canova insisted on presenting such contemporary life as they studied in classical costumes and attitudes. Thus Napoleon could only be represented as a Roman consul or emperor nude or in a toga and wearing a crown of laurel. None of Canova's French imitators, of whom the ablest in the years of the Restoration were Pradier and Bosio, approached the best of Canova's work.

A close friend of the Romantic literary men was David d'Angers, to whom both Hugo and Sainte-Beuve addressed verses. He was a man of no great originality, but one who interests us because he has left nearly five hundred excellent medallion portraits of his contemporaries. Another figure of secondary importance who is interesting chiefly because he belonged to the Cénacle of 1829 is the sculptor Jehan du Seigneur. His short career shows the close relationship between literature and the fine arts in the earlier years of the Romantic Movement. After 1830 sculpture began, in the work of Barye and Rude, — Rude first exhibited in the Salon of 1827,— to show a vital and independent development.

At no time in the century, however, was sculpture at such a level of mediocrity as under the Restoration.

Almost the same must be said of architecture. The Revolutionary government had planned many public buildings, but had built only a few. These governments lived always in a provisional state. They held their assemblies in any convenient hall, and were content with wooden sheds and plaster statues for their great festivals. Napoleon, like Louis XIV, wanted architecture to celebrate him, and under his government many great public works were undertaken. The avenues about the Arc de Triomphe were laid out, the Arc itself begun, the Vendôme Column was set up, further work was carried out on the Louvre, the rue de Rivoli was built, and all over France many public buildings were started. Regarding architecture from the point of view of a soldier, Napoleon believed that vigor, size, and regularity of lines were the attributes of beauty. The preparation of great temporary altars and temples during the Revolution, and the general taste of the time for declamation, also contributed to the elaboration of the ponderous Imperial Style.

Fontaine and Percier were Napoleon's official architects, and Fontaine remained the state architect of the restored Bourbons. They designed buildings on a colossal scale in a style that was heavy and gloomy. The Gothic, the Italian, the Baroque, and the graceful French style of the eighteenth century were all alike condemned in the name of a pure classic style modeled on the monuments of ancient Rome, especially as they were depicted in the drawings and etchings of Piranesi. The peristyle was greatly admired, and everything had consequently to be crowded behind or put inside a row of columns. After 1820 this style met severe criticism from a group of young heretics, among them Labrouste and Viollet-le-Duc. They maintained that architecture should profit by the discoveries of each new age, and that the styles of the past should be studied, not to imitate them slavishly, but to draw from them useful lessons for the present. These younger men complained that the older architects built only fronts, that the interiors of their buildings had little organic relation to the façades, and that for practical purposes they were often simply unusable. These criticisms were very just, but they received little attention until about 1840.

Fortunately there was almost no building during the Restoration. In 1820 Fontaine built the Chapelle Expiatoire on the spot where Louis XVI and Marie Antoinette had been buried. It is a heavy and uninteresting pile. A pupil of Fontaine's, Lebas, designed the Church of Notre Dame de Lorette, and another one of his followers built the Church of Saint-Vincent-de-Paul. Both are imitations of the Early Christian basilicas of Rome. They are mechanical in design, and their interiors were never decorated with the glowing mosaics that belong to the style. The Church of the Madeleine, and the Bourse, begun before 1815, were opened to the public during the Restoration.

The furniture and interior decoration of the period is equally heavy and gloomy. The gay and exquisite decorative art of the eighteenth century was proscribed unreservedly. The Bourbons made no changes in the apartments decorated by Napoleon except to remove the arms and initials of the usurper. The "Style Empire," with its abstraction and its empty dignity, lasted with certain changes until the Second Empire. Furniture was designed on simple and massive lines. Mahogany was the favorite wood. The only decorations used were appliqué designs in gilded bronze, lyres, trophies, swans, nymphs, and Cupids. The huge cabinets that designers delighted in have the air of private mausoleums. A taste for Gothic knickknacks and bric-à-brac grew during the Restoration, and some decorators executed whole Gothic interiors. The décor for the coronation of Charles X in 1825 was all done in Gothic, or what was then called Gothic. "Gothic" silverware, clocks, and furniture, and "Gothic" book-bindings with Gothic window tracing stamped on them had some vogue. This style was called the "Style Troubadour," or the "Style Cathédrale," in contrast with the "Style Empire." These Gothic pastiches, if one may judge from the present Musée des Arts Décoratifs in the Louvre, are vulgar and ugly to a degree rivaled only by the monstrosities of the Second Empire.

The products of the Gothic craze were often strangely mixed with other incongruous elements. At Chateaubriand's country home, "La Vallée aux Loups," which was originally a small brick house, he had added a portico supported by two columns of black marble and two caryatides of white marble. "For," he said, "I

ROMANTIC INTERIOR

GOTHIC REVIVAL

remembered I had passed through Athens." At one end of the house he added "simulated battlements." The amazing incongruity of it all never seems to have struck Chateaubriand's generation.

Music is the youngest of the arts, and, since many of its possibilities were still untried, it was more easily influenced by the new Romantic Movement than either literature or the fine arts. The opposition between Classic and Romantic styles in music in the later eighteenth century and the early part of the nineteenth thus represents more the gradual growth in technical mastery than the sort of artistic controversy waged between Hugo and the Classicists, or between Delacroix and Ingres. The music of the eighteenth century had been marked by two great movements, first by the gradual development of a homophonic style, in contrast with the earlier polyphonic music, which had reached its culmination in the great works of Bach, and second by the growth of the sonata form, which Haydn and Mozart had perfected in their compositions for the harpsichord and piano, the string quartet, and the orchestra. In France, which was musically more backward than Germany, the same period was marked by the great enthusiasm of the public for the melodious Italian operas which were given by the hundreds in the theaters of Paris. The more serious composers like Rameau, the greatest French composer of the eighteenth century, and the German composer Gluck, who lived for years in Paris, found it hard to get a hearing for their operas. Rameau and, later, Gluck tried to fit their music to the dramatic work they were setting forth, and both used a more elaborate and complicated orchestral accompaniment. The public found their operas dry, preferring the simple and rather vapid style of the Italian School, with its sensuous melodies and its simple harmonic backgrounds. Just before the Revolution a great controversy arose between the followers of Gluck and the advocates of the Italian opera, who took Piccinni as their leader.

The taste for orchestral and chamber music which prevailed in Germany hardly existed in France; hence any musical controversy in Paris was centered on the form of the opera. Paris was the greatest center of European opera from 1760 to 1870, and so was the scene of a series of acrimonious disputes over the nature of the opera. The questions debated were whether dramatic music should be expressive or melodious and whether harmony was to be preferred to melody in instrumental music. The critics, who were literary men with almost no knowledge of music, preferred the Italian style. Even Rousseau, who was a good musician, was a partisan of the Italians. Gluck's genius finally convinced at least a part of the public of the superiority of a more serious musical style. The performances of Mozart's *Mariage de Figaro* in Paris in 1793, of the *Magic Flute* in 1801, and of *Don Juan* in 1805 did much to strengthen the cause of a type of music of greater depth and variety. The influence of Gluck and Mozart passed in direct line through Méhul, Spontini, and Lesur to Berlioz, for whom Gluck was the "Jupiter of his musical Olympus."

The traditions of Italian opera were revived after 1810, first by Rossini and later by Meyerbeer. Rossini, who wrote nearly forty operas between 1810 and 1829, was the great showman of the Restoration, as Meyerbeer was of the period after 1830. Rossini's popularity was due to the florid style of singing he encouraged. His aim was immediate success, and no composer had ever shown greater ability in exploiting his talents. Ingres called his operas "the music of a dishonest man." His popular success was due in part to the extraordinary singing of Malibran and Sontag, for whom his writing was cleverly adapted. Rossini's operas were superior to the Italian operas of the eighteenth century, though they contributed nothing essentially new to the development of musical style. In the style of Rossini, Auber, a Frenchman, wrote his *La Muette de Portici* in 1828. Rossini's *William Tell* of 1829, however, was the greatest popular success of the Restoration. The story of Tell, with its spirit of independence and its richness in local color, made the work seem to Jeune-France the apotheosis of Romanticism. All that can be said of the work today is that it presents the Italian style of opera at its best, yet when compared with the contemporary writing of Beethoven, Weber, and Berlioz it is found to be of slight importance.

Besides this long controversy over the opera, other influences were at work which developed and enriched French musical style. One was the interesting development of the opéra-comique under a group of Frenchmen which included Boïeldieu, Hérold, Adam, and Auber.

Here the use of spoken conversation and the gaiety of the subject developed a style that was less completely melodious and much more expressive than that of the Italian grand opera. A greater seriousness and depth was, at this same time, brought into French music through the religious music of Lesueur, the teacher of Berlioz, and that of Cherubini, an Italian. Both were connected with the Paris Conservatory during the Revolution and the Empire. Their compositions are dry, but they have a seriousness and a complexity which mark a movement away from a style of purely sensuous melody. Cherubini, who lived in Paris from 1788 to 1842, was a rather narrow dogmatist, but as a teacher, and later as head, at the Paris Conservatory he insisted on a broad and thorough musical training. He once had the audacity to inform Napoleon that the reason why the Emperor preferred Italian opera to the works of Gluck and his followers was that the Italian style did not interfere with "His Majesty's thinking of affairs of state." The French public found much of Cherubini's music dull, though Beethoven had a high opinion of him. He grew so dictatorial that the younger men disliked him, and after 1820 Lesueur became the more influential of the two. In writing for church festivals Lesueur tried to make his music expressive of the meaning of the liturgy or Biblical text he used. He wrote an opera on Ossian, one of the first operas to have a Romantic subject. It was Lesueur who suggested to the young Berlioz the idea of a descriptive program for his music, as well as the use of certain themes to represent persons or ideas.

Lesueur's important place in the development of French music rests on the originality of his theoretical treatises and on the unacademic character of his teaching.

Alongside the internal development of French music through Rameau, Gluck, Cherubini, and Lesueur, there was also a steady German influence. The great masters of German music in the period from about 1770 to 1830, Haydn, Gluck, Mozart, Beethoven, Shubert, and Weber, were men of far greater genius than any of their French or Italian contemporaries. Their influence in France lay primarily in stimulating an interest in instrumental music, which had been neglected in France in favor of opera. The French reception of these German composers was very slow. This was partly due to the lack of an organization to present orchestral works. Not until 1828, with the establishment of the Société des Concerts du Conservatoire, was there any regular organization in France to present instrumental music on an adequate scale. Before this the performances of string quartets and symphonies depended entirely on temporary groups that never played together long enough to develop a concert-going public. The symphonies of Haydn, when they were performed in Paris, seemed uninteresting and dull to the French, while Mozart's symphonies were condemned for having "too many ideas." Only gradually did French taste become accustomed to music which because of its intellectual and emotional value could stand alone, without words or action.

This German influence became more marked after

1820. In 1824 the first performances of Beethoven's Fifth Symphony, played by the orchestra of the Paris Opera, and the first presentation of Weber's *Der Freischütz* show this growing attention toGerman music. Soon Beethoven and Weber played for the young Romanticists in music the same rôle that Shakespeare and Scott played in literature. Here was a great musical style that made the inanities of the Italian style ridiculous. The richness and variety of Weber's orchestration made a great impression on the young Berlioz. Weber's other operas, with their themes derived from mediæval and oriental sources, were later performed in Paris, and gradually Weber came to have a large following in France. His immediate influence, however, was on the development of orchestral music, rather than on the opera.

Beethoven stirred Jeune-France to his own sublime longing. They admired without bounds this "Mirabeau and Danton of music," who had broken with artistic rules and conventions and who in his political views was a Liberal. They recognized, too, that Beethoven had created a new set of musical forms through which he could express the ardors of his fiery soul. By 1830 Beethoven had become in certain circles a veritable cult. His growing reputation in France was due partly to the remarkable playing of Franz Liszt. Liszt was only twelve years old when he made his first appearance in Paris in 1823. For the next few years he threw himself into the new Romantic Movement. He read Rousseau and Chateaubriand, learned to know and admire

Lamennais, and with perfect Romantic inconsistency belonged at the same time to the Saint-Simonian School. Liszt's extraordinary success depended partly on the development of the pianoforte, which was supplanting the harpsichord. Mozart, who died in 1791, had used both the harpsichord and the piano, Beethoven only the piano. Liszt was the first great virtuoso to reveal the technical and interpretative possibilities of the piano to the artistic world of Paris. His playing of the Beethoven E flat Concerto in 1828 with the newly founded Société des Concerts was one of the great musical events of the Restoration. This introduction of Beethoven into France marks an epoch in the history of French music.

All these new forces found their first great expression in the works of Hector Berlioz, the one great composer who represents perfectly the Romantic Movement, not only in France, but in all Europe. The early life of Berlioz was spent in a quiet provincial village, and when he came to Paris in 1821 at the age of eighteen he had never heard either an opera or a large orchestra, or even a piano. He had been sent to Paris to study medicine, but he went often to the opera, and spent all his leisure time devouring musical scores in the library of the Paris Conservatory. Much to the displeasure of his family, as he tells us in his remarkable *Autobiography*, he quit the study of medicine and for a short time enrolled at the Conservatory as a student of Lesueur. His allowance was cut off, and he began his tragic career of hardship, which, together with his excessive sensibility and his lack of emotional poise, made his life one of the most wretched and pathetic in the history of modern music.

In these first years he was filled with a tremendous ardor to create. His idols were Shakespeare, Gluck, Weber, and Beethoven, and his great detestations were Rossini and the Italian style. His first Mass was performed in 1825. Its style is extravagant, with interesting new effects for brasses and drums. Lesueur, who heard the Mass, assured Berlioz that he was never meant to be a doctor or a druggist, but that he had the genius of a great composer. By 1827 Berlioz had begun his *Waverley*, *Le roi Lear*, and *Les Francs-Juges*. The next year he wrote his great *Romeo et Juliette*, inspired by the performances of Shakespeare in Paris by an English company, one of whose members, a Miss Smithson, he later married. The same year, 1828, he wrote the *Eight Scenes from Faust* and in 1829 a part of *Lélio*. In 1830, the year in which *Hernani* was produced, he wrote his first great work, *Symphonie fantastique*.

He was still in 1830 only twenty-seven years old, and at nineteen he had known almost no music at all. Besides his composing, he was obliged to take all sorts of work to support himself. He turned early to literary hack work, which he did amazingly well. His early reviews — especially those on Beethoven and Gluck — in the newspapers, in the *Revue musicale* founded in 1827, and in the *Gazette musicale de Paris*, founded three years later, all show his great literary capacity.

Personally he was a strange and unhappy man, a fantastic visionary, and at the same time a man filled with bitter irony. His frenzied force of ecstasy and despair and his keen thirst for experience, wherein he resembles Delacroix, mark him as one of the most vivid figures of a vivid generation. His conception of music was that Beethoven had exhausted the possibilities of abstract music and that the orchestra writing of the future would have to be in the form of program music. Berlioz remained consistent in this, and he never wrote an orchestral work without a program. This mixture of the genres, as in Hugo's *Hernani*, was to make art express with greater definiteness and flexibility all the moods and emotions of the composer. His *Symphonie fantastique*, *épisode de la vie d'un artiste* of 1830 shows his method. Here is a continuous story told in five movements which correspond to five acts. In the first movement a lover's reveries are portrayed; in the second he is at a ball; in the third the hero is taken to an idyllic countryside; in the fourth the hero-lover attempts to take his own life; and in the last there is a saturnalia of goblins and demons. The first three movements are reminiscent of Beethoven, the last two prefigure Wagner. Through the whole composition there appears and reappears the same fixed melody which typifies the beloved. The reception of the work was indifferent. No one seems to have understood it. As Boïeldieu, another composer, remarked to Berlioz, "I cannot understand half of Beethoven, and you go further than Beethoven."

Berlioz' lack of early or thorough technical training in music, as well as a certain inability to create interesting themes, make for certain limitations in his work. On the other hand, his handling of orchestral effects, especially in the brasses and wood winds, give him rank as one of the most original of all modern masters of orchestration. As Delacroix thought and composed his painting in color, so Berlioz wrote his music in terms of orchestral coloring. It is because Berlioz conceived his music in this way that one finds it impossible to understand him from a piano score. He thought and wrote orchestrally. This is the reason why most of the recent critics have regarded him as the originator of the whole modern school of orchestration, from Wagner to Richard Strauss and Debussy.

Romanticism continued to dominate French thought and expression during the July Monarchy. By 1848, however, new forces were at work, and Realism and Parnassianism in literature, and Realism in painting, were gradually taking possession of the field, though these movements were but new aspects of the same Romantic Revolt. Before it passed, Romanticism, even in its narrower sense, had revitalized style in every branch of literature, had brought undreamed-of subjects within the range of art, had created a new music, had proved the relativity of all beauty, and at the same time had insinuated itself into politics, religion, and ethics. For good or for ill, it stands as the greatest movement of the nineteenth century.

BIBLIOGRAPHICAL NOTES

BIBLIOGRAPHICAL NOTES[1]

CHAPTER I

BIBLIOGRAPHICAL WORKS

The *Catalogue de l'histoire de France de la Bibliothèque Nationale* gives a list of all the works, pamphlets, and articles on French history in the Bibliothèque Nationale at Paris up to the year 1878. The *Catalogue Lorenz*, a publishers' annual catalogue, lists all the works published in France since 1840. Its topical classifications make it useful for reference. For works published on French history from 1866 to 1897 there is P. Caron, *Bibliographie des travaux publiés sur l'histoire de France de 1866 à 1897* (1912). The works published since 1897 are listed in G. Brière and P. Caron, *Répertoire méthodique d'histoire moderne et contemporaine de la France, 1898–1906*. (7 vol. 1898 ff.). From 1910 on the *Revue d'histoire moderne et contemporaine* published a bibliographical supplement covering the years 1910–1913. P. Caron and H. Stein have supplemented the bibliography of Brière and Caron for the years 1920–1923. There is nothing at present for the years 1907–1909, 1913–1919, and 1923 to date. There is a summary bibliography of new works in French History in the section *Historical News* in each issue of the *American Historical Review*.

DOCUMENTS

The laws, ordinances, and principal regulations of the Central Government are in the *Bulletin des Lois*. Less complete, but better arranged for use, is Duvergier de Hauranne, *Collection des lois* (1824–32); also *Circulaires, instructions et autres actes émanés du ministère de l'intérieur de 1797 à 1830* (6 vol., 1821–30). The text of the Charter and important constitu-

[1] The place of publication for all French works is Paris, for all English works New York, unless otherwise noted. Works starred are of special value. This bibliography is intended to be of use apart from the book and hence it includes some titles not used in preparing the text.

tional documents may be found in a number of small and useful manuals: F. A. Hélie, *Les Constitutions de la France* (1880); L. Duguit and H. Monnier, *Les constitutions et les principales lois politiques de la France depuis 1789* (3d ed., 1920); L. Cahen and A. Mathiez, *Les lois françaises 1789–1919* (3d ed., 1927); a good collection in English is F. M. Anderson, *The Constitutions and other select Documents illustrative of the History of France, 1789–1901* (Minneapolis, 1904); also G. Elton, *The Revolutionary Idea in France, 1789–1871* (1921). The parliamentary debates are published in *Archives parlementaires*, 2d series, Vol. 12–41 incl. There is a good guide to materials in the Archives Nationales at Paris; Ch. Schmidt, *Les sources de l'histoire de France depuis 1789 aux archives nationales* (1907).

MEMOIRS

There are a great many memoirs for the period. A long list is given in S. Charléty, *La Restauration* (1921), p. 2. The most useful of these memoirs for political affairs are Barante, *Souvenirs* (5 vol., 1890); Broglie, *Souvenirs* (4 vol., 1886). Chateaubriand, *Mémoires d'Outre-Tombe* (6 vol. [ed. Bire], 1898–1900); Guizot, *Mémoires pour servir à l'histoire de mon temps* (8 vol., 1856–67); Pasquier, **Mémoires* (6 vol., 1893–4); Talleyrand, *Mémoires* (5 vol., 1891–2); Villèle, *Mémoires et Correspondance* (5 vol., 1887–90). Of these Chateaubriand's are the most interesting reading, Pasquier the most reliable and comprehensive. Almost none of the memoirs have indices. The introduction to Louis Blanc's *Histoire de dix ans* is really a memoir. I have found the list of memoirs referred to in Charléty very useful and fairly complete. One important memoir has appeared since the publication of Charléty's volume: Baron de Damas' *Mémoires* (2 vol., 1922–3).

GENERAL HISTORIES

The general histories of the period are numerous. Of the older works, the two best are Duvergier de Hauranne, **L'histoire du gouvernement parlementaire en France, 1789–1830* (10 vol., 1857–71); and Viel-Castel, **Histoire de la Restauration* (20 vol., 1860–78). Duvergier de Hauranne knew the period at first hand and made use of newspapers and unpublished memoirs. He belonged to the circle that published the *Globe* and his work is that of a profound and powerful mind. Viel-Castel was a diplomat, and his work is excellent on the diplomatic side. Of the other older works, Vaulabelle, *Histoire des deux Restaurations* (8 vol., 3d ed., 1857), is Liberal; A. Nettement, *Histoire de la Restauration* (1860), is Royalist, as is also that of Capefigue (10 vol., 1831–3). Three German works are good: Gervinus, *Histoire du XIXe siècle depuis les traités de Vienne*, tr. by Minssen (20 vol., 1864–9), A. Stern, **Geschichte Europas seit den Vertragen von 1815* (2 vol. go to 1830, 2d ed., Stuttgart, 1916), and A. Stern and others, **Die französische Revolution, Napoleon und die Restauration 1789–1848* (Berlin, 1929). A number of other general histories are mentioned in Charléty, *op. cit.*, p. 3. A good though brief interpretation of the period is in G. L. Dickinson, **Reaction and Revolution in Modern France* (new ed., 1927). For a contemporary chronicle cf. Ch. Lesur, *L'Annuaire historique universel*, (1 vol. a year, 1818–32). An interesting collection of lithographs and portraits of the period is in A. Dayot, *La Restauration d'après l'image du temps* (1902). Of recent works two are outstanding: G. Weill, **La France sous la monarchie constitutionnelle* (2d ed., 1912); and S. Charléty, **La Restauration* (1921) in E. Lavisse, Histoire de la France contemporaine. Both treat social and intellectual matters, and are easily the best manuals on the period. There is an English work, almost entirely political, J. R. Hall, *The Bourbon Restoration* (London, 1909). J. Lucas-Dubreton's *La Restauration et la Monarchie de Juillet* (1927; Eng. tr., 1929) in the series L'Histoire de France racontée à tous is the work of a journalist, as are also his lives of Louis XVIII and Charles X. More interesting and showing Royalist and Catholic leanings is P. de la Gorce, *La Restauration: Louis XVIII, Charles X* (2 vol., 1926–8). R. Viviani wrote the volume on the Restoration (1909) in Jaurès' Histoire Socialiste. There is a good account of the period in G. Weill **L'éveil des nationalités et le mouvement libéral 1814–1848* (1930) in Halphen and Sagnac's series, Peuples et civilisations.

SPECIAL STUDIES OF INCIDENTS AND FIGURES IN POLITICAL HISTORY

J. M. S. Allison, **Thiers and the French Monarchy, 1788–1848* (Boston, 1926); R. André, *L'Occupation de la France: 1815* (1924); A. Aulard, "Les adhésions aux Bourbons en 1814" in *La Révolution française* (April, 1890); Barante, *La vie politique de Royer-Collard* (2 vol., 3d ed., 1878); E. W. Shermerhorn, *Benjamin Constant* (Boston, 1924). E. Bonnal de Ganges, *Manuel et son temps* (1877). S. Charléty, "Une Conspiration à Lyon en 1817" in *Revue de Paris* (15 July, 1904); E. Beau de Lomenie, **La carrière politique de Chateaubriand, 1814–1830* (2 vol., 1929); R. de Cisternes, *Le Duc de Richelieu* (1898); E. Daudet, "Histoire de l'émigration" (3 vol., 1886–9); E. Daudet, *La terreur blanche* (1878); E. Daudet, "La dissolution de la Chambre Introuvable" in *Revue de Paris* (Feb., 1899); E. Daudet, *Le ministère Martignac* (2d ed., 1875); E. Daudet, *Louis XVIII et Decazes* (1899); H. Dumolard, *La terreur blanche dans l'Isère* (Grenoble, 1928); J. P. Garnier, *Le sacre de Charles X et l'opinion publique en 1825* (1927); L. Grasilier, *L'Aventure des quatre sergents de La Rochelle* (1929); another work on the same subject by J. Lucas-Dubreton appeared in 1929; H. Houssaye, **1814* (1898); H. Houssaye, **1815* (3 vol., 1895–1905); P. Jacomet, *Le palais (de justice) sous la Restauration* (1922); G. Lanson, "La défection de Chateaubriand" in *Revue de Paris* (Aug., 1901); L. Madelin, **Fouché* (2 vol., 2d ed., 1903); P. Mantoux, *"Patrons et Ouvriers en Juillet, 1830" in *Revue d'histoire moderne et contemporaine* (Sept.-Oct., 1901); P. Mantoux, *"Talleyrand en 1830" in *Revue historique* (1902); H. Monin, "Une épidémie anarchiste sous la Restauration" in *Revue internationale de sociologie* (1894); Paillet, "Les cours prévôtales" in *Revue des Deux Mondes* (July, 1911); E. de Perceval, *Le vicomte Lainé et la vie parlementaire au temps de la Restauration* (1927); C. H. Pouthas, **Guizot pendant la Restauration* (1923); P. Rain, **L'Europe et la restauration des Bourbons 1814–1818* (1908); A. Sorel, "Le procès du Maréchal Ney" in *Nouveaux essais de critique et d'histoire* (1895); G. Stenger, *Le retour des Bourbons, 1814–1815* (1908); H. I. Stewart and P. Desjardins,

French Patriotism in the Nineteenth Century (Cambridge, Eng., 1924), L. Léon, *B. Constant* (1930), and Noailles, **Molé* (4 vol. 1922–5). Other bibliographical details on events of the period are to be found at the beginnings of the chapters in Charléty, *op. cit.*

There is a doctoral thesis of mine on the *Polignac Ministry* in the Harvard Library and an article in the *Revue d'histoire moderne* (March–April, 1929) on "La crise des incendies de 1830 et les compagnies d'assurance" which bear on this aspect of the subject.

THE CENTRAL POLITICAL REGIME

Charter. P. Simon, **L'élaboration de la Charte* (1906), an excellent work. Some of the contemporary pamphlets on the Charter are interesting; cf. Chateaubriand, *La monarchie selon la Charte* (1816); Villèle, *Observations sur le projet de constitution* (Toulouse, 1814); B. Constant, *Réflexions sur les constitutions* (1814); Clauzel de Coussergues, *Considérations sur l'origine, la rédaction, la promulgation et l'exécution de la Charte* (1830); Guizot, *Du gouvernement représentatif et du gouvernement actuel de la France* (1815).

Parliamentary system. The best study is that of J. Barthélemy; **L'Introduction du régime parlementaire sous Louis XVIII et Charles X* (1904); cf. also Ch. Léonardi, *Le Conseil d'état sous la Restauration* (1909); L. Michon, *Le Gouvernement parlementaire sous la Restauration* (1905); J. Bonnefón, *Le régime parlementaire sous la Restauration* (1905); P. Marx, *L'évolution du régime représentatif sous le régime parlementaire 1814–1816* (1929); and M. Barbe, *L'étude historique des idées sur la souveraineté en France de 1815 à 1848* (1904). On the personnel of the Chambers, A. Robert, E. Bourloton, and G. Cougny, *Dictionnaire des parlementaires français, 1789–1889* (5 vol., 1891); J. B. M. Braun, *Tableau nominatif et raisonné de la future majorité des députés constitutionnels à la Chambre de 1830* (1829), and by the same author, *Nouvelle biographie des députés, ou statistique de la chambre de 1814 à 1829* (1830); on the personnel of the Chamber of Peers cf. Lardier, *Histoire biographique de la chambre des pairs depuis* *la Restauration* (1829). The addresses of the King are given in A. Lepage, *Les discours du trône 1814–1869* (1869). The personnel of the ministries are listed in Muel, *Les ministères français de 1789 à 1909* (1911). The same author has a *Précis historique des assemblées parlementaires, 1789–1895* (1896). A more extended work of the sort is that of E. Pierre, *Histoire des assemblées politiques en France* (1877), Vol. 1. The legislative side of public finance is studied in detail in H. Pouyanne, *Les prérogatives financières du pouvoir législatif sous la Restauration* (1911). Two useful selections of parliamentary speeches are: A. Chabrier, **Les orateurs politiques de la France des origines à 1830* (1898); and J. Reinach, *Les Conciones français* (1893).

LOCAL ADMINISTRATION

On the prefects cf. Moulard, *Le Comte de Tournon, Préfet de la Gironde* (1914); Sers, *Souvenirs d'un préfet de la monarchie 1786–1862* (1906); H. Baumont, "Girardin, préfet de la côte d'Or" in *Revue française* (Sept., 1908); Barthélemy, *Souvenirs d'un ancien préfet* (1886); Rambuteau, *Mémoires* (1905); Puymaigre, *Souvenirs* (1884); P. Leuilliot, "Le dernier préfet du Haut-Rhin sous la Restauration" in *Revue d'histoire moderne* (1929). On the local administration in general, G. Alix, "Les origines du système administratif français" in *Annals of Political Science* (1899); V. Vivien, *Etudes administratives* (1846); E. de Luze, *L'organisation administrative de la France depuis 1789* (1884); A. Descilleuls, *Histoire de l'administration parisienne au XIXe siècle* (3 vol., 1900–1); A. Rousseau, "L'idée décentralisatrice et les parties politiques sous la Restauration" in *Revue de Bretagne* (1903); and C. H. Pouthas, *"Les projets de réforme administrative sous la Restauration" in *Revue d'histoire moderne* (Oct., 1926).

The police. Froment, *La police dévoilée sous la Restauration* (1829); and two more recent works: E. Daudet, *La police politique 1815–1820* (1912), and A. de Courson, *Souvenirs d'un officer de gendarmerie sous la Restauration* (1914).

POLITICAL PARTIES

Parties of the Right. H. Michel, **L'idée de l'état* (1896), a remarkable study of the political theories of the 19th century in France; also R. Soltau, *French Political Thought in the 19th Century* (announced, 1931); F. Uzureau, "Politique de l'extrême droite sous la Restauration," a collection of letters, in *Révolution de 1848*, Vol. 17, pp. 254–64; P. Thureau-Dangin, *"L'extrême droite et les royalistes sous la Restauration," in *Royalistes et Républicains* (1874); C. de Mazade, *L'opposition royaliste* (1894); Vitrolles, **Mémoires* (3 vol., 1884); Falloux, *Mémoires* (2 vol., 1888); Frénilly, *Mémoires* (1908); de Serre, *Correspondance* (6 vol., 1876); Ch. de Lacombe, *Le Comte de Serre* (2 vol., 1881); Salaberry, *Souvenirs politiques, 1821–1830* (2 vol., 1900); Polignac, *Etudes politiques* (1845); also the Memoirs of Villèle already referred to, and the speeches of de Serre and Villèle in the *Archives parlementaires*. There are good studies of de Maistre and Bonald in E. Faguet, **Politiques et Moralistes du XIXe siècle* (1st series, 1891); and of Bonald in H. Laski, *Authority in the Modern State* (New Haven, 1919) and in J. Morley, *Miscellanies* (London, Vol. 2, 1890). There is a thorough study of Bonald in Moulinie, **Bonald* (1915). The best study of de Maistre is perhaps P. R. Rodhen, **Joseph de Maistre als politischer Theoretiker* (Munich, 1929).

Doctrinaires. Cf. Nesmes-Desmarets, **Les doctrines politiques de Royer-Collard* (1908); and Memoirs of the Duc de Broglie.

Left. Though hostile in tone P. Thureau-Dangin's **Le parti libéral sous la Restauration* (2d ed., 1888) remains the best study of the Liberal Party of the Restoration; cf. also Boutenko, *Le parti libéral sous la Restauration* (Leningrad, 1913); the text is in Russian, but the footnotes and references, which are very useful, are in French; also cf. C. de Mazade *La politique libérale* (1860); Nicoullaud, *Casimir-Périer: député de l'opposition* (1894); also J. Lucas-Dubreton, *La manière forte: Casimir-Périer* (1930); V. Bompar, *Le général Foy* (1926); special aspects of the liberal parties are discussed in Germond de Lavigne, *Les pamphlets de la Restauration*

(1879); F. Drujon, *Catalogue des ouvrages, écrits et desseins poursuivis, supprimés, ou condamnés, 1814–1877* (1878); A. Lelarge, *Paul-Louis Courier, Parisien* (1925), R. Gaschet, *Paul-Louis Courier et la Restauration* (1913); and by the same author *Les aventures d'un écrivain, Paul-Louis Courier* (1928); A. Dessoye, *Brest sous la Restauration: Le parti libéral et les missions, 1818–1827* (Brest, 1895); R. Dûpuch, "Le parti libéral à Bordeaux et dans la Gironde sous la deuxième Restauration" in *Revue philomathique de Bordeaux* (1902). Two recent works of the first order are: G. de Ruggiero, **History of European Liberalism* (Oxford, 1928); and J. M. Robertson, **History of Free Thought in the 19th Century* (2 vol., London, 1929).

The Military plots and the Carbonari. Cf. A. Calmette, *"Les carbonari en France sous la Restauration" in *Révolution de 1848*, Vol. 9, 10 (1913–4); E. Bonnal de Granges, *Les royalistes contre l'armée, 1815–1820* (1906); E. Guillon, *Les complots militaires sous la Restauration* (1895); Grasilier, *Simon Duplay et son mémoire sur les sociétés secrètes et les conspirations sous la Restauration* (1913); and by the same author, *Les quatre sergents de La Rochelle* (1929); H. Pontois, *La Conspiration du général Barton* (1877); H. Dumolard, *J. P. Didier et la conspiration de Grenoble* (Grenoble, 1928); L. Dubreuil, *Histoire des Insurrections de l'ouest 1790–1832* (1930); and two old works that are still interesting: Trélat, *Paris révolutionnaire* (4 vol., 1833–4); and de la Hodde, *Histoire des Sociétés secrètes* (1850).

The Republicans. Cf. G. Weill, **Histoire du parti républicain en France, 1814–1870* (2d ed., 1928).

Bonapartism. Cf. H. A. L. Fisher, **Bonapartism* (Oxford, 1908); A. L. Guérard, *Reflections on the Napoleonic Legend* (1924); Ph. Gonnard, **Les origines de la légende napoléonienne* (1906), and by the same author, "La légende napoléonienne et la presse libérale" in *Revue des études napoléoniennes* (March, 1912), J. Garsou, *Béranger* (Brussels, 1897); J. Garsou, *L'évolution napoléonienne de Victor Hugo sous la Restauration* (1900); F. A. Simpson: **The Rise of Louis Napoleon* (2nd ed. 1925) and J. Deschamps, **La légend de Napoléon* in *Revue de littérature comparée* (1929).

ELECTORAL SYSTEM

There is an article of mine "The Electoral System in France under the Bourbon Restoration" in *Review of Modern History* (Chicago, June, 1929), the substance of which I have reproduced here; cf. also Pilenco, **Les mœurs électorales en France — 1815–1848* (1928); George-Denis Weil, **Les élections législatives depuis 1789* (1895); Sauve, *Les dessous d'une élection législative en province en 1824* (1904); Ch. Roussel, "La candidature officielle sous la Restauration" in *Revue parlementaire* (Feb., 1899); G. Maguelonne, "L'élection de Manuel en Vendée en 1818" in *Révolution de 1848* (1912); Sibaudière, *Les élections législatives à Nantes sous la Restauration* (Nantes, 1896); Emonot, *Les élections politiques à Montbéliard et dans le Doubs, 1804–1898* (Montbéliard, 1900); P. Fauchille, *"Comment se préparaient les élections en 1818" in *Revue de Paris* (July, 1902); J. Cann, "Le régime électoral et l'opinion publique en 1814–1815" in *La Révolution française* (1919), and J. Berger, *Etude sur la législation électorale en 1820* (1903).

POLITICAL PRESS

There is a bibliography of the press by E. Hatin, *Bibliographie historique et critique de la presse en France* (1866); and by the same author, *Histoire politique et littéraire de la presse en France* (8 vol., 1859–61). A more recent history of the press, though not so detailed, has some important facts, H. Avenel, *Histoire de la presse française depuis 1789* (1900). Cf. also *Le livre du centenaire du Journal des Débats* (1889); Welschinger, "La presse sous l'Empire et la Restauration" in *Revue encyclopédique* (1893); G. Weill, *"Les journaux ouvriers à Paris 1830–1870" in *Revue d'histoire moderne et contemporaine* (Nov., 1907). The censorship is discussed in A. Crémieux, **La censure en 1820 et 1821* (1912); and Mersan, *La liberté de la presse sous les divers régimes* (1874). The pamphlet literature of the Restoration is extensive and very interesting. It is listed in the *Catalogue de l'histoire de France. Distribution of Public Opinion.* Besides the section in Charléty referred to in the text, cf. also A. Mater, *"Le Groupement régional des partis à la fin de la Restauration, 1824–1830" in *La Révolution française* (May, 1902).

CHAPTER II

BIBLIOGRAPHY

Two articles by G. Weill: *"Le Catholicisme français depuis 1802" in *Revue de synthèse historique* (1907, 1925), in addition to bibliographical works referred to in notes to Chapter I. *Documents.* **Documents sur l'histoire religieuse de la France pendant la Restauration* (1913); and Decap, La Martinière, and Bideau, **L'Instruction primaire en France aux XVIIe et XIXe siècles: Documents d'histoire locale* (1914). These two collections printed by the Comité des Travaux Historiques contain documents that bear on nearly every aspect of the clerical and educational problems of the Restoration. There is a guide to unpublished materials on the religious history of modern France by G. Bourgin, *Les Sources manuscrites de l'histoire religieuse de la France moderne* (1927).

CHURCH AND STATE

The best general study of Church and State in this period is A. Debidour, **Histoire des rapports de l'église et de l'état en France de 1789 à 1870* (2d ed., 1911). There are a great many others, among the best of which are G. Bonet-Maury, **La liberté de conscience en France 1598–1870* (1910); Desdevises du Dézert, *L'Eglise et l'Etat en France* (2 vol., 1908); G. S. Phillips, *The Church in France 1789–1848* (London, 1928); and G. Weill, **Histoire de l'idée laïque en France au XIXe siècle* (1925). Also G. Bourgain, *L'église de France et l'état au XIXe siècle* (2 vol., 1901), Catholic in point of view whereas the others, except Goyau, are all more or less anti-clerical; Baunard, *Un siècle de l'Eglise en France 1800–1900* (1901). E. Clairin, *Le cléricalisme de 1789 à 1870* (1880); G. Goyau, **Histoire de la nation Française: histoire religieuse* (1922), an excellent work but brief on this period; E. Lamy, "Les luttes entre l'église et l'état au XIXe siècle: La Restauration," in *Revue des Deux Mondes* (April, 1898); Ch. de Lajudic, "Un siècle de l'église de France 1800–1900" in *Université Catho-*

lique (1904). Ch. Jourdain, *Le budget des cultes en France depuis le Concordat* (1859); A. Lods, *Traité de l'administration des cultes* (1896); Mouret, "L'histoire générale de l'Eglise" Vols. 7, 8 (1914–21). There are many good articles in Baudrillart, Vogt, and Rouziès, *Dictionnaire d'histoire et de géographie ecclésiastiques* (1910 ff.). On the "Petite Eglise" after 1815 cf. Latreille, *Après le Concordat* (1910); Latreille, *La petite Eglise de Lyon* (1911); Gibial, *La petite Eglise à Tassaniouze* (Aurillac, 1912); and Chauvigny, *La résistance au Concordat* (1921). On the negotiations of the Concordat of 1817 cf. *La France et le Saint Siège* (2 vol., 1911); and Ph. Sagnac, *"Le concordat de 1817" in *Revue d'histoire moderne et contemporaine* (Dec., 1905 and March, 1906). On the Papal Jubilee there is a study by G. de Grandmaison, *Le jubilé de 1825* (1902). Martignac's laws against the Jesuits and the teaching orders are discussed in Latreille, "L'application des ordonnances de 1828 dans le diocèse de Lyon" in *Revue d'histoire de Lyon* (Jan., 1912). The Gallican opposition to the Church in the reign of Charles X is discussed in Bardoux, *Le comte de Montlosier et le gallicanisme* (1881). Two studies of the religious outlook of the time from the point of view of different classes: Vicomte de Guichen, *La France morale et religieuse au début de la Restauration* (1911); and by the same author, *La France morale et religieuse à la fin de la Restauration* (1912), good material but poor judgment shown in its interpretation. For facts about individual bishops, cf. Baunard, *L'episcopat français 1802–1905* (1907).

EDUCATIONAL QUESTION

Perhaps the most useful book here is L. Liard: **L'Enseignement public supérieur en France* (2 vol., 1888–94), an excellent work so far as it goes, based on a careful study of the documents. A good manual is that of G. Weill, **Histoire de l'éducation secondaire en France 1801–1914* (1921). On the relationship of the Government to the Université, G. Poirier, *"L'Université provisoire 1814–1821" in *Revue d'histoire moderne* (1926); de Riancey, *Histoire critique et législative de l'instruction publique et de la liberté d'enseignement en France*

(2 vol., 1844); V. C. Gréard, *Législation de l'instruction primaire en France depuis 1789* (3 vol., 1874). Ch. Jourdain, *Le budget de l'instruction publique et des établissements scientifiques et littéraires* (1857); L. Grimaud, *Histoire de la liberté d'enseignement* (1899); E. Bourgeois, *La liberté d'enseignement* (1902); on the rôle of Frayssinous: Hanrion, *Vie de Monseigneur de Frayssinous* (1842); and Garnier, **Frayssinous, son rôle dans l'Université sous la Restauration* (1925). On primary instruction: Documents referred to above, also: Commission de statistique de l'enseignement primaire, *Statistique comparée de l'enseignement primaire 1829–1877* (1880); Levasseur, *Statistique de l'enseignement primaire au XIXe siècle 1801–1899* (1900); F. Buisson, *Dictionnaire pédagogique*, 1st ed., has excellent articles on: "Enseignement mutuel," "Société pour l'instruction élémentaire," "Cuvier," "Frères des écoles chrétiennes," etc.; Cournot, *Des institutions d'instruction publique en France* (1864); Gossat, *Essai critique sur l'enseignement primaire en France* (1901); Compayré, **Histoire critique des doctrines de l'éducation en France* (2 vol., 7th ed. 1904). There are some bibliographical notes on the local histories of education in G. Weill, *La France sous la monarchie constitutionnelle* (2d ed., 1912), p. 294. There is a valuable summary of Guizot's famous investigation of primary education (1833) in P. Lorain, *Tableau de l'instruction primaire en France* (1837). On the Frères des Ecoles Chrétiennes cf. Chevalier, *Les frères des Ecoles Chrétiennes et l'enseignement primaire après la Révolution* (1887); and Letouzey, *Les frères des Ecoles Chrétiennes* (1924). Three contemporary pamphlets on education are especially interesting: Lamennais, *De l'Université Impériale* (1814); Guizot, *Essai sur l'histoire et l'état actuel de l'instruction publique* (1816); F. Cuvier, *Projet d'organisation pour les écoles primaires* (1815). The life of one secondary school is described in C. Dupont-Ferrier, *Du Collège de Clermont au Lycée Louis-le-Grand*, Vol. II and III (1922-1925).

RELIGIOUS ORDERS

L. Deriès, **Les congrégations religieuses au temps de Napoléon* (1929); J. Burnichon, *La Congrégation de Jésus en France*

1814–1914 (4 vol., 1914–22); P. Rimbault, *Histoire politique des Congrégations religieuses françaises 1790–1914* (1927); A. Lirac, "La guerre aux Jésuites sous la Restauration" in *Le Correspondant* (1879); Lajudic, "La société de la propagation de la foi" in *Université Catholique* (1904); Terrien, *Vie de P. de Clorievière* (1892); P. de Rivière, *Vie de Forbin-Janson* (1892); Delaporte, *Vie du P. Rauzan* (1892); G. de Grandmaison, **La Congrégation* (1889); J. M. Villefranche, *Histoire et légende de la Congrégation* (1901); L. Carné, *Souvenirs de ma jeunesse au temps de la Restauration* (1872); *Histoire des principales missions données en France en 1820 et 1821* (2 vol., 1821). *Les ordres religieuses* (series by various authors, anonymous, 1924 ff.) and Nourrisson, *Histoire légale des congrégations depuis 1789* (2 vol. 1928). On the higher clergy: cf. A. du Bourg, *La vie religieuse en France sous la Révolution, l'Empire et la Restauration: Du Bourg 1751–1822* (1907); and Baille, *Le Cardinal de Rohan-Chalot* (1904).

THE "SECTS"

Protestants: G. Weill, "Bibliographie du mouvement protestant" in *Revue de Synthèse historique* (1911); Giesseler, *Die Protestantische Kirche Frankreichs von 1787 bis 1846* (1848); Maury, *Le réveil religieux dans l'Eglise réformée* (2 vol., 1892); E. Rambert, **Alexandre Vinet* (4th ed., 1913); H. Perrenoud, *Protestantisme en France au point de vue statistique 1802–88* (1889). On the Jews: T. Reinach, *Histoire des Israélites* (4th ed., 1910), Dubnov, **Die neueste Geschichte des judischen Volkes* (3 vol. Berlin 1920–1923). On the Free-Masons: Findel, *Histoire de la franc-maçonnerie* (2 vol., 1866); A. Lantoine, *Histoire de la franc-maçonnerie française* (1925), and Gaston-Martin, **Manuel d'histoire de la franc-maçonnerie française* (1929).

THE PHILOSOPHIC MOVEMENT

A great deal has been written on this subject and there are many excellent studies. *General works:* Ch. Adam, *La Philosophie en France* (1894); F. Baldensperger, **Le mouvement des idées dans l'émigration française* (2 vol., 1924); Barbier,

Histoire du catholicisme libéral (5 vol., Bordeaux, 1923); J. Bellamy, *La théologie catholique au XIXe siècle* (2d ed., 1904); G. Boas, **French Philosophies of the Romantic Period* (Baltimore, 1925); G. Brandes, *Main currents of XIXth Century Literature, Vol. 3, *The Reaction in France* (1903)—a penetrating study; P. M. Brin, *Histoire de la philosophie contemporaine* (1886), written from the neo-scholastic point of view; A. Cresson, **Les courants de la pensée philosophique française* (2 vol., 1927); P. Damiron, *Essai sur l'histoire de la philosophie en France au XIXe siècle* (5th ed., Brussels, 1835); E. Faguet, **Politiques et moralistes du XIXe siècle* (3 series, 1891–9); M. Ferraz, **Histoire de la philosophie en France au XIXe siècle* (3 vol., 1877–87); M. Hébert, *L'Evolution de la foi Catholique* (1905); W. M. Horton, **The Philosophy of the Abbé Bautain* (1927), excellent introductory chapter; L. Lévy-Bruhl, *History of Modern Philosophy in France* (London, 1894); L. Reynaud, **L'influence allemande en France aux XVIIIe et XIXe siècles* (1922); H. Taine, *Les philosophes français au XIXe siècle* (1859); G. Weill, **Histoire du Catholicisme libéral en France* (1909).

SPECIAL AND MORE DETAILED STUDIES OF VARIOUS MEN AND MOVEMENTS

There are bibliographical indications on Chateaubriand, Bonald, de Maistre, Cousin, Comte, and Lamennais in G. Lanson, **Manuel bibliographique de la littérature française moderne* (1925). On the Catholic Revival: P. M. Masson, **Rousseau et la restauration religieuse* (1916); V. Giraud, **Le christianisme de Chateaubriand* (2 vol., 1925–8), an excellent study; G. Goyau, **La pensée religieuse de Joseph de Maistre* (1921); H. Moulinié, *Bonald* (1915); P. Bourget and M. Salmon, *Bonald* (1905); Duine, *Essai d'une bibliographie de Lamennais* (1923); C. Maréchal, *La jeunesse de Lamennais: contribution à l'étude des origines du romantisme religieux* (1913); V. Giraud, "Le cas de Lamennais" in *Revue des Deux Mondes* (1919); P. Dubois, *Victor Hugo, ses idées religieuses de 1802 à 1825* (1913); Jean de Cognets, *La vie intérieure de Lamartine* (1913); Viatte, *Le Catholicisme chez les Romantiques*

(1922). On the Idéologues: Picavet, **Les idéologues* (1910). On the scholars: C. H. Pouthas, **Guizot pendant la Restauration* (1923); Vauthier, *Villemain* (1913); Hannequin, "Un chapitre de l'histoire des mathématiciens et physiciens français de 1800 à 1851" in Etudes d'histoire des sciences et d'histoire de la philosophie (2 vol., 1908); D. de Blainville, *Cuvier et Saint-Hilaire* (1890); and two studies of A. Houtin, *La question biblique chez les catholiques de France au XIXe siècle* (1902), and *Histoire du modernisme catholique* (1913); P. Janet **Victor Cousin et son œuvre* (1885); and J. B. Saint Hilaire, **Victor Cousin, sa vie et sa correspondance* (3 vol., 1895). For Comte: Lévy-Bruhl, **La philosophie de Comte* (1900); C. Dumas, *Les deux messies du positivisme* (1905); C. Dumas, *"Saint-Simon, père du positivisme" in *Revue philosophique* (1904), an article which proves that there is almost nothing in the system of Comte that was not taken from the ideas of Saint-Simon. On the younger generation: Dejot, "L'Athénée" in *Revue internationale de l'enseignement* (1889); Calippe, *L'attitude sociale des catholiques français au XIXe siècle* (3 vol., 1911–2); Mainage, *Les mouvements de la jeunesse catholique au XIXe siècle* (1918); Rastoul, *Histoire de la démocratie catholique en France* (1913); P. T. Moon, *The Social Catholic Movement in France* (1921). There is an interesting collection of articles in English by G. Ripley, *Philosophic Miscellanies translated from Cousin, Gouffroy and Constant* (2 vol., Boston, 1838). Two other recent works on the beginnings of the Liberal Catholic Movement should be noted, C. Maréchal, *La Mennais, la dispute de l'essai de l'indifférence* (1925), F. Duine, *La Mennais* (1922), and E. Ledos, *Lacordaire* (1922). Additional bibliography on the history of science will be found in E. Picard and others, *Histoire des sciences en France* (1924), in G. Weill, **L'éveil des nationalités et le mouvement libéral* (1930) pp. 268–284 and above all in G. Sarton **An Introduction to the History of Science* Vol. I (Washington 1928).

CHAPTER III[1]

DOCUMENTS

The two most valuable collections of documents for the economic situation 1815–1830 are: *La Statistique agricole de 1814 (1914), and G. and H. Bourgin, *Le régime de l'industrie en France 1814–1830 (2 vol., 1912–21), pub. by the Société d'histoire moderne.

GENERAL WORKS

The great compend of E. Levasseur, **Histoire des classes ouvrières et de l'industrie en France de 1789 à 1870* (2 vol., 2d ed., 1903) remains a classic. An excellent manual recently published is H. Sée, **La vie économique en France sous la monarchie censitaire, 1815–1830* (1927); cf. also H. Sée, **Esquisse d'une histoire économique de la France* (1929). Other general works of value are J. H. Clapham, **The Economic Development of France and Germany 1815–1914* (Cambridge, England, 3d ed., 1928); A. L. Dunham, **The Anglo-French Treaty of Commerce of 1860 and the Progress of the Industrial Revolution in France* (Ann Arbor, 1930); H. Gibbins, **Economic and Industrial Progress of the Century* (Toronto, 1903); M. Knight, Flugel, and Barnes, *Economic History of Modern Europe* (Boston, 1928, Vol. 2); G. Martin, *Histoire de la nation française: Histoire économique et financière* (1927); F. A. Ogg, *Economic Development of Modern Europe* (1917; a later ed. has no changes for this period); G. Renard and A. Dulac, *L'évolution industrielle et agricole depuis 150 ans* (1912); H. Sée, "Stendhal et la vie économique et sociale de son temps" in *Mercure de France* (July, 1929); L. Cahen, *"L'enrichissement de la France sous la Restauration" in *Revue d'histoire moderne* (1930); and A. Zévaes, "Le mouvement social de 1789 à 1848" in *Nouvelle Revue* (1930). Two general works on economic conditions written during the Restoration are very valuable: Ch. Dupin, **Forces productives et commerciales*

[1] Consult also the bibliography of Chapter IV.

de la France (2 vol., 1829); and Chaptal, **De l'industrie française* (2 vol., 1819).

There are two general bibliographical articles of value: G. Bourgin, "L'histoire économique de la France 1800–1830" in *Revue d'histoire moderne et contemporaine*, Vol. 6; and H. Sée, "Recent work in French economic history" in *Economic History Review* (Jan., 1927). A summary bibliography of new works in French Economic History appears every January in the *Economic History Review*.

In the general histories of the period by Charléty and Weill, referred to in the bibliography for Chapter I, are excellent summaries of the economic conditions of the Restoration.

AGRICULTURE

On the question of land ownership and the Revolution: M. Marion, **La vente des biens nationaux pendant la Révolution* (1908); Loutchisky, **L'Etat des classes agricoles en France* (1911); and by the same author; *Quelques remarques sur la vente des biens nationaux* (1913); G. Bourgin, "La Révolution et l'agriculture" in *Revue d'histoire des doctrines économiques et sociales* (1911); P. Sagnac, "La division du sol pendant la Révolution et ses conséquences" in *Revue d'histoire moderne et contemporaine*, Vol. 5; and three excellent studies by G. Lefebvre, **Les paysans du Nord et la Révolution française* (1924), *"Les recherches relatives à larépartition de la propriété et de l'exploitation foncières à la fin de l'ancien régime" in *Revue d'histoire moderne* (1928), and *"Place de la Révolution dans l'histoire agraire de la France" in *Annales d'histoire économique et sociale* (1929). Other works on agriculture: Arbos, *La vie pastorale dans les Alpes* (1922); Augé-Laribé, *L'évolution de la France agricole* (1912), a short survey by an eminent authority; H. Baudrillart, **Les populations agricoles de la France* (3 vol., 1885–1903); Baudrimont, *Dictionnaire de l'industrie commerciale et agricole* (10 vol., 1834–41); N. Beaurieux, *Le prix du blé en France au XIXe siècle* (1909); G. de Buzareingues, *Essai sur la division indéfinie des propriétés* (Rodez, 1823), an interesting contemporary study; Cahen, "L'économie sociale chrétienne et la colonisation agricole" in

Revue d'économie politique (1903); T. E. C. Leslie, "Land system in France," in Cobden Club, *Systems of Land Tenure in various countries* (2d ed., London, 1870), about the only discussion that exists in English; R. Delabeigerie, *Histoire de l'agriculture française considérée dans ses rapports avec les lois, les cultes, les mœurs et le commerce* (1815); a contemporary study; F. Dreyfus, **La Rochefoucauld-Liancourt* (1903), the life of a famous philanthropist interested in improving agriculture; Ch. Dupin, *Petit producteur français*, a short-lived periodical of 1827–8 that has some good articles on agriculture and on industry; Flour de Saint-Genis, *La propriété rurale en France* (1902); J. Gaumont, **Histoire générale de la coopération en France* (2 vol., 1925); G. Hottenger, *La Lorraine économique au lendemain de la Révolution* (Nancy, 1924); F. Ponteil, *La situation économique du Bas-Rhin au lendemain de la Révolution* (Strasbourg, 1927); K. Kautsky, *La question agricole* (1900), doctrinaire but interesting; N. de Krakzak, *France agricole, industrielle et commerciale en chiffres* (1845), inadequate statistics, but about all that exists, cf. Charléty, p. 299, note for value of another body of statistics, *Statistique de la France.* Charléty's remarks apply likewise to the statistics in Moreau de Jonnès, *Statistique de l'agriculture de la France* (1848); A. Larbalétrier and A. Malpeaux, "Culture de la betterave en France" in *Revue générale des sciences* (1896); G. de Bueil, *Evolution de l'agriculture dans le Vexin normand* (Evreux, 1926); Le Névanic, "L'agriculture en Ille-et-Vilaine de 1815 à 1870" in *Annales de Bretagne* (1910); T. Leroux and M. Lenglen, *L'agriculture dans le département de l'Oise* (1909); Letaconnoux, "L'agriculture dans le département d'Ille-et-Vilaine en 1816" in *Annales de Bretagne* (1919); J. C. Loudon, **An encyclopedia of agriculture* (London, 1839); Lullin de Chateaurieux, *Voyages agronomiques en France* (2 vol., 1843); de Lavergne, **Economie rurale de la France* (4th ed., 1877), though now out of date this is still a useful work; G. Martin and Martenot, **Contribution à l'histoire des classes rurales en France au XIXe siècle: La Côte d'Or* (1909), this study includes a bibliography of all regional studies 1880–1908; Manguin, **Histoire de l'administration de l'agriculture*

(2 vol., 1877); C. Morel de Vindée, *Considérations sur le morcellement de la propriété territoriale en France* (1826), another contemporary pamphlet; R. Musset, *Le Bas-Maine* (1917); R. Musset, *L'élevage du cheval en France* (1917); J. du Plessis de Grenédan, *Géographie agricole de la France et du Monde* (1903); H. de Rocquiny, *Syndicats agricoles et leur œuvre* (1900); L. de Romeuf, *La crise agricole sous la Restauration* (1902); H. Sée, **Esquisse d'une histoire agraire en Europe aux XVIIIe et XIXe siècles* (1921); H. Sée, *"L'économie rurale en Anjou dans la première moitié du XIXe siècle" in *Revue d'histoire économique* (1927); H. Sée, "Landes, communaux et défrichements en Haute-Bretagne dans la première moitié du XIXe siècle" in *Mémoires de la société d'histoire de Bretagne* (1926); H. Sée, "La vaine pâture en France sous la monarchie de Juillet" in *Revue d'histoire moderne* (1926); G. Sion, *Les paysans de la Normandie orientale* (1909); H. C. Stutt, "Notes on the distribution of Estates in France and in the United Kingdom" in *Journal of Royal Statistical Society* (June, 1910); L. F. Tessier, "L'idée forestière dans l'histoire" in *Revue des eaux et forêts* (1905). On the tariff and agriculture cf. Tariff Regime below.

INDUSTRY

Besides the general works referred to above, there are a great many monographs on special industries and their development. On the Industrial Revolution in the eighteenth century: C. Ballot, **L'introduction du méchanisme dans l'industrie française 1780–1815* (1923), a remarkable work, unfortunately it stops in 1815.

Coal mining and the Metallurgic Industries: There is a series of studies by L. G. Gras, all published at St. Etienne: *Histoire de la quincaillerie à Saint-Etienne* (1904); *Histoire de l'armurerie à Saint-Etienne* (1905); **Histoire de la métallurgie dans la Loire* (1908), and **Histoire économique générale des mines de la Loire* (2 vol., 1922). Also, Gréan, *Le fer en Lorraine* (1908); J. Levainville, **L'industrie du fer en France* (1923); several articles in *Le Pas-de-Calais au XIXe siècle* (4 vol., Arras, 1900); L. Reybaud, **Le fer et la houille* (1874);

Vuillemin, *Le bassin houiller du Pas-de-Calais* (3 vol., 1878–9).

Textile Industries. Alazard, *"Les causes de l'insurrection lyonnaise de 1831" in *Revue historique* (Sept., 1912); L. J. Gras, *Histoire de la rubanerie à Saint-Etienne* (St. Etienne, 1906); H. Hénon, *L'industrie des tulles et des dentelles dans le Pas-de-Calais* (Calais, 1900); Houdoy, **La filature du coton dans le Nord de la France* (1903); P. Leuilliot, "Une monographie d'établissement industriel alsacien en 1826" in *Revue d'histoire moderne* (1930); R. Lévy, **L'industrie cotonnière en Alsace* (1912), an important work; E. Pariset, **Histoire de la fabrique lyonnaise* (Lyons, 1901); L. Reybaud, **La soie* (1859); L. Reybaud, **Le coton* (1863); L. Reybaud, **La laine* (1867); E. Reynier, *La soie en Vivarais* (Largentière, 1923); Société industrielle de Mulhouse, *L'histoire documentaire de l'industrie de Mulhouse et de ses environs au XIXe siècle* (Mulhouse, 1902); Truchon, *"La vie intérieure de la fabrique lyonnaise sous la Restauration" in *Revue d'histoire de Lyon* (1910); and two general surveys of Lyons: *L'économie sociale et l'histoire du travail à Lyon* (Lyons, 1900); and *Lyon en 1906* (2 vol., Lyons, 1906).

Porcelain industry. C. Grellier, *L'industrie de la porcelaine dans le Limousin* (1908).

Administration of Industry. Chambre de Commerce, *Rapport de la commission formée pour l'examen de certaines questions de législation commerciale* (2 vol., 1828); Chambre de Commerce, *L'analyse succincte des délibérations de la Chambre de Commerce de Paris 1803 à 1836* (1838); L. J. Gras, *Le Conseil de commerce de Saint-Etienne et les industries locales au commencement du XIXe siècle* (St. Etienne, 1895); and a comprehensive study by G. Bourgin, *"Législation et organisation administrative du travail sous la Restauration" in *Revue politique et parlementaire* (Oct., 1910), an article which, with some modifications, is reprinted in the introduction to Vol. 2 of *Le régime de l'industrie en France 1814–1830* (1921). The **Manuel des agents de change, banques, finances et commerce, 1804–1893* (1893), gives most of the commercial laws and regulations of the period. On technical education cf. L. Guillet, *Cent ans de l'école central des arts et manufactures* (1929).

Industrial expositions and Inventions. O'Reilly, *Annales des arts et manufactures contenant les découvertes modernes dans les arts, les manufactures et le commerce* (1st series, 56 vol., 1800–15; 2d series, 5 vol., 1815–7); L. S. Normand and J. G. M. de Moléon, *Annales de l'industrie nationale et étrangère* (27 vol., 1820–7); de Moléon, *Annales de l'industrie manufacturière agricole et commerciale* (55 vol., 1827–44). These works are particularly valuable for their full description of the processes of manufacturing. For the Expositions 1819, 1823, and 1827, *Rapports du Jury central 1819* (2 vol., 1824); *L'exposition de 1827: Rapport du Jury départemental de la Seine* (2 vol., 1829); *Voyage dans la Cour du Louvre, ou guide de l'observateur à l'exposition des produits de l'industrie française* (1827); A. de Colmont, *Histoire des expositions de l'industrie française* (1855); A. Blanqui, **Histoire de l'exposition des produits de l'industrie française en 1827* (1827); and Poncelet, *Rapport sur les machines et les outils à l'exposition universelle de 1851* (1851).

BANKING AND PUBLIC FINANCE

Banking. "L'or et l'argent dans l'encaisse de la Banque de France" (after 1814) in *Bulletin de statistique et de législation comparée* (1887), Vol. 21; Capefigue, *Histoire des grandes opérations financières* (4 vol., 1855–60), Vol. 2 is on banks, and Vol. 4 on industrial companies; A. Courtois, *Histoire des banques en France* (2d ed., 1881); Flour de Saint-Genis, *La Banque de France à travers le siècle* (1896); Gautier, "Banques et institutions de crédit," in *Encyclopédie du Droit* (1839); *La compagnie générale des assurances, 1819–1919* (1919); O. Noël, *Les banques d'émission en Europe*, Vol. 1 (1888); L. de Lavergne, "Banque de France et les banques départementales" in *Revue des Deux-Mondes* (15 April, 1864); G. Ramon, **Histoire de la Banque de France* (1929); C. Juglar, **Des crises commerciales et de leur retour périodique en France, en Angleterre et aux Etats-Unis* (1889); and E. de Laveleye, *Le marché monétaire et ses crises depuis 50 ans* (1865).

Bourse. Bresson, *Des fonds publics et des opérations de la Bourse de Paris* (6th ed., 1830); A. S. G. Coffinières, *De la*

Bourse et des spéculations sur les effets publics (1824); and A. Liesse, "Jacques Lafitte, sa vie et ses idées financières" in *Revue des Deux-Mondes* (Nov., 1907).

Public Finance. R. Arnaud, *La débâcle financière de la Révolution: Cambon, 1756–1820* (1926); d'Audiffret, *Souvenirs de l'administration du Comte de Villèle* (1855), a defence of Villèle; d'Audiffret, *Le système financier de la France* (6 vol., 1863–70), documents; A. Bacon, *Le Ministère des Finances: organisation et attributions* (1906); J. Bresson, *Histoire financière de la France* (2 vol., 1840); Calmon, **Histoire des finances sous la Restauration* (2 vol. 1868–70); Ganihl, *De la science des finances et du ministère de M. de Villèle* (1825), an attack on Villéle; C. G. Gignoux, *Vie du Baron Louis* (1928); M. Marion, **Histoire financière de la France* (Vol. 4, *1797–1818*, 1925; Vol. 5, *1818–1825*, 1928), a definitive work; Ministère des Finances, *Etats détaillés des liquidations faites par la commission des indemnités* (9 vol., 1827–9); de Montmoillon, "Thiers et la politique financière de M. de Villèle" in *Revue historique* (1926); de Nervo, *Les finances françaises sous la Restauration* (4 vol., 1865 ff.); H. Pouyanne, *Les prérogatives financières du pouvoir législatif sous la Restauration* (1911); F. Sancholle, *Les finances de la France depuis 1815* (1872); Stourm, **Le budget, son histoire et son mécanisme* (5th ed., 1906), C. Sudre, *Les finances de la France au XIXe siècle* (2 vol., 1883); M. Ruini, *Corvetto ministro 1756–1821* (Bari, Italy, 1929); and A. Gain, **La Restauration et les biens des émigrés* (2 vol., Nancy, 1928).

TARIFF REGIME

A. Armauné, *Le commerce extérieur et les tarifs de douane* (1911); L. Amé, **Etudes sur les tarifs de douane et sur les traités de commerce* (2 vol., 1876); W. Ashley, **Modern tariff history* (3d ed., London, 1920); E. Boizard and H. Tardieu, *Histoire de la législation des sucres 1664–1891* (1891); Cochut, "La politique du libre-échange: Le régime économique de la France de 1815 à 1860" in *Revue des Deux-Mondes* (1861); P. Clément, *Histoire du système protecteur en France depuis le ministère de Colbert jusqu'à la Révolution de 1848* (1854); F. L.

Ferrier, *Du gouvernement considéré dans ses rapports avec le commerce* (1821), the best contemporary protectionist pamphlet; Ch. Gouard, *Histoire de la politique commerciale de la France* (2 vol., 1854); E. Levasseur, *"Le système protecteur sous la Restauration" in *Revue internationale du commerce et de l'industrie*; H. O. Meredith, **Protection in France* (London, 1909); cf. pp. 271 and 291, notes in Charléty for other contemporary pamphlets on the tariff question.

COMMERCE

Bères de Gers, *Les causes de l'affaiblissement du commerce de Bordeaux* (1835), a contemporary pamphlet; A. von Brandt, **Beiträge zur Geschichte des Französichen Handelspolitik* (Berlin, 1896); E. Levasseur, **Histoire du commerce de la France de 1789 à nos jours* (1912), the work of a great scholar but much less complete than his history of industry; Malvezin, *Histoire du commerce de Bordeaux* (4 vol., Bordeaux, 1892); Ministère du Commerce, *Statistique du commerce extérieur au Ministère des finances* (yearly after 1819); Ministère du Commerce, *Un siècle de commerce entre la France et le Royaume-Uni* (1908); Ministère de l'Intérieur, *Tableau général du commerce de la France avec les colonies et les puissances étrangères* (annual after 1825); O. Noël, *Histoire du commerce extérieur de la France depuis la Révolution* (1881); C. Périgot, *Histoire du commerce français* (1884); H. Pigeonneau **Histoire du commerce de la France* (2 vol., 1887–9); du Vaublanc; *Du commerce de la France en 1820 et 1821* (1822), and du Vaublanc, *Du commerce de la France, examen des états de M. le Directeur général des douanes* (1824), two contemporary pamphlets.

Retail Trade. H. d'Almeras, *La vie parisienne sous la Restauration* (1910); and A. Franklin, *Les magasins de nouveautés* (4 vol., 1894–8).

Colonial Policy. Bajot, *Annales maritimes et coloniales ou recueil des lois et ordonnances royales* (94 vol., 1816–45); M. Dubois and A. Terrier, *Un siècle d'expansion coloniale 1800–1900* (1902); Gaffarel, **La politique coloniale en France de 1789 à 1830* (1908); C. Schefer, **La France et le problème colonial* (Vol. 1, 1906), the last two are excellent; also cf.

C. Schefer, *Instructions générales données de 1763 à 1870 aux gouverneurs et ordonnateurs des établissements français des côtes d'Afrique* (2 vol., 1921–7); G. Tramond and A. Reussner, **Eléments d'histoire maritime et coloniale contemporaine 1815–1914* (1925); R. Valet, *L'Afrique du nord devant le parlement au XIXe siècle* (Algiers, 1924), C. Schefer, *L'Algérie et l'évolution de la colonisation française* (1928), G. Hardy, *Histoire de la colonisation française* (1928), and G. Hanotaux and A. Martineau, **Histoire des colonies françaises*, Vol. I (1929).

Means of communication. Audigaine, *Les chemins de fer aujourd'hui et dans cent ans* (2 vol., 1858); Breitmayer, *Le Rhône, sa navigation depuis les temps anciens jusqu'à nos jours* (1904); A. Colin, *La navigation commerciale au XIXe siècle* (1901); A. Courtois, "Notices historiques sur les canaux entrepris en vertu des lois de 1821 et de 1822" in *Journal des économistes* (1851); J. Dutens, *Histoire de la navigation intérieure de la France* (2 vol., 1829); Ernest Charles *Les chemins de fer en France pendant le règne de Louis-Philippe* (1896); A. D. Evans, *History and Economics of Transport* (London, 1915); G. Lefranc, *"French Railroads 1823–42" in *Journal of Economic and Business History* (1930); and by the same author, *"La construction des chemins de fer et l'opinion publique vers 1830" in *Revue d'histoire moderne* (1930); Foville, *La transformation des moyens de transport et ses conséquences économiques et sociales* (1880); J. Letaconnous, *La transformation des moyens de transport* in Les divisions régionales de la France; A. Picard, **Les chemins de fer* (1918), a good manual; P. Truchon, *"Les transports et voies de communication au service du commerce lyonnais sous la Restauration" in *Revue d'histoire de Lyon* (1911); M. Wallon, "Les Saint-Simoniens et les chemins de fer" in *Annales des sciences politiques* (1908); L. J. Gras, *Histoire des premiers chemins de fer en France* (St. Etienne 1924); and two works on the post office: A. Belloc, *Les postes françaises* (1886); and *Livre de poste* (annual).

CHAPTER IV[1]

GENERAL WORKS

The best introduction to social conditions in this period are in some of the general histories, especially Chapters III and VII of G. Weill, **La France sous la Monarchie Constitutionnelle* (2d ed., 1912), and Book III, Chapter III, in S. Charléty, **La Restauration* (1921). There is a collection of studies of types of French life by contemporary authors which is full of interesting material: **Les Français peints par eux-mêmes* (2 vol., 1840–1). Other works that touch on a number of aspects of French society are: James Fenimore Cooper, **Gleanings in Europe: France* (new ed. Oxford, 1928); Lady Morgan, *France* (2 vol., London, 1817); *France in 1829* (London, 1830); and *My Autobiography* (London, 1859) two works of Heine, *De la France* (1873), and *Allemands et Français* (1899); L. Madelin, *La France de l'Empire* (1928); and C. H. C. Wright, **The background of Modern French Literature* (Boston, 1926), confusing in its presentation but dense with facts. There is likewise a good deal about social conditions in the works of Clapham, Gibbon, Knight, Levasseur, Martin, Ogg, Renard and Dulac, and Sée referred to in the section "General Works" in the bibliographical notes for Chapter III.

PARIS

Here the most useful works are: H. d'Alméras, **La vie parisienne sous la Restauration* (1910), and Ch. Simond, **Paris de 1800 à 1900* (3 vol., 1901); Simond's volumes are particularly good. The appearance of Paris during the Restoration is shown in two studies of M. Poëte, **Une promenade à Paris au temps des romantiques* (1908), a pamphlet, and in the pictures of his **Une vie de cité: Album* (1925). Other general books on Paris, 1815–1830, are: R. Boutet de Monvel, *Les Anglais à Paris, (1800–1850)* (1911); L. Barron, *Paris pittoresque 1800–1900* (1899); M. Barroux, **Essai de bibliographie critique des généralités de l'histoire de Paris* (1908), and

[1] Consult also the bibliography for Ch. III.

by the same author, **Le Département de la Seine et la Ville de Paris, notions générales et bibliographiques pour étudier l'histoire* (1910); P. R. Broemel, *Paris and London in 1815* (London, 1929); L. Dubech and P. d'Espezel, **Histoire de Paris* (1926), an admirable manual; Forster, *Quinze ans de Paris* (2 vol., 1848); Heine, *Lutèce* (1892); F. M. Marchand, *Le nouveau conducteur de l'étranger à Paris* (1830); Mrs. John Mayo, *An American Lady in Paris 1829*, ed. by Mary M. Crenshaw (Boston, 1928); Montigny, *Le Provincial à Paris* (3 vol., 1825); Prudhomme, *Voyage historique et descriptif de l'ancien et du nouveau Paris* (2 vol., 1821); Frances Trollope, *Paris and the Parisians in 1835* (1836); Verfèle, *Pélérinages d'un Childe Harold parisien* (1825).

Parisian Theaters. M. Albert, *Les théâtres des boulevards 1789–1848* (1902); N. C. Arvin, **Eugène Scribe and the French Theater, 1815–1860* (Cambridge, Mass., 1924), excellent; G. Cain, *Anciens théâtres de Paris* (1906); C. M. Des Granges, **La comédie et les mœurs sous la Restauration et la Monarchie de Juillet* (1902), an important study; D. O. Evans, **Le drame moderne à l'époque romantique* (1923); A. Flamand, *Une étoile en 1830: Malibran* (1928); C. Gével and J. Rabot, "La censure théâtrale sous la Restauration" in *Revue de Paris* (1913); J. Guex, *Le théâtre et la société française de 1815 à 1845* (Vévey, 1900); A. Joannides, *La Comédie-Française, 1680–1900, dictionnaire des pièces et des auteurs* (1901); T. Muret, **L'histoire par le théâtre 1789–1851* (3 vol., 1864–5); P. Tisseau, *Une comédienne sous la Restauration* (1928).

The Court. The books on Louis XVIII and Charles X by Lucas-Dubreton referred to in the bibliography of Chapter I give many details of court life. J. Turquan has written a life of the *Duchesse d'Angoulême* (1901), and one of *Charles X* (1929), which contain court chit-chat aplenty. There is material also in the Memoirs of the Duchesse de Gontaut (1892), de Saint-Chamans (1896), de Reiset (3 vol., 1900–2), de Sosthène de la Rochefoucauld, Duc de Doudeauville (2d ed., 15 vol., 1861–5).

Old Nobility. *Mémoires* of Vitrolles (3 vol., 1883–4); Chateaubriand, **Mémoires d'Outre-Tombe* (ed. Biré, 6 vol., 1898–

1900); Comtesse de Boigne, *Mémoires* (4 vol., 1907–9); de Castellane, *Journal* (4 vol., 1895–6); D'Haussonville, *Ma Jeunesse* (1885); Daniel Stern, **Mes Souvenirs* (1877); d'Alton-Shée, *Mes Mémoires* (2 vol., 1869).

Salons. Nearly all the memoirs of the period give some information about the salons of the time. Also cf. Ancelot, *Un salon de Paris, 1824–1864* (1865); Madame de Bassanville, **Les Salons d'autrefois* (4 vol., 1862); F. de Bondy, *Une femme d'esprit de 1830* (1928); Duchesse de Broglie, *Lettres 1814–1838* (1896); R. Capefigue, *La Comtesse de Cayla, Louis XVIII et les salons du Faubourg Saint-Germain sous la Restauration* (1866); E. Herriot, *Madame Récamier et ses amis* (1905); Kozmian, *"Le carnet d'un mondain sous la Restauration" in *Revue de Paris* (15 Jan., 1900), very interesting; H. Malo, *Une muse et sa mère* (1924), about Delphine Gay; M. Martin, **Le Docteur Koreff, un aventurier intellectuel* (1925); Stendhal, **Armance, ou quelques scènes d'un salon de Paris en 1827* (Frankfurt, 1920); M. E. Elkington, **Les relations de société entre l'Angleterre et la France 1814–1830* (1929); and G. Stenger, *Les grandes dames du XIXe siècle: chronique au temps de la Restauration* (1911).

BOURGEOISIE

A. Bardoux, **La bourgeoisie française 1789–1848* (1886). The novels of Balzac are particularly valuable here, for the people Balzac knew best were the bourgeoisie in both Paris and the provinces. There were few memoirs written by the members of the bourgeoisie except those who were very wealthy and moved in the highest Parisian society. There are extracts about the bourgeoisie of the Restoration in **Les français peints par eux-mêmes* (11 vol., 1840–1), referred to above. Cf. also P. Gaulot, *L'indiscrétion d'un bourgeois de Paris* (1928). Many of the plays of the period discussed problems of the bourgeoisie, such as marriage, place-hunting, etc.; for these plays cf. the works of Des Granges and of D. O. Evans referred to above under "Theaters," for types in the novel cf. Ch. Brun, *Le roman social en France au XIXe siècle* (1910).

Fashions. H. Bouchot, *Le luxe français; La Restauration*

(1893); J. Boulenger, *Les dandys* (1907); O. Fischel and M. von Boehn, *Modes and Manners of the Nineteenth Century* (4 vol., London, 1927); Grand-Carteret, *Les élégances de la toilette sous le Directoire, l'Empire et la Restauration* (1911); and two quite remarkable studies by Maigron, **Le romantisme et les mœurs* (1910), and **Le romantisme et la mode* (1911). Also W. Sombart, **Le bourgeoisie* (1926) and B. Groethuysen, *Origines de l'esprit bourgeois en France*. Vol. I (1927).

Romanticists. Besides the work of Maigron referred to above cf. also J. Bertaut, *Villégiatures romantiques* (1927); M. Bouteron, *Muses romantiques* (1926); P. Jarry, *Etudiants et grisettes romantiques* (1927); J. Maison, *Bohème romantique* (1929); and M. Pailleron, *Les auberges romantiques* (1929), and also the bibliography for Chapter V.

PROVINCIAL CITIES

Boucher de Perthes, **Sous dix rois* (7 vol., 1863–4), a curious and interesting collection of bits about provincial life; Delautre, *Dunkerque à l'époque de la Restauration* (1902); Guépin et Bonnamy, *Nantes au dix-neuvième siècle* (1835); E. Jouy, **L'ermite en province* (3 vol., 1818–27); Lebas, *Histoire de la ville de Dieppe de 1830 à 1875* (Dieppe, 1900); Lady Morgan, *France in 1829–1830* (2d ed., 2 vol., London, 1831); Stendhal, **Mémoires d'un touriste* (2 vol., 1837), excellent; P. de Vaudreuil, *Promenade de Paris à Bagnères de Luchon* (1820); and also by the same author, *Promenade de Bagnères de Luchon à Paris* (1820); also Marceline Tinayre, *Une provinciale en 1830* (1928). The novels of Balzac are full of extraordinary studies of life in the provincial towns. The provincial histories, of which there are a number for nearly every French province, usually have little material on the Restoration. There are further bibliographical details on the subject in G. Weill, *La France sous la monarchie constitutionnelle*, p. 296.

Provincial Nobility. There is much of interest in Comte de Comminges, *"Souvenirs d'enfance" in *Revue de Paris* (15 Sept., 1909).

Professions. Cf. Gaudry, *Histoire du barreau de Paris* (1864); Pinard, *Le barreau au XIXe siècle* (2 vol., 1865);

Henri-Robert, *Un avocat en 1830* (1928); Poumiès de la Siboutie, *Souvenirs d'un médecin de Paris* (1910).

WORKING CLASSES

The literature on the working classes is enormous. The best introduction to the subject will be found in sections of the general works of Levasseur, Sée, and Clapham referred to above. Perhaps the most useful single volume on the subject is P. Louis, **Histoire de la classe ouvrière en France depuis la Révolution* (1927). Other general works are: M. R. Clark, **History of the French Labor Movement* (Berkeley, 1930); J. Godart, *Travailleurs et métiers lyonnais* (Lyon, 1909); P. Leroy-Beaulieu, *La question ouvrière au XIXe siècle* (2d ed., 1881); H. D. Lockwood, **Tools and the Man, a Comparative Study of the French Workingman and the English Chartists 1830–48* (1927); E. Martin Saint-Léon, *Histoire des corporations de métiers* (3d ed., 1923); P. Truchon, *"La vie ouvrière à Lyon sous la Restauration" in *Revue d'histoire de Lyon*(1912).

Studies of Income, and Living and Working Conditions. Bigot de Morogues, *De la misère des ouvriers et de la marche à suivre pour y remédier* (1832); A. Blanqui, **Les classes ouvrières en 1848* (2 vol., 1849); E. Buret, **De la misère des classes laborieuses en France et en Angleterre* (1846); E. Chevallier, **Les salariés au XIXe siècle* (1887); J. D. M. Cochin, *De l'extinction de la mendicité* (1829); Duchâtellier, *Essai sur les salaires et les prix de consommation de 1202 à 1830* (1830); Ch. Dupin, **Discours sur le sort de la classe ouvrière* (1827); Fodéré, **Essai historique et moral sur la pauvreté des nations* (1825); P. Leroy-Beaulieu, *Essai sur la répartition des richesses* (2d ed., 1883); P. Leroy-Beaulieu, *Le travail des femmes au XIXe siècle* (1888); H. Mansion, **Essai sur l'extinction de la mendicité en France* (1829); Ch. Rist. *"Durée du travail dans l'industrie française de 1820 à 1870" in *Revue d'économie politique* (1897); Rubichon, *Du mécanisme de la société en France et en Angleterre* (2d ed., 1833); Fr. Simiand, *Le salaire des ouvriers des mines en France* (1904); Statistique de la France, Vol. 2, *Territoire et population;* also 2d series, Vol. 11, *Prix et salaires à diverses époques;* Villeneuve-Bargemont, **Economie politique chrétienne* (3 vol., 1834), and L. R. Villermé, **Tableau d'état physique et moral des ouvriers* (2 vol., 1840).

Strikes. M. Blanchard, *"Une émeute ouvrière dans l'Isère en 1819" in *Revue d'histoire de Lyon* (1914); C. Schmidt, "Un épisode de l'histoire du mécanisme en France," in *Révolution française* (1903); also Ch. Schmidt, "Encore un document relatif à l'histoire du mécanisme en France" in *Révolution française* (1903).

Labor Organizations. General: Office du Travail, **Les associations professionnelles ouvrières* (Vol. 1, 1899); J. Drioux, *Etude économique et juridique sur les associations, les coalitions d'ouvriers et de patrons de 1789 à nos jours* (1884); O. Festry, **Le mouvement ouvrier au début de la monarchie de juillet* (1908); P. Louis, **Histoire du mouvement syndical en France* (3d ed., 1920); L. Levine, **Syndicalism in France* (2d ed., 1914); G. Weill, "Les journaux ouvriers à Paris de 1830 à 1870" in *Revue d'histoire moderne* (1907).

Compagnonnage. J. Connay, *Le compagnonnage* (1909); A. de Bersancourt, *"Le compagnonnage pittoresque" in *Grande Revue* (Sept., 1924); J. Godart, "Le compagnonnage à Lyon" in *Revue d'histoire de Lyon* (1903); E. Martin Saint-Léon, *Le compagnonnage* (1901); A. Perdiguier, **Mémoires d'un compagnon* (Moulins, 1914); A. Perdiguier, **Le livre du compagnonnage* (1839).

Société Philanthropique. "Annuaire philanthropique," an annual, and the annual "Comptes-rendus des assemblées générales de la société philanthropique" give details about mutual aid societies; cf. also O. Festry, *"La société philanthropique et les sociétés de secours mutuels" in *Revue d'histoire moderne* (1911); also E. Bayard, *La caisse d'épargne et de prévoyance de Paris 1818–1900* (1909).

Memoirs of workingmen. S. Commissaire, *Mémoires* (2 vol., 1888); and Nadaud, *Mémoires de Léonard* (1895).

PEASANTS

Cf. references to agriculture for Chapter III, also Balzac's **Les paysans*, *Le médecin de campagne*, and *Le curé de village;*

Bouquet, *De la moralité dans les campagnes depuis 1789* (Châlons, 1860); G. Cahen, "L'économie sociale chrétienne et la colonisation agricole sous la Restauration et la monarchie de Juillet" in *Revue d'économie politique* (1903); Castez, *Le paysan, type national* (1839); Champollion-Figeac, "Le département de l'Isère sous la Restauration" in *Revue du Monde Latin* (1892); Dutouquet, *De la condition des classes pauvres à la campagne* (1846); and an excellent novel by Eugène Le Roy, **Jacquou le croquant* (1899), translated into English (1919), a wonderful picture of peasant life during the Restoration.

SOCIAL AND ECONOMIC DOCTRINE

Here again the literature is very extensive. Most outstanding as a general work is Ch. Gide and Rist, **Histoire des doctrines économiques* (Eng. tr., 1915). A work of less value is L. H. Haney, *History of Economic Thought* (2d ed., 1920). There is some discussion of social and economic theories in the remarkable work of H. Michel, **L'idée de l'état* (1896). There are a whole series of histories of French socialism: C. C. Bouglé, *Chez les prophètes socialistes* (1908); G. Bourgin, *Le socialisme français, 1789–1848* (1912); E. Fournière, *Les théories socialistes au XIXe siècle* (1904); G. Isambert, *Les idées socialistes en France de 1815 à 1848* (1905); P. Janet, *Les origines du socialisme contemporain* (1883); T. Kirkup, *History of Socialism* (London, 1892); H. W. Laidler, *History of Socialist Thought* (1927); P. Louis, **Histoire du socialisme en France* (new ed., 1925); L. von Stern, **Geschichte des sozialen Bewegung in Frankreich* (1850); W. Sombart, **Der prolétarische sozialismus* (2 vol., Jena, 1924), an important work; Warshauer, *Zur Enturcklungsgeschichte des Sozialismus* (Berlin, 1909).

J.-B. Say. Allix, *"J.-B. Say" in *Revue d'économie politique* (1910); J. M. Clark and others, *Adam Smith, 1776–1926* (Chicago, 1928), especially Chapter V, *"Introduction of Smith on the Continent"; Liesse, *J.-B. Say au Conservatoire* (1901); E. Teilhac, **L'œuvre économique de J.-B. Say 1927.*

Sismondi. A. Aftalion, *L'oeuvre économique de Sismondi*

(1894); M.-L. Tuan, **Sismondi as an Economist* (1927); R. Jeandeau, *Sismondi, précurseur de la législation sociale contemporaine* (Bordeaux, 1913), and H. Grossmann, *Sismondi et ses théories économiques* (Warsaw 1924).

Saint-Simon. C. Bouglé, **L'oeuvre de Saint-Simon* (1925), a useful selection of texts; G. Brunet, *Le mysticisme social de Saint-Simon* (1925); M. Leroy, *Vie de Saint-Simon* (1925); M. E. Halévy, *"La doctrine économique de Saint-Simon" *in Revue du mois* (1907–8); G. Weill, **Un précurseur du socialisme: Saint-Simon et son œuvre* (1894), an admirable work; J. H. Jenks, *"Saint-Simon" in *Essays in Intellectual History* (1929); and P. Janet, **Saint-Simon et le Saint-Simonisme* (1878).

Saint-Simonian School. J. d'Avray, *L'aventure Saint-Simonienne et les femmes* (1928); C. Bouglé and E. Halévy, **Doctrine de Saint-Simon, exposition première année 1829* (new ed. with commentary, 1924), very useful; S. Charléty, **Histoire du Saint-Simonisme* (1896), based on the sources, an important study; G. Pinet, "L'Ecole polytechnique et les Saint-Simoniens" in *Revue de Paris* (1894); G. Weill, **L'Ecole Saint-Simonienne* (1894); H. R. d'Allemagne, **Les Saint-Simoniens 1827–37* (1930); and W. Spühler, *Der Saint-Simonismus* (Zurich 1926).

Fourier. H. Bourgin, **Fourier, contribution à l'étude du socialisme français* (1905); Ch. Gide, *Oeuvres choisies de Fourier* (1890 series of texts with a brilliant introductory essay, Eng. tr., London, 1901); E. S. Mason, *"Fourier and Anarchism" in *Quarterly Journal of Economics* (Feb., 1928), excellent.

CHAPTER V

THE LITERARY MOVEMENT

Bibliography. There are two excellent bibliographies of modern French literature: G. Lanson, **Manuel Bibliographique de la littérature française moderne* (last ed., 1925); and H. Talvart and J. Place, *Bibliographie des auteurs modernes de la langue française de 1801 à 1927* (Vol. 1, 1928); cf. also: G. Brunet, *Manuel du libraire* (1860 ff.); and H. P. Thième, *Bibliographie de la littérature française de 1800 à 1906* (1907). Each March there appears in the *Pub. of the Mod. Lang. Ass.* a summary bibliography of new works in the history of French Literature, written by Americans; cf. also current bibliographies in *Revue d'histoire littéraire de la France*.

General Histories. The standard manual of the history of French Literature is G. Lanson, **Histoire de la littérature française* (20th ed., 1929). Other general works are F. Brunot and others, **Le romantisme et les lettres* (1929), a series of lectures; G. Brandes, *Main Currents of Nineteenth Century Literature, Vol. 5, *The Romantic School in France* (1903); E. Faguet, **Etudes littéraires du XIXe siècle* (1887); J. Giraud, **L'école romantique française* (1927); excellent survey; A. Nettement, *L'histoire de la littérature française sous la Restauration* (2 vol., 2d ed., 1858); G. Pellisier, **Le mouvement littéraire au XIXe siècle* (1889); Sainte-Beuve, **Causeries du Lundi* (16 vol., 3d ed., 1857–72), and **Nouveaux Lundis* (13 vol., 2d ed., 1864–78); D. Sauvageot, *Le romantisme*, Vol. 3 of Petit de Julleville's, Histoire de la littérature française (1899 ff.); M. Souriau, *Histoire du Romantisme en France* (1928). From 1904 to 1914 there was a review of Romanticism, *Les annales romantiques* ed. by L. Séché. A special number of *La revue de littérature comparée* (Jan.–Mar. 1927) is devoted to Romanticism.

Pre-Romanticism. F. Baldensperger, **Le mouvement des idées dans l'émigration française* (2 vol., 1925–7), and "Genre troubadour" in *Etudes d'histoire littéraire* (1907); Lady Blennerhasset, **Frau von Stäel*, (3 vol., Berlin, 1887–9, tr. also in French, and English, 1890); E. Estève, *Etudes de littérature préromantique* (1923); M. B. Finch and E. A. Peers, *The Origins of French Romanticism* (London, 1920); P. Hazard, *"Tendances romantiques dans la littérature de la Révolution" in *Revue d'histoire littéraire de la France* (1907); H. Jacoubet, *Le genre troubadour et les origines françaises du romantisme* (1929); D.Mornet, **Le romantisme en France au XVIIIe siècle* (1912), the later edition has no changes and omits the illustrations, an admirable book; A. Mouglond, *Vies préromantiques* (1925); Sainte-Beuve, **Chateaubriand et son groupe littéraire* (2 vol., 1860); J. Texte, **Rousseau et les origines du cosmopolitisme littéraire* (1895); a very important study; A. Schinz, **La pensée de Rousseau* (1929); P. Van Tieghem, *La poésie de la nuit et des tombeaux en Europe au XVIIIe siècle* (1921), and *Le préromantisme* (2 vol., 1924).

Foreign Influences. England. F. Baldensperger, *"Shakespeare en France" in *Etudes d'histoire littéraire* (1907) and *Young et ses "Nuits" en France* in *Etudes d'histoire littéraire* (2d ser., 1910); E. Estève, **Byron et le romantisme français* (1907); R. W. Hartland, *Walter Scott et le roman frénétique* (1929); A. Killen, *Le roman terrifiant et son influence sur la littérature française* (1924); E. Partridge, **The French Romantics' Knowledge of English Literature 1820–1848* (1924); L. Reynaud, **Le romantisme, ses origines anglo-germaniques* (1926), an excellent survey, but written with a nationalist bias; A. C. Thomas, *Moore en France 1819–1830* (1911); P. Van Tieghem, **Ossian en France* (2 vol., 1916).

America.. G. C. Bosset, *Fenimore Cooper et le roman d'aventure en France vers 1830* (1929).

Germany. F. Baldensperger, " Lénore' de Bürger dans la littérature française" in *Etudes d'histoire littéraire* (1st ser., 1907), and **Goethe en France* (1904); L. Cazamian, *"Le romantisme français et l'esprit germanique" in *Etudes de psychologie littéraire* (1913); E. Eggli, **Schiller et le romantisme français* (3 vol., 1928); L. Reynaud, **L'influence allemande en France aux XVIIIe et XIXe siècles* (1922), the best general study; J. Texte, "L'influence allemande dans le romantisme français" in *Etudes de littérature européenne* (1898); H. Tronchon, *La fortune intellectuelle de Herder en France* (Vol. 1, 1920); P. Van Tieghem, "Les idylles de Gessner et le rêve pastoral dans le préromantisme européen" in *Revue de littérature comparée* (1924), and V. Tibal, **L'influence allemande en France au temps du romantisme* in *Mélanges Andler* (1924).

Spain. E. Martinenche, *L'Espagne et le romantisme français* (1922).

Italy. A. Bisi, *L'Italie et le romantisme français* (Milan, 1914); R. Noli, *Les romantiques français et l'Italie* (Dijon, 1928).

Growth of Romantic Doctrines. Collections of texts: H. F. Stewart and A. Tilley, *The Romantic Movement in French Literature traced by a series of texts* (Cambridge, Eng., 1910); and F. Vial and E. Denise, *Idées et doctrines littéraires du XIXe siècle.* The story of the fight between Classicism and Romanticism, 1820–1830, is told in detail in J. Marsan's **La bataille romantique* (1912). Other useful studies are: E. Asse, *Les petits romantiques* (2d ed., 1909); E. Biré, **Hugo avant 1830* (1883); J. L. Borgerhoff, *Le théâtre anglais à Paris sous la Restauration* (1913); E. Dupuy, **La jeunesse des romantiques* (1907), and *Alfred de Vigny* (2 vol., 1910–2); E. Faguet, *La jeunesse de Sainte-Beuve* (1913); T. Gautier, *Histoire du romantisme* (1874), a collection of reminiscences; H. Girard, **Un bourgeois dilettante à l'époque romantique: Emile Deschamps 1791–1871* (1927); J. A. Henning, *"L'Allemagne" de Mme. de Staël et la polémique romantique* (1929); A. Michiels, *Histoire des idées littéraires en France au XIXe siècle* (2 vol., 4th ed., 1863); M. Salomon, **Charles Nodier et le groupe romantique* (1908); L. Séché, **Le cénacle de la "Muse Française" 1823–1827* (1908), and **Le cénacle de Joseph Delorme 1827–30* (2 vol., 1912); M. E. Smith, *Une anglaise intellectuelle en France sous la Restauration: Mary Clarke* (1927); P. Souday, *Les romantiques à l'académie* (1928), the discourses of the great Romanticists at their admission to the French Academy; P. Trahard, *La jeunesse de Mérimée* (2 vol., 1924), Larat, *La tradition et l'exotisme dans l'œuvre de Nodier* (1923).

Literary Press. Des Granges, **La presse littéraire sous la*

Aulard, "Les premiers historiens de la Révolution française" in *La Revue française* (1909); Courajod, *Lenoir* (2 vol., 1878) and also *"L'influence du musée des monuments français sur le développement de l'art et des études historiques" in *Revue historique* (1886), an excellent article; Galley, "Fauriel" (1909); Guérard, "Notice sur Daunou" (1855); Guizot, *Barante* (1867); Laborde, *Les archives de France pendant la Révolution et l'Empire* (1867); G. Lanson, *"La formation de la méthode historique de Michelet," in *Revue d'histoire moderne et contemporaine* (1905–6); *Livret de l'école des Chartes, 1821–1891* (1891); G. Monod, **Michelet, sa vie et son oeuvre* (2 vol., 1923); E. Petit, *Mignet* (1889); C. H. Pouthas, **Guizot pendant la Restauration* (1923); A. Rambaud, "Thiers, historien de la Révolution française" in *Revue politique et littéraire* (1878), J. M. S. Allison, **Thiers* (Boston 1926).

FINE ARTS

General works. The outstanding survey of French art in this period is in Vol. 8, Part I of A. Michel's, **Histoire de l'art* (1926). Other general works are: L. Bénédite, *Histoire des beaux arts 1800–1900* (1909); L. Gillet, *Histoire des arts*, Vol. 11 of Histoire de la nation française (1922). L. Hautecœur and others, **Le romantisme et l'art* (1928), a series of lectures; L. Hourticq, **Art in France* (1910); A. Fontainas and L. Vauxcelles, **Histoire générale de l'art français de la Révolution à nos jours* (3 vol., 1922); P. Petioz, *L'art et la critique en France depuis 1822* (1875); R. Schneider, **L'art français au XIXe siècle, du classicisme davidien au romantisme* (1929). On the art of the Revolution and the Empire: F. Benoit, **L'art français sous la Révolution et l'Empire* (1897); and L. Rosenthal, *David* (1905).

Painting. L. Rosenthal, **La peinture romantique* (1900), the best study; also L. Dimier, **Histoire de la peinture française au XIXe siècle* (1914); H. Focillon, **La peinture au XIXe siècle* (Vol. 1, 1927); P. Dorbec, *L'art du paysage en France* (1925); P. Dorbec, *Rousseau* (1910); P. Dorbec, *"La peinture française de 1750 à 1820 jugée par le factum, la chanson, et la caricature" in *Gazette des Beaux Arts* (1914), and a second article by same author which carries his study down later, in the same magazine; Gruffrey, *L'œuvre de Prud'hon* (1924); Geoffroy, *Corot* (1924); L. Hourticq, *Ingres* (1928); Maier-Graefe, **Delacroix* (2d ed., Munich, 1923); R. Escholier, **Delacroix* (3 vol. 1926–1929); R. Régamy, *Géricault* (1926).

Sculpture. The best recent study is that of Luc-Benoit, **La sculpture romantique* (1928); cf. also Etex, *Pradier* (1859); and H. Jouin, *David d'Angers* (1878), and by the same author, *David d'Angers et ses relations littéraires* (1890).

Architecture. Architecture, like sculpture and painting is discussed in the general works on French art; cf. also Gromont, *L'histoire abrégée de l'architecture au XIXe siècle* (1924).

Decorative Art. R. Clark, **The Gothic Revival* (London, 1928); C. Hussey, **The Picturesque* (1927); R. Lanson, **Le goût du Moyen-Age en France au XVIII siècle* (1926); L. Maigron, **Le romantisme et la mode* (1911); J. Robicquet, *L'art et le goût sous la Restauration*; and P. Schommer, **l'Art décoratif au temps du romantisme* (1928), this work, like those of Lanson and Maigron, has excellent illustrations.

MUSIC

The best recent history of music is that of J. Combarieu, **Histoire de la musique* Vol. 2 (1913), and Vol. 3 (1919) cover this period. Other general works in English are: E. Dickinson, **The Study of the History of Music* (new ed., 1926); G. Grove, **Dictionary of Music and Musicians* (new ed., 5 vol., 1921); C. H. Parry, **The Evolution of the Art of Music* (new ed., 1929); and **The Oxford History of Music* (6 vol., Oxford, 1901–5), the first volume of a new ed. appeared in 1929. On the French Romantic period there is an excellent monography by A. W. Locke, **Music and the Romantic Movement in France* (London, 1920). The evolution of French music is the subject of H. Lavoix, *La musique française* (1890); A. Coquard, **La musique en France depuis Rameau* (1891); and A. Hervey, *French Music in the Nineteenth Century* (London, 1903). The opera is discussed in A. Choquet, **Histoire de la musique dramatique en France* (1873); Choquet wrote the article on *"Rossini" in Grove's *Dictionary of Music and Musicians*; also E. Newman, *Gluck and the Opera* (1895); H. T. Finck, "Italian and German Vocal Styles" in *Chopin and Other Musical Essays* (1889). *Mozart and Weber*, *Weber's Memoir* by Simpson (2 vols., London, 1865). On the pianoforte, O. Bie, **History of the Pianoforte and Pianoforte Players* (1899); W. J. Henderson, *How Music Developed* (1898); J. Tiersot, *Liszt* (1911); and J. Kapp, *Franz Liszt* (2nd ed., 1909). For the history of the orchestra, A. Dandelot, *La société des Concerts du Conservatoire 1828–1897* (1898); and F. A. Coerne, *The Evolution of Modern Orchestration* (1908). Berlioz has been much written about. The best work is A. Boschot, **Berlioz, histoire d'un romantique* (3 vols., 1906 ff.); Boschot has recently published a one volume life of Berlioz, *Une vie romantique* (1919). Berlioz' letters, 1819–1842, have been published in J. Tiersot, *Les années romantiques* (1904); and there is a translation of Berlioz' *Autobiography* in Everyman's Library. The two best short studies are those in E. Newman, *Musical Studies* (London, 1910); and Romain Rolland, **Musiciens d'aujourd'hui* (4th ed., 1908), of which there is an English translation. Other works on musical conditions of the time are: P. Hollenberger, **Sensibilité musicale et romantisme* (1925); M. Boucheron, *Dante et musique romantiques* (1907); H. F. Chorley, *Music and Manners in France and Germany* (3 vols., London, 1841); C. Lalo, *La vie musicale au temps romantique* (1929); L. de la Laurencie, **Le goût musical en France* (1905); and J. d'Ortigue, *De la guerre des dilettanti ou de la révolution opérée par M. Rossini dans l'opéra français* (1829), an interesting contemporary study.

INDEX